READER'S DIGEST
CRIME FILES

READER'S DIGEST

CRIME FILES

Published by the Reader's Digest Association Limited

London • New York • Sydney • Montreal

CONTENTS

FOREWORD

"Am I my brother's keeper?"

In five now immortal words, the world's first murderer, Cain, sought to evade an admission that he had just killed his own brother, Abel. Since then, man has been more fascinated by crime than by any other subject. The concept of wickedness and evil, parlayed into violent crime; of detection by skill, stealth and cunning; and of retribution by an outraged society—all have not just shelves dedicated to them but entire libraries.

From the medieval Brother Cadfael, through Sherlock Holmes to DNA, we rejoice to see the tiny clues spotted, collected and used to unmask the guilty. And we still love dotty Miss Marple and Hercule Poirot's little grey cells, just as we relish the laconic cynicism of Philip Marlowe. Fashions come and fashions go, yet crime, detection and retribution remain right up among the league leaders in thriller fiction.

But a word of warning: anything fiction can do, real facts can do better. This is where *Reader's Digest Crime Files*, successor to *Crime Casebook*, comes in. Here are 26 real crime stories not from the fevered imagination of a thriller novelist but from the files of true life. And what a variety! They range from solving the enigma of how a 2,000-year-old mummy really died, in 'Secrets of the Mummy', to uncovering the secret obsession of a mild-mannered family doctor—the power of life and death—in 'A Tragedy of Trust'. His elderly patients thought the world of him, but Harold Shipman was probably the most prolific serial killer in British history. In another story, 'The Silent Witness', the villain was convinced he had got away with it until, years later, a new investigator, fresh evidence and revolutionary technology finally caught up with him.

Some of the cases in this selection are already "cases célèbres"; others are hardly known to the general public. Almost all have the same challenge: *track him down and prove he did it.*

Leading the list of these stories for topicality must surely be 'The Judge Who Cracked Al Qaeda', featuring the French judge-turned-detective who first discovered the identity and true global spread of the terror group we now know as Al Qaeda. Recalling the horrors of Nine Eleven, we might think it was the FBI that was first on the scene. But it was the methodical pipe-chewing Frenchman, Jean-Louis Bruguière, who could easily pass for Simenon's Commissaire Maigret. Bruguière followed up some outrages perpetrated by north Africans in France and realised that the tentacles went back to a place called Afghanistan. It is only now that we are aware of the huge contribution made to Al Qaeda by these north African fanatics.

In the United States, the lone killer who has probably destroyed the most lives was Timothy McVeigh, whose story also appears in this anthology of 26 cliffhangers. 'Into the Mind of Terror' explores the life and twisted mind of this man who planted a bomb in the William Murrah Building in Oklahoma City, causing the death of 168 people and the lifelong mutilation of many others.

And so, it seems, the old adage that "truth is stranger than fiction" still holds up. Let me add mention of another case, not in this anthology, in which the sheer oddity of coincidence causes the observer to shake his head. My new novel, *Avenger*, recalls the 1985 hijacking of the Italian cruise liner *Achille Lauro* off the Egyptian coast, and the brutal murder of a passenger—the elderly, wheelchair-bound New Yorker, Leon Klinghoffer—by four Palestinian terrorists. My research told me that the real mastermind, Abu Abbas, had got away and was still at liberty. Writing in the winter of 2002, I had no choice but to say so. On March 20, 2003, American forces moved into Iraq. Twenty-five days later, Green Berets, acting on a tip-off, raided a villa in west Baghdad. And there he was: retired, fresh papers, but still Abu Abbas.

As Ronald Reagan once said: "You can run but you can't hide." The stories in this excellent volume prove that, with modern technology and a bit of help from Lady Luck, it is getting harder and harder to do so.

Frederick Forsyth, September 2003

MISSISSIPPI
JUSTICE

Bobby DeLaughter

Moved by a widow's plea, Bobby DeLaughter, a young prosecutor in Jackson, Mississippi, sets out to solve a 26-year-old murder. In the process, he puts his career and his life at risk—and forces a community to revisit its darkest moment. DeLaughter was haunted by the case of Medgar Evers—a young father and a civil rights pioneer—who was gunned down outside his home, leaving his wife, Myrlie, and their three young children, to face life without him.

t was just after midnight on a warm June evening in Jackson, Mississippi. A full moon illuminated the driveway of 2332 Guynes Street as a powder-blue Oldsmobile pulled in.

Inside the house, a woman and three young children heard the familiar sound of the motor. "There's Daddy," the youngsters said. They had waited up for him—long past their bedtime.

Just then, the peace of the night was shattered by a terrible blast. The two eldest children grabbed their little brother, dropping to the floor as their father had taught them to do. The woman ran to the door, flung it open and found her husband lying before the steps with his keys in his hand, blood everywhere. She screamed uncontrollably, as the children, rushing up behind her, called out to their mortally wounded father.

Strewn around the fallen man and clutched in his hand were T-shirts that bore the words "Jim Crow Must Go."

Neighbors soon arrived on the scene. Some of them put the wounded man on a mattress and into a station wagon to take him to the hospital.

Other well-meaning friends restrained the victim's wife from going with her husband. It was something she would never get over—that she did not make that last journey with him.

Someone called the victim's physician, Dr A. B. Britton, who rushed to the emergency room.

"When I first came in," he recalled later, "some of them spent a little time trying to prevent me from getting in. This was 1963 and all of the hospital doctors were white males. So, naturally, it was a common reaction to want to know what in the world I, a black man, was doing in there.

"One of the physicians recognized me and said, 'Come on, Doctor, we're trying to get a drip started.'"

As Dr Britton pushed down on the dressing on the wounded man's chest to try to stop the flow of blood, he spoke to him: "This is Dr Britton. Do you know who shot you?"

But all the other man said was, "Oh, Doc, Doc, oh . . . "

Then he expired.

Medgar Evers, civil rights pioneer, husband and father, was dead.

On the other side of town, in a white neighborhood, a nine-year-old boy slept, unaware of the assassination and of how his life would be profoundly affected by it 26 years later.

I was that boy.

Making Headlines

On the morning of October 1, 1989, clad in robe and slippers, I made my way out the front door and picked up the Jackson *Clarion-Ledger*. Back inside, I settled on the couch in the early morning quiet.

My wife, Dixie, wasn't at home. She was gone a lot since taking a job in the *Clarion-Ledger*'s circulation department. That morning it was up

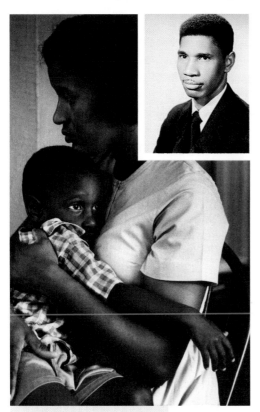

to me to rouse our three kids: Burt, 10, Claire, 6, and Drew, 4. I usually couldn't linger too long reading the paper, but today the front-page headline caught my eye: "State Checked Possible Jurors in Evers Slaying."

The reporter, Jerry Mitchell, who I knew well, had obtained access to some revealing records. These implied the Sovereignty Commission, a government body established in the 1950s to promote racial segregation, had, in 1964, run secret background checks on the jury during the second trial of Byron De La Beckwith for the murder of Medgar Evers.

I had been too young to remember much of those events from my early boyhood. Beckwith, a slight, unprepossessing man in his mid-forties, seemed an unlikely player for so large a drama. But he

Cold comfort—Myrlie Evers holds her son, James Van Dyke, after civil rights leader Medgar Evers (inset) was murdered.

was an unrepentant racist, consumed with his own importance and eager to share his views. On his way to and from court each day, he would smile and joke with reporters, acting more like a movie star than an alleged murderer. I vaguely recalled my parents' friends talking about him during the first trial. Someone said he was guilty, but the state couldn't prove it.

Sure enough, the trial resulted in a hung jury—and so did a subsequent one. Though he'd have another brush with the law, Beckwith was never again tried for the murder. And for the last 25 years, he had openly mocked law enforcement for its futile efforts to pin the crime on him.

I didn't think much about the *Clarion-Ledger*'s article—I was an assistant D.A. for Hinds County, Mississippi, and in the middle of another prosecution. But Tuesday morning, I unfurled the paper and saw that

A family's loss—Myrlie Evers and two of her children, Reena and Darrell, view the body of Medgar Evers at a Jackson funeral home.

Jerry had written a follow-up piece. This one said that Myrlie Evers, widow of the slain civil rights leader, wanted the case reopened.

I went to talk to Ed Peters, my boss. The county D.A. for the past 17 years, Ed was tall, lanky and known for his formidable presence in the courtroom. His southern drawl and pleasant manner have lured many defendants into carefully laid traps during cross-examination.

When I asked him for his response to the article about Myrlie Evers, he was typically direct. Without new evidence, there was no constitutional way to reopen the case.

Made sense to me. After all, it had been 26 years since the Evers murder, and our Mississippi Supreme Court had reversed verdicts in criminal cases prosecuted after delays of only a few years. There was no way we'd be allowed to go to trial again unless there was new and dramatic evidence. The flurry of renewed interest in the Evers murder will just go away, we thought.

We couldn't have been more wrong.

Dream of Justice

To my surprise, public reaction to the articles was immediate and divisive. For our reluctance to rush out and reindict Beckwith, Ed Peters and I were labeled by some as racists. Conversely, I received calls and letters from people who fervently hoped we were not considering reopening the matter. "The case is too old," they said. "It will cost too much money." "It will open

A widow's grief—a tear drops down the face of Myrlie Evers at her husband's memorial service in Jackson.

up an old wound." To this group, Beckwith's guilt was not an issue. I was repeatedly told, "We know he's guilty, everybody knows that, but that's not the point."

As misguided as that feeling was, it was there. After some 25 years of integration, some people couldn't get beyond race and harbored a subterranean rage I could only try to imagine. But if I didn't find a way to deal with it, there was no hope of ever winning over a jury that included people like this.

In the end, Ed asked me to look into the allegations of misconduct concerning the jury. Unfortunately, I couldn't go to the file room and pull out a folder bearing Beckwith's name. Our records went back only as far as 1972.

We had no court minutes, no case files, no crime-scene photos, no exhibits. We had zilch. However, I was able to find out the names of the original jurors and began to set up interviews. Tentatively, I made a beginning.

Part of my effort consisted of sending a letter to Myrlie Evers asking if it would be possible for us to meet in our office and talk about what we planned to do, as well as to receive feedback and information from her. I didn't really believe Mrs Evers would come. But on the morning of December 4, I was in the office pouring coffee when Ed approached me. "Myrlie Evers is coming here in about an hour."

"Today?" I asked, spilling hot coffee over my hand and the floor.

> "Myrlie Evers is coming here in about an hour." I pictured a confrontation and dreaded the prospect.

Great. Just great, I thought. I pictured an in-your-face confrontation and dreaded the prospect. I expected Mrs Evers to hammer us for not going after Beckwith, notwithstanding that we had no evidence.

I felt about the coming meeting much the same way I imagined a condemned prisoner would prepare for a firing squad. All I could think was *Let's get this over with.*

At the appointed time I was summoned to Ed's office and introduced to Myrlie Evers. As we shook hands, her eyes drew my attention. They were haunted and sad, but hopeful.

13

Clearly she was still burdened by the knowledge that, after 26 years, her husband's alleged killer, Byron De La Beckwith, was still free and continued to boast of his freedom to whomever would listen.

Unfortunately, Ed did not have good news for her. The accounts from the jurors we had interviewed fell far short of proving jury tampering or any misconduct. "Mrs Evers, there is no case," Ed told her. "We have no physical evidence from the 1964 trials: no gun, no bullet, no photographs. Lord knows where the witnesses have scattered to, if they are still alive. And there's the problem posed by the constitutional guarantee of a speedy trial. There is nothing speedy about 26 years."

I had expected Myrlie Evers, political activist, to speak. Instead, I heard Myrlie Evers, wife and mother, tell us of her dream that one day justice would be done. That one day the coward who had killed her unarmed husband would be brought to justice.

There was strength in her, but not only in her words. I listened, mesmerized, as she told her story. "I opened the door and saw Medgar lying in a pool of blood, pulling himself across the carport toward the door.

"The children had gotten to the door by that time and were crying, 'Daddy, get up! Get up!'"

She described the events of that dreadful June night, with her children wailing as they watched their father dying, and images of my own children flashed through my mind. Wouldn't anyone want the same thing the Evers family wanted?

I knew that after the murder, Myrlie Evers had refused to succumb to despair. She had taken her kids to California, finished her education, and through hard work had become a commissioner of the public works department in Los Angeles.

Brave spirit—Myrlie Evers refused to let her children (from left) James Van Dyke, Darrell and Reena be destroyed by one man's hatred.

She raised all three children into fine adults. All outward appearances suggested they had not merely survived but had overcome their tragedy.

But what about inside? I sensed the pain in Myrlie Evers's eyes would not recede until justice was done.

After our meeting ended, I saw her to the elevator. She turned, grasped my hand and said, "Mr DeLaughter, please keep me informed."

That night, after I tucked my kids into bed, I sat in the den, lights out except for the warm glow in the fireplace.

I recalled Mrs Evers stating in the police report that when the first shot rang out, her children hit the floor and lay still for a moment, just as their daddy had taught them to do. Baseball, dolls, fishing and cartoons—those are the things that should occupy youngsters' minds, not what to do when gunfire erupts.

I was also thinking about something Mrs Evers had said earlier that day. Mississippi needed justice in this case as much as her family did.

I love my state. My roots run deep here, and I have never planned on living anywhere else. I wanted Mississippi to be known as a place where law-abiding people—no matter what race—live and raise their families in peace and safety. That was the legacy I wanted to leave to my children.

Crucial Clues

I knew that involving myself in this politically hot, divisive case might jeopardize my hoped-for career in public office. I knew, too, that larger issues than my career prospects were at stake if we moved forward.

My mother expressed her apprehension one day when the kids and I were at her house for dinner.

"For your sake and the children's, I would just as soon that nothing comes of this Beckwith thing," Mama said. "There are all kinds of kooks out there, and Beckwith is one of the kookiest."

I promised to be careful.

Dixie also seemed less than happy about my work on the case. Some people had made derisive comments about my involvement with it. I attributed her apparent uneasiness to embarrassment, but in my gut I sensed that there was some deeper reason, though I wasn't sure what.

"There are all kinds of kooks out there," Mama said, "and Beckwith is one of the kookiest." I promised to be careful.

Despite my own and my family's reservations, I knew I couldn't look myself in the mirror if I knowingly let a man get away with murder. So I pressed on. In the process I learned a lot about Medgar Evers.

Back in 1954, when the US Supreme Court ruled that schools could no longer be racially segregated, Evers was working as an insurance salesman in the Mississippi Delta.

A young war veteran and graduate of Alcorn A&M College (where he'd met

Picket arrest—a young Medgar Evers (centre), NAACP field secretary, is arrested outside a Woolworths store in Jackson.

Myrlie), he traveled the Delta back roads, seeing first-hand the desperate living conditions of the black populace. He could never shake those images from his mind or his heart.

Evers's resolve to make a difference only deepened after he was denied admission to law school at the University of Mississippi. In time, he became the first field secretary of the National Association for the Advancement of Colored People (NAACP) in the state.

As the struggle for equal rights intensified, Evers became the point man on the NAACP team—and a lightning rod for segregationists.

Immediately, the family began receiving threatening phone calls, forcing them to get an unlisted number.

Asked once about threats on his life, Evers said he could not be swayed from his fight for racial equality. "If I die, it will be in a good cause. I've been fighting for America just as much as the soldiers in Vietnam. I'm determined [that] we be accepted as human beings with dignity."

By the time of his murder, Evers had become the leading civil rights activist in Mississippi.

The murder weapon—not even Beckwith's fingerprint on the gun (right) could persuade two juries. New evidence was needed.

Bullet proof—a hole in the window of the Evers home was chilling evidence of gunshots.

Reading the Jackson Police Department's report on the case, I knew the officers fully appreciated the political powder keg they were sitting on. If the assassin wasn't caught, it wouldn't be because of a lack of effort on their part. The evidence they had gathered against Beckwith was strong. They found the murder weapon, a 1917 .30-06 Enfield rifle, hidden in a thicket in a semiwooded area near the Evers house. Analysis revealed a fingerprint on its scope.

A young Delta planter named Thorn McIntyre, who saw a picture of the weapon in the local paper, contacted the police. He told them that he had traded a 1917 .30-06 Enfield rifle about three years earlier to a man by the name of "Mr De La Beckwith, Greenwood, Mississippi." According to the police report, McIntyre said that Beckwith "is very radical on this racial problem and he [McIntyre] would not be surprised as to what this man might do."

An employee of a hangout called Joe's Drive-In, which adjoined the area where the gun had been found, told detectives that around 8.30 on the night of the murder, a white Plymouth Valiant had pulled into the parking lot. She remembered it had a long, whiplike aerial on the back. Beckwith had a car like that.

A cab driver named Lee F. Swilley had come forward to say that he and another driver, Hubert Speight, had been parked in front of the bus station the weekend before the killing. A white male walked up to them, asking if they knew where "the Negro Evers lived." He said it was important he find the house in the next couple of days. Neither man could help.

Meanwhile, the FBI crime lab advised police that the bullet recovered from inside the Evers house was a .30-caliber that could have been fired from the Enfield.

Other important evidence was still to come. After Beckwith's arrest, a booklet advertising ammunition was found in his home. Interestingly, some promotional information about the power of .30-06 bullets had been circled. Detectives also picked up Beckwith's white Plymouth Valiant, which had, as described, a long, whiplike aerial.

And most damning of all, once Beckwith was fingerprinted, police determined the print on the scope of the murder weapon matched his.

Valuable as this was, I knew we still were missing other critical evidence.

Fortunately, we got a break a couple of days after Myrlie Evers's visit. It was a call from David Adams, a police photographer. "I want to show you something," he said.

When I got to his office, he flipped the switch to a light box on which he placed an array of negatives. The first showed the front of a ranch-style house bearing the number 2332. The Evers home. As I looked at each of the other frames, the reality sank in. I was viewing the crime-scene photographs from 1963. "Where did you find these?" I asked David.

"In here." He picked up a slide carousel box. "It was in the bottom of that closet over there. The closet hasn't been used in years. I was cleaning it out yesterday."

I was dumbstruck. But an even more dramatic discovery awaited.

As I looked at the frames, the reality sank in. I was viewing the crime-scene photographs from 1963.

In my effort to find relevant documents, I spoke to a man who had been a deputy court clerk in the 1960s. He had no knowledge of where the trial transcripts—which were still missing—would be. He had heard, though, that the judge eventually got custody of the murder weapon. "Back in those days," he said, "it wasn't unusual for things like that to be taken."

I called a grandson of Judge Leon Hendrick, who had presided over the Beckwith trial. As I anticipated, he had never heard Judge Hendrick mention any such rifle. It seemed to be a dead end.

Then one day, shortly after Christmas, I was poring over the evidence we had accumulated when a memory slowly seeped from my subconscious: I had once seen a rifle in the house of my father-in-law, Judge Russel Moore. At the time, I had asked Russel about the gun. It had been part of an old civil rights case was all he would say.

Russel had died the previous year. I called Carolyn Moore, my mother-in-law, told her what was nagging me and asked if I could come over. Before leaving, I jotted down the serial numbers of the rifle and scope.

Carolyn greeted me at the door, and took me upstairs to a bedroom closet where Russel had kept some rifles. "I think there are two or three up there," she said, pointing to a shelf.

Yep, there were several weapons. I pulled down the first two and saw they were nothing like the Beckwith gun. As the third one eased over the edge of the shelf, my heart quickened. It appeared to be an old gun with a scope and a short wooden stock. On the weapon I saw some etchings: "OML 6/12/63."

My hands were shaking as I pulled the paper from my shirt pocket. OML were the initials of O. M. Luke, the detective who had found the weapon 26 years ago. Then I compared the serial numbers. The hair on the back of my neck stood on end. "Carolyn," I said, "this is it."

Things were coming together: the crime-scene photos, the fingerprint comparisons and the murder weapon from my father-in-law's house. It was a trumpet blast to me to have faith and keep pressing ahead with the case.

I passed along news of my find to R. D. "Doc" Thaggard, one of our veteran investigators. "That's good," he said, "but they had that 25 years ago. You better hope you get something else."

Just before going to sleep that night, I read a *Time* article about Beckwith and the reinvestigation. *The whole thing was a joke to him,* I thought. I could picture him at his home in Signal Mountain, Tennessee, having a big laugh about our efforts.

R. D. Thaggard was right: the physical evidence wasn't enough. If we were to get Beckwith, we still needed witnesses: someone who could place him at the crime scene or had heard him admit his guilt.

Chilling Conversations

On May 1, 1990, I received a call from a lawyer friend in town, Jack Ables. Jack was representing Orion Pictures in a defamation suit filed by an alleged Ku Klux Klan member, who was upset with his portrayal in Orion's *Mississippi Burning.* The movie dramatically retold the 1964 murders of three civil rights workers. Jack had spent months reading everything he could find on the case.

One book, *Klandestine: The Untold Story of Delmar Dennis and His Role in the FBI's War Against the Ku Klux Klan* by William H. McIlhany II, was a biography of a Methodist minister, Delmar Dennis, who joined the Klan and soon afterward agreed to become an FBI informant. In time he worked his way up to a trusted position in the organization. "There is one paragraph on page 38 that might interest you," Jack said:

> "Once at a training session, Dennis and other Klansmen allegedly heard Byron De La Beckwith speak. The accused killer of Jackson NAACP official Medgar Evers is reported to have fully admitted his guilt in that crime.
>
> "'Killing that nigger,' Beckwith boasted, 'gave me no more inner discomfort than our wives endure when they give birth to our children . . . So, let's get in there and kill those enemies, including the President, from the top down!'"

After testifying against those involved in the murders of the civil rights workers, things got more difficult for Dennis. He went into seclusion somewhere in Tennessee.

I had just hung up the phone when it rang again. It was Jerry Mitchell, the newspaper reporter. "Folks are beginning to wonder how serious your office is in pursuing the Beckwith case."

I felt trapped. "I can't comment."

"We're trying to help," he continued.

"OK. You want to help? You can help me find a guy named Delmar Dennis."

"Hang on, I've got his number right here."

I nearly dropped the receiver.

I reached Dennis in Sevierville, Tennessee, without trouble, though he quickly let me know that he wanted no part of our case. He was scared to death of Beckwith and the Klan. But after shameless begging on my part, he agreed to meet me if I made the trip to Sevierville. I told him I would leave first thing the next day.

My adrenaline was flowing. This was our first chance to obtain evidence the prosecution did not have in 1964. Suddenly I remembered something else. Tennessee was where Beckwith lived. I located an atlas. I would have to drive right by the town of Signal Mountain on my way to see Dennis.

What did I have to lose? I picked up the phone and dialed directory assistance. The number was listed. When Beckwith answered, my stomach was doing flip-flops. Acting more confident than I felt, I explained who I was.

"Yes, suh, Mr DeLaughter," he replied, "I'm delighted to hear from you. Tell me what's going on down there with all this tomfoolery."

I played along with him.

"Well, Mr Beckwith, we've been backed into a corner on this thing. I don't just want to hear one side of the story. We certainly want to be fair, and would like to come up and visit with you. Would Friday morning at around 10 be OK?"

"That would be fine, but first we need to clear up the preliminaries."

"Preliminaries?"

"Yes, suh. You know I don't allow riffraff up here. I don't let anyone on my property that isn't white Caucasian Christians. Now, you sound white. Are you?"

He grilled me until he was satisfied. I then mentioned that I would have two investigators coming along, and he demanded to know their race and religion as well. Finally, he gave me the directions to his house.

When I arrived home that evening, Dixie was holding the kitchen phone in her hand, covering the mouthpiece, a horrified look on her face. "It's Byron De La Beckwith for you!"

I wasn't alarmed, but I didn't have time to explain everything to Dixie. "Hello," I said into the receiver.

"Mr DeLaughter, I wanted to let you know that you and your investigators are no longer welcome here at my home." His entire demeanor had changed. "My wife and I have talked with our lawyer, and he advises against it."

"Well, Mr Beckwith, we don't have to meet at your home. We can meet anywhere you like."

"I'll tell you what I would be willing to do," he said. "If you wish to come alone and meet me wherever I say, I'll be glad to do that." It was the only time in the conversation that he laughed. I felt a cold chill.

> "Come alone and meet me wherever I say," Beckwith said. It was the only time that he laughed. I felt a cold chill.

I told him I couldn't do that because I would be putting myself in the position of being a possible witness. He hung up with a curt, "Good day, suh."

It was difficult going to sleep that night.

Matters of Trust

On a bright May morning, I drove to interview Delmar Dennis with my two investigators, Charlie Crisco and Benny Bennett. The trip took most of the day. We met Dennis at a restaurant the next morning. He was an imposing figure, at least six foot two and in the 300-pound range.

I asked Dennis where he'd like to talk.

"If you boys don't mind riding for about 20 or 30 minutes, I know a place that will be just right."

"We're all yours," I said. Since Dennis insisted that we follow him in his pickup, we got in our car and drove behind him out of town. Soon a large brown sign greeted us: "Welcome to the Great Smoky Mountains National Park." We started winding our way up one of the mountains. Dennis left the main road, and we followed, encountering less and less traffic, until we had only him in sight.

"Where do you think he's taking us?" Crisco asked between gulps of antacid.

"I got a guess for you," said Benny. "He could be so scared of Beckwith and the Klan that he's leading us into a trap. Hell, the SOBs could be hiding anywhere along here for a perfect ambush. Don't you think it's funny he wouldn't ride with us?"

I was getting a little uneasy myself. Soon the brake lights on Dennis's truck flashed. He killed his engine and got out.

> "I got a guess for you," said Benny. "He could be so scared of Beckwith and the Klan that he's leading us into a trap."

We then followed him on foot along a path. Benny and Crisco, I could tell, were scanning the landscape—for snipers, I supposed. We came to a clearing among the trees and found a place to sit. Then, with our tape recorder running, we listened as Dennis told his story.

"For three years, from '64 through '67, I worked undercover in the White Knights of the Ku Klux Klan of Mississippi for the FBI. I was primarily gathering information that was later used in the trial of Klansmen accused of killing the three civil rights workers in Neshoba County."

Dennis then repeated his account of Beckwith's address before the Klan when he spoke of killing Medgar Evers. Crisco asked, "Did he make it clear he was talking about Evers?"

"Yes. There was no doubt. We all knew. That's why he was invited to speak. He was a Klan hero."

I asked why the FBI never came forward with this information in the Evers murder. Presumably, he said, because they didn't want him to surface until he could testify in the Neshoba case.

How about now? "If we rounded up enough evidence and came to you and said, 'Mr Dennis, will you testify?' would you?"

He was reluctant. "I did that 25 years ago and I have suffered for it ever since."

"He's just an old man," Benny said of Beckwith.

"That old man is probably the most dangerous of anybody I ever knew in the Klan," Dennis retorted.

But he didn't say no outright. Was he telling me he would testify if subpoenaed? Only time would tell.

Crime images—the drive-in from where the killer set out for the Evers home, and Byron De La Beckwith's distinctive white car.

On the ride back, the three of us rarely stopped talking. We still had a lot to do to get Beckwith, but the mood had shifted from "what if" to "when."

The following day was spent returning phone calls and answering letters. Then, around 4.45pm, the reporter Jerry Mitchell called, saying he wanted to see me. When he arrived, he had a large briefcase with him. "I have something here I think you would be interested in."

He opened the case, revealing three large binders. He handed one to me. I flipped it open and read, "State of Mississippi *v.* Byron De La Beckwith, VI, Transcript of First Trial."

I stumbled backward into my chair. "Where in the world did you get this? I've been looking everywhere for it."

"Myrlie Evers."

"What?"

Apparently, Mrs Evers had managed to get hold of the transcript years earlier. But after being disappointed so many times by the legal system, she hesitated to turn it over to Ed and me. She did, however, trust Jerry, and he had decided to share a photocopy of the transcript confidentially with me.

Several months later, I was moved and gratified when Mrs Evers personally gave me the original, which would prove critical at the trial. As she would explain to the *Los Angeles Times*, she deliberately waited till she was satisfied with our efforts.

I understood her caution after all she had been through. I had already begun calling her every Friday, regardless of our progress on the case. As time went on, my calls became more frequent. I knew Mrs Evers and I needed to trust and depend on each other if we were to succeed in bringing Beckwith to justice.

Throughout that spring, Crisco and I pored over the transcript, listing the witnesses and noting the substance of their testimony. Then Crisco renewed his effort to locate everyone, including James Holley and Hollis Creswell. These two men had been police officers in Greenwood, a town 90 miles from Jackson, at the time of the Evers murder.

At the trial they provided Beckwith with an alibi, saying they had seen him about 1am at a gas station in Greenwood, getting fuel. This would have placed Beckwith too far from the crime scene to be considered a likely suspect.

Some of the jurors we interviewed indicated that they didn't believe the cops' testimony, because neither Creswell nor Holley had said anything to the FBI or the Jackson police about the alibi until the actual trial. And Holley later admitted to us that he only did so then because "De La's lawyer contacted us."

How Beckwith's attorney had known to contact these officers who had not publicly come forward with their information was a mystery.

We met with Holley a few days later. Then 61, he had retired from the Greenwood Police Department. We didn't find him a convincing witness. His answers were inconsistent with earlier statements. I was determined to subpoena both officers in any retrial.

As we headed toward a new indictment, media coverage heated up. The local news station, Channel 3, ran a two-part special. The national show "Primetime Live," which had taped interviews with Ed and me, aired a segment on June 14, 1990.

> As we headed toward a new indictment, media coverage heated up. Public response was not all positive.

Public response to the broadcast was not all positive. A woman in Texas wrote a letter to Ed: "I have never seen a more blatent [sic] frame of anyone in my life . . . The same people that killed Kennedy killed Evers, not Beckwith." My secretary told me that the phone lines were buzzing with calls of a similar nature.

When I talked with Mrs Evers shortly after that, she wanted to know if I was feeling pressure from the constant media scrutiny. I said I was, but assured her that I was more determined than ever to see this thing through.

"You remind me a lot of Medgar," she said. "He was so determined to do a good job, especially when things got tough. He was quiet, he was dignified, but he was strong. It was an inner strength. And, Mr DeLaughter, I sense that in you."

If we'd been talking face-to-face I would have given her a great big bear hug. Instead I said, "Mrs Evers, that's one of the nicest things anyone has ever said to me, and it couldn't have come at a better time. Thank you."

A Killer's Boast

Ed and I had two murder trials out of town on changes of venue, so it was September before I was able to return full throttle to the Beckwith case.

Despite steady progress, we were still a long way from having an airtight case, and then—out of the blue—we got a big break.

A woman named Peggy Morgan telephoned and asked to talk with us. So on September 6, Benny, Crisco and I headed south to interview her.

Though now divorced, she had married a man named Lloyd Morgan in 1964. They had moved from place to place around the Delta, settling for a time in Greenwood. At one point, a new neighbor moved into an apartment across the street: Byron De La Beckwith.

Lloyd's brother was serving time, and some Sundays Peggy and her husband drove to the prison to visit him. A few days before one such trip, she recalled, Beckwith asked to join them.

"He told us the guy he was going to see had helped him destroy something. I guess he saw the look on my face, 'cause he then said he had killed a nigger but nobody was ever able to prove it, so we had better keep our mouth shut after this visit."

"Or the same thing would happen to you?"

"He didn't say it, but that was the implication."

All these years later she was still scared. I told Mrs Morgan how appreciative we were and assured her that her information would be strictly confidential until an indictment was returned.

Again, I was out of town that fall when more good news arrived. A woman wrote me to say, "During the summer of 1967, Byron De La Beckwith was introduced to me in a Greenwood restaurant as the man who killed Medgar Evers. If my testimony will be helpful at this late date, I will gladly offer it."

Crisco and I arranged to take a statement from the woman as soon as we returned. Mary Ann Adams, a 47-year-old IRS employee, related that she and a male coworker were seated in the restaurant as Byron De La Beckwith left with some other men. Since members of the group knew Adams's coworker slightly, they stopped at the table to say hello.

"One gentleman said something to the effect, 'Do you know who this is? He's the man who killed that animal Evers.'

"Beckwith was agreeing, you know, nodding his head and smiling, and saying, 'That's right.' He stuck his hand out for me to shake, but I refused. I told him I wouldn't shake the hand of a murderer. He got angry, and we got into a heated exchange. He was so brazen about it. A little man with a big ego."

Testimony like this only deepened my commitment to retry the case. After two and a half more weeks of hard work, Ed Peters and I decided we were ready. We knew we now had more evidence than was found in many contemporary homicides.

On December 14, 1990, we took the case to the grand jurors and asked for a murder indictment against Byron De La Beckwith.

Myrlie Evers waited in my office during their deliberation. After several anxious hours, I got the jurors' answer and hurried to see her. By law, I wasn't allowed to tell her the final vote, until the defendant, if indicted, was taken into custody. Fortunately, words weren't necessary.

All eyes were focused on me as I came into the room. Mrs Evers's gaze was penetrating. I stayed resolutely silent, but a big grin spread across my face, and I opened my arms wide.

"Yes!" she exclaimed, jumping out of her chair.

The vote had been 17 to one in favor of indicting Beckwith—only 12 votes had been needed. The lone holdout was a woman who didn't think the case should be reprosecuted after so much time.

As Mrs Evers and I embraced, I felt her weeping.

"Oh, Bobby," she said, "I can't believe it. We've come such a long, long way."

"Yes, we have, Mrs Evers, but we've got a long way yet to go."

"Well, then, let's get the SOB."

"My pleasure, ma'am."

Hoax or Threat?

Byron De La Beckwith was arrested on December 17. A month later I got a phone message from his wife, Thelma. My receptionist had transcribed it: "You and Ed ruined their family's holiday, and you will be punished for this."

Worse was to come. I should have seen the signs, but I didn't. After 17 years my marriage disintegrated. Dixie moved in with her mother, and on February 11, she agreed to an order awarding temporary custody of our three children to me. I agreed to a no-fault divorce.

The next few months were hard on all of us, but gradually we settled into a routine. One night the kids and I arrived home after one of my son Burt's Little League games.

While he undressed to shower, the younger kids, Claire and Drew, climbed into bed. I sat down to take off my sneakers and noticed the message light flashing on the bedside answering machine.

"I'm nearby watching," began the male voice on the machine. I jerked up and stared at it. What the hell? "I wouldn't miss this for anything. I hope you don't. You see, there's a bomb in your house. It's set to go off at 10 o'clock. Ha! Ha! Ha!"

> "I'm nearby watching," began the male voice on the answering machine. "I wouldn't miss this for anything . . . You see, there's a bomb in your house."

The clock was steadily ticking on a nearby shelf. Seven minutes before 10. My mind raced. A hoax or a serious threat? Whatever the reality, my heart was screaming, "You can't take a chance, get out!"

I jumped up, barefoot, and sprinted through the house. I burst into the bathroom and told Burt to pull his pants on and run to the truck.

Claire and Drew were up by then, wanting to know what was wrong. I picked up Drew with one arm and grabbed Claire with the other hand. "Nothing's wrong, sweetie, we're just seeing how fast we can make it to Granny's house.

"It's a drill," I added, my gut wrenching at the thought of being watched as the message had said.

Was there a bomb, or was the call a ruse to flush us out, like a covey of quail from their brush, only to gun us down? We made it to the truck, no shots. Well down the street, I slowed and listened. It was straight-up 10 o'clock, but no explosion came.

Once at my parents' house, I sent the kids to bed. My father was already asleep, and in hushed whispers I related the message left for me to my mother.

"Have you called the police?"

"No. It was a hoax, Mama."

"This time."

"If I call the police or tell anybody about this, the media is going to get wind of it. That'll only give the idea to other crackpots."

The kids spent the night there, and I returned home. I searched our property thoroughly. The house was intact, the neighborhood quiet.

It was a hoax, but nonetheless I felt violated, angry and afraid for my family. Was I making the right decision about not reporting it?

I said more than one prayer that night, and from then on, I kept my Smith & Wesson .38 close by.

To See His Father's Face

Not long afterward I met world-renowned forensic pathologist Dr Michael Baden at a Mississippi Prosecutors' Association conference. My boss, Ed Peters, was a long-time friend of Baden's, and after the conference the subject of the Evers case arose. Ed and I explained to Baden some of the problems caused by the passage of time.

Baden suggested an exhumation and second autopsy. "You don't have the bullet," he explained, "but a high-caliber rifle like a .30-06 frequently leaves a starburst pattern of fragments from the bullet if it hits bone." These, he said, could be recovered. "Also, since you don't have photos or X-rays from the first autopsy, you will be able to get pictures."

Ed secured a court order for the exhumation, and Dr Baden and I both talked to Myrlie Evers. After her initial shock, she gave her consent, but added a condition.

Her 31-year-old son, Van, the youngest of the children, had no recollection of his father. His only memories were those passed along by his mother and older siblings, Darrell and Reena. He insisted on being present when the casket was opened. It was, in his mind, his only chance to cast his eyes on his father.

"But, Mrs Evers," I pleaded, "after 28 years this probably isn't the image of his dad he needs to have burned into his memory."

"Bobby, oh, how I know that," she replied. "And I've said as much to him, but he's so like Medgar. He's not giving an inch, and this is his call to make."

The autopsy would take place at Albany Medical Center in New York. Crisco and I would attend. Dr Baden had spoken to Van Evers and agreed to a compromise. Van would not be on hand when the casket was first opened.

Once the condition of the body was known, Dr Baden would telephone him at his hotel in downtown Albany. Van would then make the final decision on whether to come in, but I suspected he already knew he would.

The moment arrived. As Dr Baden opened the casket lid, a collective gasp sounded through the room. The body was in pristine condition. Medgar Evers looked as if he had just been placed in the coffin. His son was called. He said he would head in immediately.

While we waited for Van, Dr Baden explained that the perfect condition of the body might be explained by several factors, such as skillful embalming or the 12-foot depth of the grave that had kept moisture from the body.

"I'm a man of science, and that's the scientific explanation," he said. "Beyond that, all I can say is . . ." He paused a moment. "Are you a religious man, Bobby?"

I nodded. "Then you can appreciate the unscientific explanation."

Indeed I did.

Excited chatter was quelled as Van entered the room. The youngest child of Medgar Evers edged up to the coffin and looked on the visage that death had withheld from him for all these years.

I watched as he reached out and just for a moment gently stroked his father's hair.

By the end of the five-hour autopsy we had X-rays showing the starburst pattern of the lead fragments left by the bullet. We also had a vial of these fragments, which Baden had meticulously removed.

Just as important were the photographs of Medgar Evers. A homicide victim must be humanized for the jury. The photos taken that day filled the void. The jurors would see the face of the man, the face that his assassin had refused to see.

I had promised to call Myrlie Evers, so I telephoned her from Dr Baden's office. "It was a remarkable day," I told her. "It was an emotional risk for you, I know, but it paid off."

"Bobby, I spoke with Van this afternoon, and this has been so good for him," she told me. "It's like Medgar was saying, 'This is the final thing that I can give you: myself. Now take it and go do justice for me, my family, and the Mississippi I dreamed of.'"

> "This is the final thing that I can give you: myself. Now take it and go do justice for me, my family, and the Mississippi I dreamed of."

Yet after all Myrlie Evers had been through, this strong woman would now have to draw on additional reserves of fortitude and endurance as our journey to trial was agonizingly slow. Three years of legal delay ensued as we fought off legal challenges from Beckwith's attorneys.

During this time, my personal life took a turn for the better. I met Peggy Lloyd at a local hospital where she worked as an emergency-room nurse. My daughter, Claire, had suffered a head injury at the school gym. Treating her, Peggy got my immediate attention. She was gentle, caring and humorous. I learned that she was divorced and had three teenage sons.

Our relationship blossomed, and we were married in 1993. God sent me a companion and a soul mate when I needed one most.

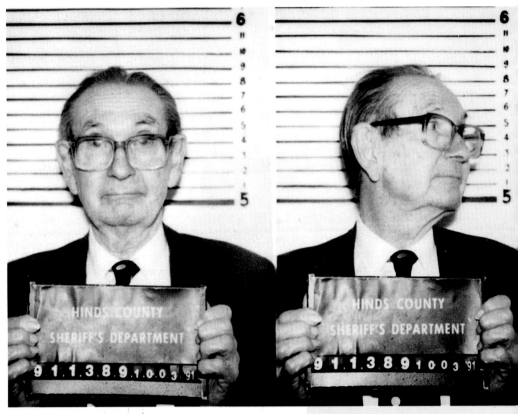

Hidden evil—to some, Beckwith appeared to be just a harmless old man, but others believed him to be the most dangerous Ku Klux Klansman of all.

Over the next difficult months, Peggy bolstered me with her unwavering support. She was there with me when the defense's legal maneuvers were at last exhausted, and the trial opened on January 27, 1994.

Finally, after 28 years, the Mississippi justice system would once more be put to the test.

Startling Testimony

Although we were sharing duties in the trial, Ed Peters trusted me to prepare and present our case. The responsibility weighed heavily on me. A hung jury in 1994 would be as much a defeat for Mississippi as an outright acquittal.

Beckwith seemed confident as ever of the outcome. Each day he came to court smiling to the crowds and chatting freely with the reporters. His cockiness only made me more determined to prove our case.

One by one, we called our witnesses. Myrlie Evers was the first. She told about meeting her husband in college, about his efforts on behalf of the NAACP, about the night of his death. The jury was visibly moved by her testimony.

During a recess on the second day, my office gave Crisco a message slip with the name of Mark Reiley and an out-of-state phone number on it. I told Crisco to check it out.

Reiley, a 36-year-old air-traffic controller in Chicago, had recognized Beckwith through television news coverage of the trial. It turned out the young man was yet another witness to Beckwith's "bragging" confession to murder. Ed OK'd bringing Reiley to Jackson, and put him on the stand on February 1.

Reiley testified that he had last seen Beckwith at Long Hospital in Baton Rouge, Louisiana, in late 1979. At the time, Reiley was a guard at Angola State Penitentiary and his job was seeing to inmates sent to the prison ward of the hospital.

Beckwith was then serving a five-year jail term (which was later vacated) after being arrested, in the early 1970s, while transporting a bomb in his car from Jackson to New Orleans. His alleged target was the home of Adolph Botnick, regional head of the Anti-Defamation League.

Over the next several weeks, while Beckwith was a patient in the hospital, a close relationship developed between the young guard and the older inmate, Reiley said.

"He knew I was lacking a father-type figure, and he seemed like he would be willing to fill that role."

Beckwith openly discussed his beliefs with him. "He explained to me that just as you might have to kill a deer or catch a fish for food, because that was their place, the blacks were there to sow the field and take care of the earth for the chosen people, so if they got out of line, you should kill them and not in any way feel guilty about it."

One time, Reiley recalled, Beckwith summoned a nurse. When a black nurse's aide responded, Beckwith told her to "get a white person."

Naturally the comment angered the woman, and they were soon yelling at each other. "He was screaming 'If I could get rid of an uppity nigger like Evers, I would have no problem with a no-account nigger like you.'"

It was startling testimony, and the defense was unable to shake it.

On February 4, 1994, I delivered the summation. I had waited more than four years for this moment, and I was ready.

First, I reviewed the prosecution's case: the reports of witnesses and the physical evidence that connected Beckwith to the crime.

It was "his gun, his scope, his fingerprint, his car, and lastly, but not least, his mouth" that confirmed his guilt, I told the jury. "When he thought he had beaten the system 30 years ago, he couldn't keep his mouth shut with people he thought were going to be impressed by him.

"And so not only do we have his car, his gun, his scope, his fingerprint, his mouth, we've got his own venom, which has come back to poison him.

"And why did any of this happen? For what reason was Medgar Evers assassinated? For wanting to be called by name, instead of *boy*. To go to a restaurant, to go to a department store, to vote, and for his children to get a decent education in a decent school; for wanting some degree of equality for himself, his family, and his fellow man, and for them to be accepted as human beings with some dignity.

"When that kind of murder happens, ladies and gentlemen, no matter who the victim, no matter what his race, there is a gaping wound laid open on society as a whole.

"Is it ever too late to do the right thing? For the sake of justice and the hope of us as a civilized society, I pray that it's not."

Jury deliberation began at noon. After five hours they had yet to reach a decision, and the judge sent them to their hotel.

Unlike in some other parts of the country, our juries rarely deliberate more than a few hours. *What in the world could be hanging them up?* I wondered. I felt alone, worn out in every sense of the word.

I reached the D.A.'s office a few minutes after nine the next morning, expecting a long day. But at 9.35, the phone rang.

They had a verdict.

Everything, for a few seconds, stopped: my heart, my breath and time itself. The verdict had to be "not guilty." If the jurors were unable to unanimously convict by the end of the previous day, I reasoned, it would take longer than 35 minutes this morning for the majority to change the minds of any holdouts.

We quickly assembled in court, and at 10.15 the jury filed in. My palms were sweating and my insides convulsing.

"The clerk will read the verdict," Judge L. Breland Hilburn said. I closed my eyes.

"We, the jury, find the defendant guilty, as charged."

There was a brief outburst from the audience. A stern look from the judge restored silence, but as deputies relayed the verdict outside, jubilant cheers and thunderous applause erupted in the packed hallways.

Judge Hilburn continued. "Will the defendant please rise and come forward for sentencing?"

Gone was Beckwith's smirk as he was sentenced to life imprisonment.

Dream fulfilled—as Myrlie Evers addressed the media after the trial, the pain that Bobby DeLaughter once saw in her eyes had finally lifted.

After a brief meeting with the press, Ed and I returned to our office. There I met the one person I wanted to see most: Myrlie Evers. She wore the biggest smile I had ever seen.

Tears streaked her cheeks, but her eyes were no longer sad and haunted. She swept me up in her arms in a warm hug, and I could feel her shaking with emotion. "Thank you, Bobby. Thank you so much for me, my family and for Medgar. He can rest in peace now."

Bobby DeLaughter is currently a county judge in Hinds County, Mississippi.

Byron De La Beckwith appealed the verdict, and the case went all the way to the Mississippi Supreme Court. In 1997 the court issued a statement, applauding the "voices, both present and past, who showed the courage and will to state the truth . . . Their voices cannot be ignored. We affirm the finding of the jury that Byron De La Beckwith murdered Medgar Evers on the night of June 12, 1963."

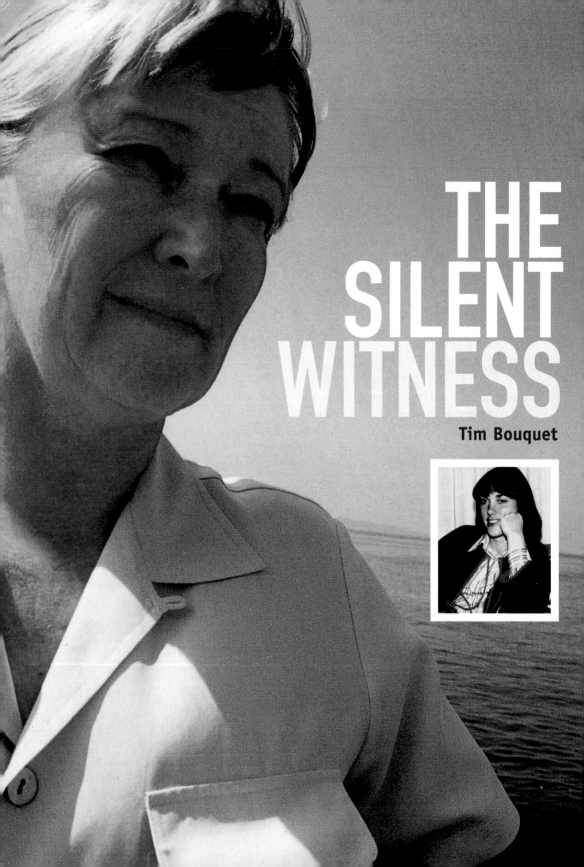

THE
SILENT
WITNESS

Tim Bouquet

Could the work of two courageous and determined women—one a brilliant British scientist, the other a relentless cop—find the vital evidence to end a 15-year-hunt for a murderer? The scientist, Dr Helena Greenwood (pictured inset opposite), was the victim, and Laura Heilig (opposite) the Californian detective who never gave up in her quest to bring an evil man to justice.

Helena Greenwood made sure the two cats were in and that all the doors were locked. Although it was still only April, it had been warm enough to put the mosquito screens over the windows of the single-storey wood and stucco home on Walnut Avenue in Atherton, California, about an hour's drive south of San Francisco.

As the young scientist made her way to the bedroom she glanced at the calendar. Only a couple of days to go and her husband would be back from his business trip. Helena couldn't wait to see him.

It was a Saturday evening and, as usual, she had had a tough week at Syva, a market leader in the medical diagnostics business, where she worked in international marketing. Around 10pm she put aside her book, turned out her bedside lamp and snuggled down for the night. Twenty minutes later she was woken by a shape in the half-light. Her brown eyes shot open. The shape was dark and tall and it filled her bedroom doorway.

The figure took a silent step forward. Its right hand was holding a torch. In its left hand, Helena could see the gun. Instinctively, she rose to her knees and pulled the bedclothes tightly round her.

"Take your clothes off!"

Terrified, Helena removed her T-shirt and briefs. Thinking fast, she tried to pacify the man with the offer of money. He followed her to the study where she tipped the contents of her handbag onto the floor. "Anything I have, you can have," Helena told him. But all she could find was 75 cents.

"Go back to the bedroom," the man commanded.

There he told her to switch on the light and sit down on her bed. His head was completely hooded, revealing only his eyes. He approached and placed both hands on her shoulders.

She managed to struggle upright.

"No!" she shouted, pushing him away. "I can't go through with this! I don't want to do this."

He pushed her back. She felt the power in his arms. "Don't get awkward or I'll have to get my gun out again," he said as she backed closer to the bed.

"Come on now," he said, shoving her down towards her pillows. "I'm as afraid as you are." Helena stared in horror as the man unzipped his jeans.

Sergeant Steve Chaput of Atherton Police Department, who was leading the investigation into the attack, had Helena Greenwood go through her story one more time. It was now April 9, 1984, two days after it had happened.

Even though she'd never seen her assailant's face, Helena reckoned he was aged between 22 and 28. She was tall at five foot ten but he had still towered over her. She estimated him at around six foot three, more than 14 stone and of an athletic build.

Daddy's girl—Helena on holiday as a baby with her father Sydney Greenwood.

"What colour were his eyes?" Chaput asked.

"Dark, piercing, I can't be sure what colour. The skin around his right eye was very smooth. It had no wrinkles."

"Anything else you noticed?"

"He had quite an educated voice," Greenwood continued. "He didn't use slang."

She paused, suddenly remembering something else. "Oh—his underclothes were perfumed."

Greenwood was clearly shaken but Chaput was moved by her bravery. In his experience, most women did not even report a sex crime, let alone relive it in front of a detective. She'd even had the presence of mind to look round the house when she returned to collect some clothes the day after the attack.

Outside the kitchen window there was an upturned crate on which the man must have stood to remove the mosquito netting before climbing in. Not far away on the garden decking she spotted her favourite teapot. Usually it sat on the windowsill. Realizing she must not touch it, she had called the police immediately.

Chaput now had the fingerprint the attacker had left on the teapot. It did not match with anyone on police records, but he stayed upbeat.

"When we catch this man, will you take the stand and give evidence?" he asked Helena.

He feared she'd back off.

"Yes," she said without a flicker.

Family days—Helena's boyfriend Roger spends time with her parents. Inset: relaxing away from the lab.

A Smart and Lovely Girl

When Helena Greenwood was a student she asked her father Sydney, "Do you often worry about what's going to happen next?"

"How do you mean?"

"Maybe this country's time has passed and the future's in America?"

Sydney, a scholarly and creative man, was head of Design and Fine Art at Southampton College of Art. He and his wife Marjorie, a teacher, had brought up their daughter to have an enquiring mind. They knew an only child could be a lonely child, so they made sure Helena's childhood, in and around the New Forest in the 1950s, involved meeting people and mixing widely through sea scouts, drama groups and art classes.

She took to leadership from an early age. As a 14-year-old she was always first to take the tiller during sailing races off Portland Bill. She also looked after the other children while encouraging them to give their best.

Helena did well at school, excelling at sciences. It was now the 1960s and while her contemporaries were fashioning flower power and protest, Helena took A levels, then worked white-coated in a local hospital pathology lab. She longed to follow in the footsteps of Francis Crick, James Watson and Maurice Wilkins, men bold enough to look beyond their fields and unlock the secret of life, discovering the double helix of DNA in 1953.

After taking a biochemistry degree at Sheffield, Helena married a man she had met while in the sixth form. Roger Franklin was dashing, clever and obsessed with boats and the outdoor life. He had soon fallen in love with this accomplished girl with the mane of dark hair and

Wedding day—Helena and Roger looked forward to an exciting future together.

infectious laugh. They moved to London in 1972. Roger took a town-planning job on the construction of the Thames Barrier and Helena enrolled to study her PhD at St Bartholomew's Hospital's medical school, which was part of the University of London.

There she worked on the development of an immunoassay, a technology that helped determine the effective dose of a drug.

In 1976, at the age of 27, Helena became Dr Greenwood. Her supervisor Professor John Landon describes her as one of the best PhD graduates he's ever had. "Not only was she very bright, with great drive and determination, she was very sociable and popular, and worked extremely well with others."

Helena recognized not just the academic and humanitarian benefits of medical research but also the commercial possibilities. Why shouldn't scientists profit from their medical advances by taking them from the lab to the market?

It was this thinking that led her to take a research and development job with Syva in Palo Alto, near San Francisco.

The hours were long and the demands unrelenting. Helena was often in a hurry, her expensive clothes just that little bit beyond the fashionably crumpled. During this period, Roger completed a master's degree in landscape architecture.

After two years, Helena started a new job in the international marketing department. She flew round the world finding out from doctors and scientists the kind of diagnostic products they needed to detect and treat disease. Being a scientist, she spoke their language. Being a natural networker, she convinced the medics to buy Syva products. Even when Syva lost 50 per cent of its share of the US market to a rival company, Helena managed to maintain its leading slice of the international market.

Helena's sights, though, were on a new technology that, if commercially applied, held the promise of saving lives in just three letters: DNA.

"Daddy," she told Sydney excitedly in one of her frequent letters home, "this is going to change the world. And one day there will be genetic databases which will help police prove guilt and innocence."

At the time her father had no idea what she was going on about. "I was just proud that we had produced such a smart and lovely girl."

Looking for a Break

Eleven months on, Steve Chaput still had no leads on what looked like a one-off, random crime. He was leafing through bulletins from the California Law Enforcement Information System when a report from a neighbouring police district caught his eye.

A man had been arrested for masturbating outside the bedroom window of a 13-year-old girl. He was also wanted for prowling, indecent exposure and attempted sexual assault in the homes of other young women.

Significantly, the suspect, now out on bail, had worn a hood or sweatshirt pulled down over his head so only his eyes were visible.

This might be my guy! Chaput hoped as he sent the print from Helena's teapot to the crime lab. It matched the suspect's perfectly.

Chaput sent the fingerprint to the crime lab. It matched the suspect's perfectly.

A year to the day after Helena's attack, Chaput knocked on the door of a flat in an upmarket apartment and sports complex in San Mateo, in the Bay Area of San Francisco.

"David Paul Frediani?"

"That's me," said the tall, fit, olive-skinned man.

"We need to talk."

David Frediani, it emerged, was a 30-year-old financial controller for a property management company. He had a degree in accounting and administration from Eastern New Mexico University. Sporty, but with few friends, he made good money and lived with his common-law wife Audrey. He also cruised bars and had had a string of girlfriends.

"Are you familiar with Atherton?" Steve Chaput asked him.

Frediani's breathing quickened and he seemed to be "pumped up".

"I know where it is, but I'm not familiar with it." He said that his company's vice-president lived there.

"Have you ever sexually assaulted a female in a house in Atherton?"

"No."

"You see," Chaput continued, "we've had a serious sexual assault case in Atherton. The attacker came through the kitchen window, but before he could do that he had to move a teapot off the sill. He left a fingerprint on that teapot. And, Mr Frediani, that print is yours."

Chaput watched the breath vanish from Frediani. "It was as though I'd slugged him," he later said. Chaput had also obtained a serology analysis from sperm on Helena's pillow. Its donor was blood group O, the same as Frediani's. Pre-DNA analysis, this was as good as it got.

By now Helena and Roger had moved 500 miles to San Diego, where in 1984 three young, entrepreneurial scientists had set up a company called Gen-Probe, to pioneer a special DNA probe that could diagnose infectious diseases quickly and accurately.

But who could help them crack that conservative nut, the American medical research establishment? Helena Greenwood was the obvious choice. Aged just 35, she jumped at the chance to be vice-president of this exciting new company. She went to work with characteristic zeal and won the doctors over. Gen-Probe became so successful that a cluster of high-rise mirror-glass buildings sprouted from the rugged canyon landscape around San Diego. Now home to more than 200 biotech companies, it became known as "Biotech Eden".

"She didn't lose sight of the outside world," says Sam Morishima, who worked with Helena at Syva and was recruited by her to work at Gen-Probe. "She knew that most people using test kits in labs were women, yet the kits were bulky and cumbersome. Without compromising the science, Helena had us make smaller, lighter kits. She wanted to make a DNA test as simple as it could be."

Helena also went to many meetings with other companies to develop another of her dreams, DNA forensic testing.

She and Roger enjoyed an idyllic life, skiing in California's Yosemite National Park or hiking up the mountains of the High Sierra. At the house they rented above the coastal town of Del Mar, Helena hung some of her father's accomplished landscapes and held parties for a growing band of friends and colleagues.

Sydney and Marjorie visited frequently. They had never seen their daughter happier.

Then, one evening in April 1985, the phone rang. Roger took the call. When he returned Helena saw the worry on his face.

"It's Sergeant Chaput," he said, taking her hand. "They've arrested a man. You have to give evidence in three weeks' time."

Alone on the Stand

For more than an hour, defence attorney Craig Collins relentlessly cross-examined Helena at the preliminary hearing to determine whether David Frediani should stand trial. At every turn Collins tried to show that Helena's description of her attacker did not fit his client. He worked through a list of physical characteristics, from skin tone to the colour of his pubic hair, and even suggested the glass of beer she'd had that evening "might have had an impact on your power of perception".

Her emotions finally broke the surface when she blurted: "I was not trying to make an identification of the person, I was trying to survive!"

Frediani sat impassively throughout. His eyes met hers just once, when she asked him to stand up so she could confirm he was of the same height and build as her assailant.

The suspect—David Frediani's fingerprint matched the smudge left on Helena's teapot.

Helena's testimony, combined with the scientific and fingerprint evidence, was enough to convince the judge that Frediani should stand trial for sexual assault and carrying a gun. A date was fixed for September 1985, when Helena would be called again to give evidence.

But Helena put the trial to the back of her mind when, in late May, she rushed to England to nurse her mother through the final stages of leukaemia. A few days after the funeral in a small, tranquil New Forest churchyard, Sydney, now 72, flew back to California with Helena. Both in shock, neither had much to say, but they found comfort in the quiet closeness between them.

Only two months earlier Helena and Roger had moved into another rented house in Del Mar. Home was now a flat-roofed, single-storey house in 23rd Street, a cul-de-sac just a block and a half from the Pacific Ocean. Even though it was close to surfing paradise, Helena did not much like the house. The railway line ran right beside it, forming a barrier. A six-foot-high fence of split bamboo surrounded their patio, which was further shadowed by dense trees. But it would suit until she and Roger could move into the home they had agreed to buy.

Sydney didn't like the house either. Several times as he went out for a walk while Helena was at work, he sensed he was being watched. Once, he sneaked round the back in the hope of catching someone. There was no one there but it made him nervous.

As he packed to return to England at the end of July 1985, he said to his daughter, "I'm worried about this trial. Are you sure you don't want me to be there?"

Helena hugged him. "Don't worry Daddy. You'll see me again soon."

Shocking news

The sun was already streaming through the windows as Helena and Roger got up at 6.15am as usual on August 22. They breakfasted together, then Helena dressed quickly in a light blue linen skirt and jacket over a black blouse.

Just before 8am, she and Roger walked arm in arm through the garden and out to his car, where she kissed him before he drove to work. Fixing the security latch on the six-and-a-half-foot-high garden gates, the only entrance into the property, Helena went back indoors to make a few calls before going into the office.

It was early afternoon when Helena's secretary came into Sam Morishima's office. "Do you know where Helena is?" she asked him. "She's missed one meeting and now she's late for another."

Morishima had never known Helena miss any meeting, let alone two. Maybe she was ill. But he had been at a barbecue at her house only the night before to welcome a new member of staff and she had been fine then. They had talked excitedly about the future: Helena believed Gen-Probe now had the team to make it a world leader.

"Have you called her home?" Sam asked the secretary.

"There's no answer."

"If she doesn't turn up in five minutes, give Roger a call at his work."

At 1.30pm Roger Franklin ran from his office in San Clemente, 45 minutes north of Del Mar, jumped into his car and drove home as fast as he could. He was terrified that Helena had been in a traffic accident. When he saw her sports car sitting outside he let out a sigh of relief.

The garden gates wouldn't open. Roger pushed harder but he couldn't budge them.

"Helena!" he shouted out. *Maybe she's had an accident in the house.* "Helena!"

Finding something to stand on, he shinned up the fence and peered over the top. Six feet beneath him he could see his wife. She was sprawled on her back with her head to one side. The contents of her handbag were strewn around her, her shoes were off and her papers were blowing around the deck.

She must have taken ill and passed out, Roger thought, dropping to the ground. Kneeling beside her he saw that her face and neck were black and blue. He touched her hair. It was matted with blood and dirt.

He ran indoors to the phone.

"Nine-one-one emergency."

"Yes, this is an emergency, please. My name is Roger Franklin."

"What's the problem, sir?"

"Uh, my wife's been attacked. She's lying in the garden. I think she's even been killed."

"Can you repeat that, sir?" The line crackled and hissed.

"I think that my wife has been murdered."

Roger Franklin never heard the paramedics demolish part of the fence to get in. He was kneeling by Helena, gently brushing the ants from her swollen lips.

Crime scene—an officer notes details of the garden deck where Helena lies dead.

A Stolen Life

His wife had been beaten and strangled. Judging by the blood on her clothes and the welts and lacerations on her head, neck and body, she had put up a desperate fight. But Helena had not been robbed or sexually assaulted. Nor had the house been burgled.

Roger called Sydney at his house in Lymington, a small, pretty town overlooking the Isle of Wight.

"I failed to protect her, I've failed you," he told Helena's father. Sydney didn't blame Franklin. He just did not know what to say. They were two men devastated and alone. Eventually he spoke: "We both loved her so much."

Up in northern California, Sergeant Chaput was also in shock. It was barely three weeks before Helena was due back in court to give evidence. Now there was no victim, how could there be a trial?

"Do you think Roger did it?" one of the San Diego homicide detectives asked him.

"I think that's very unlikely," replied Chaput. "He loved her. I'd lay my money on David Frediani."

Detectives had discovered that Frediani, who was on extended leave from work pending his trial, had been in southern California in the week of

Helena's murder. Telling both the girl he was seeing and Audrey, who had recently delivered him twin sons, that he needed a holiday, Frediani said he was taking off for Lake Tahoe, a mountain resort 170 miles from San Francisco.

Instead, he drove his white BMW some 340 miles south to Los Angeles, where on August 15 he was involved in a car crash. Asked why he had changed plans, he said: "I suddenly realized there was nothing in Tahoe for me to go to."

Returning to San Diego three months after the murder, Sydney Greenwood found the investigation bogged down, so much so that Gen-Probe had hired its own private investigators. They found a neighbour of Frediani's who claimed to have seen Frediani after August 22 with heavy scratches on his face and neck. But the car smash, the scratches and the credit card billing in southern California were not enough to place David Frediani in Helena Greenwood's garden the morning she was murdered.

"Why can't you use this new DNA test?" Sydney pleaded to detectives, hoping the science that had so excited his daughter might hold the key to her death. No chance, they said. In 1985 forensic DNA testing of tissue and body fluids was still in its infancy. Samples had to be much bigger than anything found on Helena's body. The courts would not accept it.

For a father whose only daughter had returned home in a metal box in the hold of an aircraft, and who had buried her ashes next to his recently departed wife, this was almost more than Sydney could bear.

He and Roger walked up 23rd Street, knocking on every one of the nine doors. As each opened he said: "I am Sydney Greenwood, Helena's father. Can you remember seeing anything the day she died?" Nobody did, although the next-door neighbour, who had been getting ready for work at about 8.45, "heard a sound I'll never forget. It was like a muted scream." By the time he'd dressed and rushed out to the street the scream had stopped and there was nobody around.

Sydney was convinced Helena's killer made his getaway along the railway track and jumped on the next train.

Sydney was convinced Helena's killer made his getaway along the railway track and jumped on the next train out of Del Mar station half a mile away. Reluctantly he realized that there was little chance of anyone being charged. One of the detectives told him: "I am very sorry Mr Greenwood, but I think you have to try to get on with your life."

Sydney went back to England, alone with his grief. He remembered a day when Helena was six years old and she, Sydney and Marjorie had walked hand in hand along a pier. Helena was clutching her favourite rag doll. Sydney had painted its face and Marjorie had made the clothes. Suddenly the wind gusted and Helena dropped the doll into the water. A boatman rescued it, but when the doll was handed back to her Helena screamed. The water had washed its face away.

For a long time, Helena had once admitted, she had a fear that she too would be washed away.

Rescued from the Archives

It was April 1998 and Deputy Sheriff Laura Heilig of the San Diego homicide detail slid open a metal filing cabinet in her cluttered office. She took out three bulky, brown folders marked "Helena Greenwood Deceased".

Heilig, a 49-year-old veteran of more than 100 murder investigations, had displayed a rare persistence and talent for tracking down killers who for years thought they'd got away with it.

She was now in charge of the archive section—a grim collection of 300 unsolved murders dating back to 1934.

The softly spoken detective, a shade over five feet, with warm eyes and her blonde hair pulled back in a ponytail, was no ordinary investigator. For a start, her grandsons thought a granny who went to work with handcuffs and a gun was a big deal. She also had a notice on her desk reading: "I can do all things through Christ who strengthens me".

Laura came late to crime. When the husband she'd put through college walked out on her and their two teenage children, Laura, a high-school dropout, had to earn more money to bring up her family.

She became an offset printer, a ditch digger and a welder. But the work was seasonal and there were no benefits. Her sister suggested police work: it carried a regular salary and a pension.

She got into the police academy and joined the sheriff's department at the age of 32, quite happy to spend the rest of her life driving a patrol car. By chance she got involved in a major body-dumping case and from then solving deaths became her life.

Heilig had heard about the Greenwood case in the late 1980s. She knew Roger Franklin had moved back to northern California, where he'd eventually remarried and had two children. Sydney Greenwood had gone back to his painting and a solitary life in England.

David Frediani did stand trial for sexually assaulting Helena. Twice the prosecutors, who used her preliminary-hearing testimony, won convictions. Twice he appealed the verdict and won. Just before a third trial he entered a plea bargain of no contest. This allowed him to accept the charges without

New to the case—the softly spoken Laura Heilig stands outside Helena's house, 13 years after the unsolved murder.

admitting guilt. Where once he faced 11 years, he was sentenced to six, but was out in three.

In 1990 he'd taken a masters business degree and was now working as a financial analyst for Pacific Bell in San Francisco and living with a girlfriend in the comfortable commuter suburb of Burlingame.

A neighbour, whose children called Frediani "Uncle Paul", commented, "If my plumbing broke he'd be under the sink for eight hours fixing it. That's just the kind of guy he is."

Opening Up the Past

Thirteen years after her murder Helena was still sprawled out on the garden deck, frozen in the crime-scene photos now littering Laura Heilig's desk. Every angle was shown and not a single detail of her body and her belongings was missed. Gruesome autopsy pictures emphasized the severe beating she had taken before being strangled.

As she read the old notes it was clear to Heilig that Frediani had every motive for killing Helena. Told by his company he could have his job back if acquitted and with a pregnant girlfriend it was in his interests to stay out of jail. His initial defence to detectives—"I was really drunk when I did those things"—wasn't going to save him in court against Greenwood's testimony. On leave of absence, he had the time and opportunity to silence the prosecution's key witness, believing that if there was no victim there could be no trial.

Maybe Helena can still help us to put him in jail, thought Heilig as she walked towards the police property store where all of Helena's belongings were stored in boxes. *Maybe a silenced witness is not so silent after all.*

"Cases don't affect me until I get the suspect," Laura Heilig often said. "It's when all the pieces are in place and the guy's in jail that I have a hard time emotionally." But going through the clothes Helena wore the day she died was strangely haunting. The shoes, the ripped tights, the belt she never had time to put on, a stud ripped from an ear in her struggle to live.

Evidence revisited—would the contents of Helena's bag reveal any fresh clues?

Heilig hoped the contents of Helena's handbag might hold clues, so she sent off lipsticks, a powder compact and any other metal or plastic items for vacuum metal deposition, a process that, even after all this time, could find fingerprints. The suspect might have touched these during the struggle.

The results were negative.

Then Heilig came across two envelopes, sealed for 13 years. She opened one of them and inside was another, and inside that was another. Finally she came to a clear plastic box. It contained the fingernails clipped at autopsy from Helena's right hand.

The other package produced an identical box, this time containing the nails from Helena's left hand, cut so that bloodstains on them could be tested for blood type. There was something else: a toothpick and what looked like a tiny wood-shaving, no bigger than two pinheads. This and the debris that had been scraped, using the pick, from under Helena's fingernails before they were cut.

Even though not enough blood had been found to test, all the samples had been packaged and kept. Heilig was amazed. Had someone had a hunch that technology would catch up one day?

The very technology Helena had been working to develop could now analyse the tiniest scraps of human DNA and identify an individual's unique genetic make-up. In one case, Laura had found a cigarette butt in a beer can which had been sitting in the property stores since 1980. The DNA still on it had led her directly to a killer.

In January 1999 she sent Helena's fingernails and the scrapings to the Serological Research Institute (SERI) in Richmond, California, hoping that DNA testing might yield a clue to the killer. She also needed a genetic profile for Helena to compare with any DNA found on the nails. A dozen of Helena's hairs, with roots, had been removed at autopsy. Heilig also sent these to SERI, along with a bloodstained swatch from Helena's jacket.

She feared that, after all this time, any DNA might be too degraded to get any meaningful result. DNA is a long, linear molecule, like spaghetti. If you threw spaghetti against a wall, some of it would break into smaller pieces. Over time DNA behaves in much the same way.

But Heilig was in luck. Five of Helena's hair roots carried sufficient DNA for testing. Now armed with Helena's own genetic profile, forensic DNA analyst Gary Harmor at SERI could test the bloodstained wood-shaving. The blood was Helena's alone.

Harmor now tested the fingernails from her right hand. There was evidence of a "small amount of someone else's DNA mixed with Helena's", but not enough to be significant. He moved to the left hand. The box contained four nails given evidence numbers GH 4 #6 to #9. Clipping number 4 #6 again had a small amount of DNA similar to Greenwood's profile. Nail 4 #7 also indicated "someone else being present . . . but the results are too weak".

Harmor moved on to item GH4 #10, the debris scraped from under the nails on Helena's left hand. It had the consistency of skin and was the colour of dried blood. Was it tissue with blood on it, or just dirt?

On September 20, 1999, Laura Heilig got an answer. "The nail debris found on the left hand was Helena's flesh stained with blood," said Gary Harmor. "The blood is not hers."

Heilig felt a surge of triumph. Was GH 4 #10 going to be the smoking gun she needed? She contacted the Department of Justice upstate in

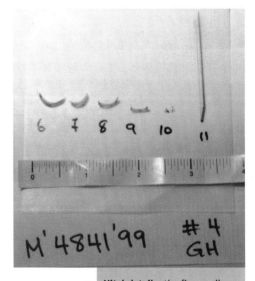

Vital detail—the fingernail scrapings, GH4 #10, from Helena's left hand.

Berkeley, which carries blood samples of all registered sex offenders. It agreed to send David Frediani's to a lab in Maryland for DNA analysis. This avoided accusations from the defence lawyer that samples from victim and suspect could have been contaminated and so were unreliable evidence.

The Waiting Game

Laura's team was beginning to get frustrated at the slow progress on the tests. "Laura, it's about your sample," said Mary Buglio, a police forensic scientist at the homicide detail, as she went into Heilig's office. It was November 9 and Buglio had just put the phone down on the labs testing Frediani's blood and Helena's fingernail scrapings. The normally bubbly Buglio looked glum.

"Now what?" said Heilig.

"It's a match," her colleague grinned. "It's a match!"

The six genetic markers in Frediani's blood matched those on the scrapings taken from Helena's left hand. From beyond the grave Dr Greenwood was trapping her killer.

But Laura still had reservations. "What are the chances of it not being him?" she wanted to know.

"Around one in 800," said Buglio.

"We need bigger numbers," said Heilig. The chances of the killer being anyone other than David Frediani had to be so low that no jury could fail to convict him. She could not get those pictures of Helena out of her head. *This man must not be allowed to do this to anyone else.*

Heilig decided to try something else. A new DNA test called STR—Short Tandem Repeat analysis—could not only provide 10 additional genetic markers to the six they already had, but could break down each one in far greater detail. Armed with a more detailed genetic profile from Frediani's blood sample, Gary Harmor tested the DNA from the fingernail scrapings again.

Once more the tiny debris from Helena's left hand did not let Laura down. "How many people on this earth share the same profile?" she asked Harmor when he had completed the second test.

"It's about one person in every 2.3 quadrillion." That's 23, then 14 zeros.

"Wonderful numbers," grinned Heilig as she filed a request for David Frediani's arrest warrant.

A Reason to Live

Sydney Greenwood didn't recognize the voice he heard on the other end of the telephone. It was female and American.

"My name is Detective Laura Heilig and I am about to arrest the man who murdered Helena." There was a pause. She sensed his shock.

To Sydney Greenwood, now 87, a door had suddenly opened to a place he no longer wished to enter. He suddenly felt his daughter near him, almost close enough to touch. On the living-room wall of his sparsely furnished house was a portrait he had painted of her as a teenager in blue dungarees.

Then his curiosity got the better of him. "How did you catch him?" Heilig told him all about the DNA testing. "She would have been fascinated," said Sydney with pride. "She knew DNA was the future. Helena believed science contained the answer to every mystery." Sydney was now in full flow, happy to talk about his daughter. "You know that this man previously broke into her house and robbed her?"

A father's love—Sydney Greenwood was devastated by his daughter's death.

He doesn't know, Laura realized. *Helena had kept the sexual assault a secret from her father.*

Sydney told Laura that Roger Franklin had died just months previously of pancreatic cancer. He himself had cancer of the prostate. His breathing came in short, sharp bursts. "Helena's awful death was like ripples on a pond. They spread outwards and ruin the lives of so many people."

In spite of a grim medical prognosis, Sydney remained fiercely independent. He was still driving his car to go shopping and refusing all offers of institutional care. Now Heilig's call had given him a renewed grip on life. He vowed he would survive to see her killer face justice. After that he would be free to join her.

"I can't thank you enough," Sydney said to Laura, then added quizzically. "A lady murder detective you say? Who would have thought it?"

That Sunday, Laura went as usual to the rural community church near her home with Robert, her second husband. There she prayed that Sydney Greenwood would live to see Frediani jailed.

At Christmas she sent Sydney a card. "You are in my prayers," she wrote. Out of the blue a parcel arrived from England. Sydney had sent one of his pictures, a watercolour of fishing boats in a Cornish village.

"It's where we used to spend our holidays when Helena was a child," he told her.

"It's a conspiracy . . ."

David Frediani emerged from the lift into the underground car park beneath his apartment complex and walked towards his black Lexus. He was wearing a dark business suit. The previous evening he had attended the black-tie opening performance of *The Nutcracker* by the San Francisco Ballet. It was now 8am.

"Mr Frediani?" A small woman who barely came up to his chest barred his path.

"Yes."

"I'm Detective Heilig of the Sheriff's Department. I have a warrant for your arrest."

He had nowhere to run. She had six men with her. Frediani stared at each one of them in turn. He started when he saw Steve Chaput. Hoping that one day Frediani would have a case to answer, the sergeant had kept all the evidence from the assault case and had turned it over to Heilig.

"What's all this about?" Frediani asked Heilig.

"Turn around and I'll tell you," she said, snapping cuffs on his wrists.

"I am arresting you for the murder of Helena Greenwood."

Detective Laura Heilig watched all the colour drain from Frediani's face.

Frediani didn't say one word. Nothing. He just stared straight ahead. Heilig watched all the colour drain from his face. "You got the wrong guy. I didn't do it," he insisted.

Heilig fed him a line, hoping to wrong-foot him. "Maybe it happened this way," she suggested. "You came to talk to Helena to say, 'Hey, I can't have this thing going to court, it's going to ruin my name, it's going to cost me my job,' and she attacks *you*. Maybe you're the victim, you panicked . . ."

"I didn't do it!"

Heilig confronted him with the DNA match-up. "We found your DNA on her body."

He stared coldly at Heilig. "It's a big conspiracy. Back in '84 and '85 the cops were after me and now you're still after me."

Building a Picture

After the arrest, Heilig drove out to Del Mar. She was joined at Helena's house by Rod Englert, a top forensic consultant. If Heilig could get this case to court she wanted the jury to know exactly how Helena had died—that she was a real person, not just an archive statistic.

"Please would you kneel down," Englert asked her as they stood by the gates where Roger Franklin had found his wife's body.

Grievous wounds—Heilig was sure that the killer had smashed Helena's head against the latch, causing her blood to spatter the gates (left).

Nobody had come up with the weapon that had inflicted two deep cuts on the back of Helena's head. One measured about an inch and a half, the other was a quarter of an inch long.

Heilig placed the back of her head so it was level with the protruding metal latch four feet off the ground. The dimensions of the latch matched exactly the wounds on Helena's head. Helena's tights had been ripped at the knees and her flesh bruised and cut. Englert had detected bloody patterns on the shoulders of Helena's jacket where her killer had grabbed her. He must have forced her down to the decking, where he smashed her head against the latch while he strangled her.

But the varying velocity shapes of the blood spatters on the gates—which Englert had studied in the police photographs and observed on her clothes—showed Helena had also bled while standing up.

With Heilig taking the part of Helena and David Decker, the original investigating officer, posing as the killer, Heilig now produced a bizarre mime under Englert's direction.

"She was up, she was down, and she lost," said Englert. "The evidence here indicates that she resisted very, very violently."

Each time Helena had tried to stand up she would have found it more difficult as her strength ebbed. At one point she had trodden in her own blood and left a footprint on one of her papers.

It probably took about ten minutes for Helena Greenwood to die. For six minutes, until the blood left her brain and she began to lose consciousness and her sight, she must have been staring into the eyes of her killer.

He had left a calling card too. "The position she was found in is not consistent with strangling," Englert told Heilig. Laura remembered vividly one picture of Helena—flat on her back, her skirt pushed up to her waist to reveal her underwear and her legs parted as wide as they could go, knees bent and feet touching, in a frog-like position.

Under powerful lighting Englert had shown Heilig two faint but distinct bloody handprints on the ankles of Helena's tights.

"She's been posed?" Heilig asked. "The final insult."

Judgement Day

"Can you identify the man you arrested?" asked the prosecutor.

"That man, sitting at the end of the table," said Laura Heilig, pointing to David Frediani, who was sitting at the front of the small, crowded courtroom.

It was January 2001 and Frediani had spent most of his trial to date gazing nonchalantly ahead at the insignia above the judge's bench.

Now he turned and stared straight at the detective who had hunted him down. Their eyes met. Heilig felt herself shiver. She glanced at a figure in a light blue linen skirt and blazer over a black blouse—a shop mannequin dressed in the clothes Helena Greenwood wore the day she died.

Deputy district attorney Valerie Summers was prosecuting. The raven-haired 39-year-old lawyer had done her usual impressive job preparing the case. She had 10 boxes of documents, photo-boards and charts. With Laura Heilig she had rounded up 25 strong witnesses: DNA experts, forensic scientists, crime-scene paramedics, several of Helena's former colleagues and a building contractor who was able to testify that Frediani

Legal and true—Deputy D.A. Valerie Summers backed Frediani into a corner.

had leant on him for a fake alibi to get him off the 1984 sexual assault charge.

But it was the science that took centre stage. Summers was thorough and to the point. She explained the intricacies of DNA to the largely female jury in everyday words anyone could understand.

As Rod Englert used stage blood to show how different kinds of blood-spatter patterns were caused, he pointed out to them that strangulation was the most intimate kind of murder, the raw hatred of the killer passing through his hands to the victim's neck.

At every turn over the two-week trial Summers reminded the jury that, even though the murder had happened in 1985, Helena Greenwood was a real person whose blameless life was ripped away. By now she would have been 51. Colleagues such as Tom Adams reckoned that she would have become the head of her own biotech company. She would also have been a millionaire on the value of her Gen-Probe shares alone: the company she helped put on the map was sold in 1989 for $110 million.

Laura Heilig's thoughts seldom left Sydney back in England. From regular phone calls with him she knew it was touch and go whether he would survive to hear a verdict.

Suddenly David Frediani opted to give evidence. Laura was thrilled. It gave Valerie Summers the chance to show the world the kind of man he was.

Summers was determined to force Frediani to admit in public for the first time what happened when he broke into Helena Greenwood's house in 1984, an event which would lead to her death.

"Mr Frediani, on April 7, 1984, did you break into Dr Greenwood's house and force her to orally copulate you?"

Backs straightened, ears perked up. The defendant was being put under pressure—a flat-footed boxer trapped in the corner of a ring.

His parents flinched.

"I said I pled no contest to that charge."

"That's not an answer to my question, sir," Summers snapped. "Did you force Dr Helena Greenwood to orally copulate you?"

"Isn't saying 'no contest' an admission of guilt?" returned Frediani.

Summers asked the question again. Frediani turned in his seat and faced towards the jury.

"For the purposes of these proceedings, I will admit guilt so we can get past this, 'cos this has nothing to do with the murder."

Summers pressed him once more. He declined a straight answer. "I'm accepting responsibility, what do you want from me?"

"I want the truth. The truth is that you forced Dr Helena Greenwood to orally copulate you. Isn't that true?"

"Yes. That is true."

Laura Heilig felt her eyes start to moisten.

Summers summed up for the jury. "You can see him in there," she said, holding high a picture of the nails that had been clipped from Helena's left hand. "You can see the dirt and blood."

Laura Heilig dialled a familiar number. Sydney Greenwood, now barely conscious and unable to speak, was too ill to come to the telephone, explained a neighbour who was nursing him.

"Please tell him that Helena's killer has been found guilty. He will never, ever get out of prison. And please," she added, "tell Sydney that he is still in my prayers."

Shortly afterwards Sydney Greenwood opened his eyes and, for a moment, he seemed to be alert. As Laura Heilig's message was relayed to him, he nodded his head. He understood.

Eleven hours later he died.

As Laura Heilig drove home to her family, one thought went through her mind. *Thank you for helping us give Sydney the only gift he craved.*

TO SAVE
AND TO
HEAL

David Moller

Attractive, petite and blonde, Gabriella Mazzali had arrived in Australia to start a new life. Trained as a nurse in London, and while still only 24 years old, she had beaten a thousand others to secure a job as a community nurse. But the dream turned into a living nightmare. Then, when she was desperately ill, a complete stranger reached out to help her.

E arly on the morning of February 4, 1998, 27-year-old Gabriella Mazzali was admitted to Sydney's Concord Hospital as little more than a pitiful, blackened, open wound. With burns to over 90 per cent of her body, only her face, head, the palms of her hands and some areas of her stomach had escaped serious injury. Each of her vital functions—heart, lungs, kidneys—took it in turns to fail, before being coaxed back into action by the intensive care team of doctors and nurses. Then, after battling desperately for several days to save her life, Dr Peter Haertsch informed Gabriella's mother and stepfather, Sandra and Terry Cooling, summoned from their home in Britain, that it looked as if doctors were losing the struggle.

An attractive, petite, honey blonde, Gabriella had arrived in Australia just over two years earlier. She had trained as a nurse at the Royal Free Hospital in London and, while still only 24, had beaten the competition of about a thousand others to secure a job as a community nurse. Australia seemed to offer everything she wanted in life. She had her own car and a one-bedroom flat not far from her work. She luxuriated in Sydney's sunny, temperate climate. There were picnics on the beach with her friends almost throughout the year.

She was with her friends at a party on Sydney's harbourside on St Patrick's Day in March 1997 when she got talking to a total stranger. An expat like herself, Stephen Rae had been in the country about the same length of time—teaching English to migrants. Chunkily built and not handsome in the conventional sense, he had an easy charm and wry wit.

Originally, the 32-year-old had come from Crieff, in Scotland, but, widely travelled like

In happier times—Gabriella and Stephen Rae shared much in common before they fell apart.

Gabriella, he had also taught in Taiwan for four years. Neither of them had any family in Australia. They seemed to have a lot in common. Before the evening was out, the two exchanged telephone numbers. A week later they began going out together.

But there were problems with the relationship. As time went on, Stephen became controlling, critical of Gabriella's friends and her appearance. Whenever she tried to speak of some form of long-term commitment, he would change the subject.

Convinced that the relationship was going nowhere, Gabriella decided to end it for good in January 1998, after an earlier failed reconciliation. She had the locks changed in her apartment, but Rae refused to leave her alone. He telephoned seven or eight times a day and began appearing in the pubs and restaurants where she was meeting friends. Just after midnight on February 4, 1998, Gabriella was jolted awake by a pounding on her door, then the splintering of wood. Suddenly, Rae was in her flat and he was holding a two-litre milk carton—with some liquid inside it. The smell was unmistakable—petrol. But before Gabriella could run from the room, the liquid was on her.

Frantic, she fled the flat, screaming for help. Rae was right behind her. A neighbour, Steve Swain, alerted by Gabriella's screams, rushed out and attempted to grab Rae in a bear hug.

Gabriella heard a noise like thunder and she was engulfed by flames.

Too late. Even as the two men struggled, Rae wrested a lighter from his pocket. A click. Another click. Gabriella heard a noise like thunder and she was engulfed by flames. She teetered at the head of a flight of stairs. If she threw herself down the stairs perhaps that would douse the flames, end the pain, end everything. She landed at the bottom in a crumpled heap, still smouldering.

The wail of an ambulance siren soon pierced the suffocating night air. Gabriella's only bit of good luck at that moment was to be near one of the world's top burns units—at Concord—the very hospital at which she was based. In the hospital's second-floor intensive care unit, she was quickly intubated and put on a ventilator to keep her lungs working. Intravenous lines were inserted to administer sedation and painkillers, and to make up for the fluid loss suffered by her body.

Doctors made long scalpel cuts—escharotomies—along the length of her arms and legs, round her neck, chest and waist to make sure that, with the contraction of burnt tissue, the blood supply was not cut off to her extremities or any other part of her body. As Dr Peter Kennedy, who would have overall responsibility for Gabriella, observed the pitiful, blackened figure, just two things gave him hope. Her face and the palms of her hands were relatively unscathed. *At least there would be some quality of life. She would have a reasonable appearance. There would be some things that she could do for herself—if she survived.*

The normal rough calculation was to add the percentage of burns to the victim's age: 100 was considered about the upper limit for survival. Gabriella's rating: 117.

For over a week, her resuscitation seesawed perilously up and down. The doctors' major concern soon became the removal of burnt tissue. As long as this tissue remained on the victim, it would be releasing more toxins into her body and there was thus the constant risk of multiple organ failure. The surgeons were not able to débride all the blackened flesh in one fell swoop, for the simple reason that Gabriella had minimal donor sites left to provide grafts for the open wound areas from which the burnt skin had been taken.

In the past, major burns had been covered temporarily by grafts from blood

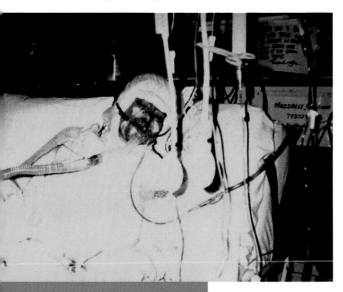

relatives or even cadaver skin. But even if there were no problems with infection, such grafts tended to be rejected within three or four weeks. With burns of this extent, Kennedy and Dr Peter Haertsch, a plastic surgeon who would be taking the lead in much of the grafting and reconstructive surgery on Gabriella, realized that some infinitely more radical solution would be needed if she were to survive.

Expensive treatment—surgeons sought government permission to use groundbreaking techniques to treat Gabriella's severe burns.

Synthetic Grafts

By good fortune, just days before Gabriella's injuries, the two doctors had sought permission from Australia's Therapeutic Goods Administration (TGA) for the use of a new synthetic skin pioneered in the United States: TransCyte. Its enormous advantage—being seeded with deep-frozen human fibroblasts (cells collected from babies' foreskins)—was that it could produce the wound-healing and tissue growth factors Gabriella needed. It was, however, costly: some $2,350 for two sheets about the size of a standard greeting card.

Within hours of Gabriella's admission, the doctors had got back to the TGA for the specific permission needed for its first clinical use in Australia. Within a few more hours, a batch of the crucial product was on its way to Sydney by air.

In their first operation—10 days after Gabriella's admission—the surgeons removed nearly 40 per cent of the damaged skin from both legs and part of her back. After removing the blackened tissue down to the fat or exposed muscle, they attached the two-millimetre-thick sheets of TransCyte, whose outer silicon layer was like a thickened film of cellophane.

This would stay on until Gabriella had grown a fresh supply of skin on her scalp—from which grafts had also been taken. The operation lasted one and a half hours. Then Gabriella was returned to intensive care.

For Gabriella, the nightmare was unending. She would often dream that Rae was still coming to get her. She could hear his voice. "I've come to kill you. I've come to kill you."

With the intubation tube in her throat, she couldn't speak or cry out. With her arms splinted out in a medical crucifixion to stretch the skin and prevent later contractures from the burnt or grafted areas, she couldn't summon help with a buzzer or bell.

She was swathed in bandages—soaked with the blood and serous fluid that continually leached from her tortured body. She could convey terror or pain only with her eyes. Gabriella was no longer in danger from Stephen Rae, however. He was in a coma in a different hospital. After the assault, he had stumbled off into the night and 45 minutes later presented himself at Ashfield police station.

"I have done a very bad crime," he had blurted out before collapsing from the effects of smoke inhalation. He had sustained 10 per cent burns to his arms, right leg and throat.

In operation after operation, Haertsch and Kennedy worked swiftly to remove more of Gabriella's burnt skin and cover the fresh wound with either the TransCyte synthetic skin or with grafts from her scalp.

"We're not going to be able to take that many more grafts from her head," warned Haertsch. Each time her scalp was harvested from its regrown outer epidermis of skin, they were forced to take a minuscule amount from the crucial lower dermis. This has the blood supply vital in temperature control and the epithelial elements that are responsible for the durability of the skin and that are able to help heal a cut or ulcer.

Problems abounded. Grafts refused to take. Infections set in. Her airway occluded—and she had to be rushed back into intensive care. When she contracted pneumonia, it became agonizing to breathe. Again her life hung in the balance.

One evening in early March, a month after her admission, she was moved to a room with another patient. "You'll be able to hear from him how to get better," a nurse pointed out. A young man who had suffered serious burns was to be her new room-mate. But the next day his condition suddenly deteriorated. He suffered a cardiac arrest and died soon after.

At home in Wingham—Donna Carson's youngest son, Bodean, was only a toddler when she suffered her own tragedy.

A heavy pall descended. *Could it happen to me?* Gabriella wondered. *Could I too just slip away in the night?* At times, she wished she would. It seemed the only conceivable escape from the draining, gnawing pain.

Towards the middle of March, she was back in intensive care with septicaemia from an infection in her left leg. It was possible that she could lose it. Gabriella passed her 28th birthday, on March 18, in a feverish state.

Helping Hand

Some days before, out of the blue, Gabriella had received a card from a stranger, a woman named Donna Carson. The card said: "Dear Gabriella, thinking of you and wishing you the strength to continue on. You are one brave lady. Keep your chin up. You're very special."

In all of Australia there were probably few better exemplars of the strength of the human spirit than Donna Carson. A slim, red-haired, 41-year-old mother of two, she had been through much of what Gabriella had been through—and in many ways, far more. Living in Wingham, New South Wales, some 320 kilometres north of Sydney, she had read only the sparse details of Gabriella's case in *The Daily Telegraph*—but knew then that Gabriella was someone she could help.

For Donna too had been grievously burnt by a former boyfriend—by someone she'd once loved and trusted, and with whom she had wanted to share part of her life. But within a matter of horrifying minutes she had lost her health, her looks, her career, her home. With 65 per cent body burns, she had endured 19 operations, and spent five and a half months in Sydney's Westmead Hospital. She had been down that long, draining road that stretched ahead of Gabriella but, if Gabriella wished, Donna believed that she could help spare her some of its trauma and anguish.

Within a matter of horrifying minutes Donna had lost her health, her looks, her career, her home.

Sandra Cooling, Gabriella's mother, responded to Donna's card, and then heard from Donna that she would be in Sydney in mid-March. Would they like to see her? Sandra grabbed at the opportunity. She was at about her lowest ebb. By then, Gabriella had been through six major operations. Sandra wanted to ask Donna questions about Gabriella's condition—and future prospects.

For four hours, Sandra poured out her heart to Donna in a small waiting room at Concord Hospital, asking questions no one else seemed to have the time or ability to answer.

"Very often the medics simply don't know the answers," Donna pointed out. "It's a new field. It's only in the last few years they have been able to save such major burns victims." In a breathy, husky voice that was a legacy of burns injuries to her airway and lungs, Donna calmly answered all the questions Sandra put to her.

A week after they met, Donna received another letter from Sandra, pleading with her to come back to Sydney. "Gabriella asks for you and desperately wants to see you," Sandra wrote.

On Sunday, March 22, Donna made her way to the seventh floor of Concord Hospital. All that she could see of Gabriella were the tips of her fingers and toes and a small part of her face. Eventually, Gabriella stirred. "How do I make the pain stop?" Donna told her that she couldn't. Tears formed in Gabriella's eyes. "I thought that you would be able to make the pain go away." Despite her own experience, Donna was unprepared for the utter helplessness she now felt at another being's suffering. For an hour and a half, she sat at Gabriella's side. Occasionally, she touched the skin beside Gabriella's nostrils—the place where she herself had once been soothed. "You've got such beautiful eyes. Such lovely, long lashes," she said.

Gabriella's blue-green eyes glistened with tears. "You're doing so well, Gabriella," Donna added. "The worst is going to be over soon. It won't be much longer." In fact, Donna knew only too well that there would be several more months of surgery, of horrendous daily changing of dressings, of tense moments between patients and staff who could do practically nothing without inflicting more pain.

Tough Regimen

Hours after Gabriella's arrival at Concord, senior burns physiotherapist Frank Li, a lithe, 37-year-old from Hong Kong, had started administering the passive percussion exercises needed to keep her lungs working—to move any phlegm to the main airway where it could be aspirated out. Li and his team manipulated her hands, feet and limbs to prevent the build-up of calcium deposits that could fuse the joints if she remained immobile too long. But none of this engendered any love between burns victims and physios—known as the torturers.

Above all, it was crucial to stretch the newly grafted skin. Arms had to be splinted out at night to prevent the contractures that could leave the body in some grotesque, incapacitating distortion. As time went on, the contractures often seemed worse.

Gabriella would often cry out, "I can't do that. I'm just not ready for that yet."

"Just go with the flow, Gabriella. Go with the flow," nurses would advise her as they rubbed her fragile, aching body down with moisturizing cream. Whenever Gabriella had at last found a relatively pain-free position in bed, a nurse would arrive to turn her so that her lungs would be kept free of phlegm and to prevent her developing pressure sores.

Donna was now Gabriella's model. On her second and later visits, Gabriella watched closely as Donna walked about the room and moved her arms. She marvelled at the fact that she could wear high heels, that she could reach up to a high shelf. She touched her skin to see what it felt like. She bombarded her with questions. Could she squat down? Donna said she could. "Show me." Could she reach behind her back? "Let me see."

Donna was now Gabriella's role model. If Donna could do something, one day, Gabriella would too.

Notwithstanding the highly experienced cajoling of nurses and physiotherapists, they had never suffered serious burns. Donna had. If Donna could do something, Gabriella became determined that one day she would too.

As well as giving physical encouragement, Donna was determined to nourish Gabriella's soul—to bring something of the outside world into the grey monochrome of hospital. Knowing how much Gabriella had enjoyed the sea,

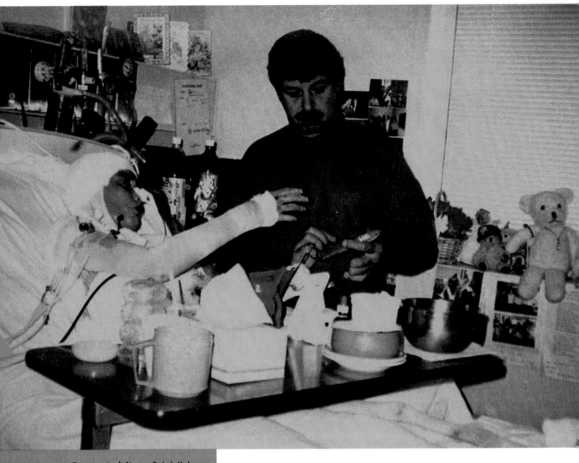

Frequent visitor—Gabriella's stepfather, Terry Cooling, was often at her bedside at the Burns Unit in Concord Hospital.

she brought a poster for her room showing the sun setting on a beach with palm trees.

She got her six-year-old son, Bodean, to do drawings for her. She sent frequent cards from her own short trips to the nearby towns of Taree and Coffs Harbour. Donna wrote of going out on a boat, and the sound of the boat as it plied through the water—the feel of the wind on her body and the effect of the sun as it shone down on the sea. "These simple things are just going to blow you away when you get out of hospital," she wrote. She sent a pretty hat for Gabriella to wear until her hair grew back.

To Gabriella, the Concord burns unit regimen continued to seem robustly brutalistic. Although it would have taken nurses no more than 10 minutes to feed Gabriella breakfast, the meal was now dumped down just about within her reach. This forced her to lean over, somehow open the little packets of cereal, haltingly lift a cup, guide a spoon from the bowl to her mouth—and over the course of an hour make the most fearful mess.

But Gabriella was beginning to understand what the system was all about. Her yells of anguish at what a physio was doing would alternate with a brave, "Do what you have to do. Just do what you have to do." There was still real horror to come: the tilt table. This was the contraption on which Gabriella was for the first time to be gradually brought upright. It had a ledge for feet. But after weeks of being horizontal, the pain of blood flowing into the legs and feet was excruciating—despite the painkilling medication. It would take several sessions before nurses could at last manhandle her onto her feet.

Donna always noticed and commented on whatever progress had been made. "You are sitting up now. The last time I saw you, you weren't able to do that." She hadn't been a primary school teacher for nothing. She encouraged Sandra to take photos of Gabriella at each visit, to stress the changes that were taking place. She drew attention to the fact that Gabriella had been able to ease her feet into slip-on shoes months earlier than she had.

Voice of Experience

In addition to this running support, Donna was also now advising Gabriella and her family on the legal aspects of their case. Her advice was based on the fruits of her own bitter experience. At her first meeting with Gabriella's mother and stepfather, she had urged them to get photographs taken of Gabriella and her injuries immediately.

"I know it's a long way ahead, but the person who did this to Gabby may not be facing trial for another year or more. By then, she will be walking and talking. Her hair will have grown back. She will be looking completely different." At that point, it would be that much easier for defence counsel to argue that the defendant hadn't really intended what had happened, that it was all an unfortunate mishap. "But look at your daughter in there now. That's what the court needs to see." Sandra and Terry Cooling seemed nonplussed. They assumed the police or hospital or someone would have taken photos. Donna quickly disabused them. They should take photographs—even video film—immediately. "There's plenty of sympathy for you and Gabriella now. But don't ever assume that that is going to translate into effective action within the judicial system." As Donna got to know Gabriella better, she told her more of her own story and problems—many of them ongoing. In her early thirties, she had been an attractive and highly effective teacher at Orana Heights primary school in Dubbo, some 400 kilometres north-west of Sydney. Her private life, however, was slowly deteriorating.

Donna felt she received little support from her husband and was left to teach, shop, cook, clean and bring up two boys on her own. She also learned to mow lawns, chop wood, put up shelves and do electrical repairs. After 14 years of marriage, Donna decided she'd be better off alone.

After she and her husband split, she was on her own for a year. Then friends across the road from her single-storey home in Geurie, near Dubbo, introduced her to Garry Clynes.

Quiet, wiry, strong, Clynes helped his brother run a nearby farm. Though 12 years younger than 36-year-old Donna, he seemed reliable and industrious and got on well with her two boys: 12-year-old Coe and Bodean, then a two-and-a-half-year-old toddler. Eventually, Garry moved in with her in early 1994 and for a couple of months all seemed well. Soon, however, Donna knew the relationship was not going to work out. It was just a question of choosing the best time to tell him.

April 1, 1994, was Good Friday and the day after Donna's 37th birthday. It was a warm autumn evening, and she was in the garden, barefoot, in jeans and a light blouse, before going in to prepare dinner.

In the dusk, she noticed Garry siphoning petrol from her car into a four-litre container. When she asked what he was doing, she heard that the petrol was going into another car that she knew was not fit to be driven. As Donna remonstrated with him, she suddenly found herself being pushed so violently that she was bouncing off the brick sidewall of her bungalow home.

Then the petrol was on her. She rubbed her face to clear her eyes. When she could open her eyes again, she couldn't believe what she was seeing: Garry holding a lighter up about 30 centimetres away from her face. She could hear a click, click.

Instantly, she was on fire and began to run and then to roll on the ground. Alerted by her screams, a neighbour, Trevor Dunn, quickly scrambled over the fence to help hose her down. Coe dashed into the house to call the emergency services. Donna was flown by helicopter to Westmead Hospital. In an unguarded moment, a member of the medical staff murmured to Donna's mother, "In some ways, it might be more humane if she dies. You'll never take your daughter home."

Defiantly, her mother responded, "You don't know our Donna."

But there were worse shocks in store for Donna—at the hands of the judicial system. Indeed, one of the reasons why she was so keen to help Gabriella was because of the treatment she herself had received. To Donna, it seemed an eternity before the police investigation got under way. Her fragile health meant it was nine months before she was able to make a full statement to the police and charges were finally laid.

Terror of Garry Clynes, and his family and associates, had driven her from Geurie to a new home in Wingham. So it was only by chance that an old Geurie friend sent her a clipping from the Dubbo *Daily Liberal*. Garry Clynes had pleaded guilty to negligently inflicting grievous bodily harm.

Donna couldn't believe her eyes. Immediately, she telephoned the office of the Director of Public Prosecutions (DPP). How come the original charge—specifying maliciously—had been changed to negligently? she demanded. "That's what he's pleaded guilty to, and that's what we accepted," a DPP lawyer told her.

An attempt on her life had now been reduced to an act of negligence——an accident.

Donna was so appalled that she drove the 580 kilometres from Wingham to Dubbo to speak with the DPP lawyers in charge of her case. There, she confronted a DPP solicitor who denied the suggestion that there had been a plea bargain in the case. He informed her that photos and a letter she had submitted were legally irrelevant.

Donna was horrified to realize the courts would not be interested in knowing her as a person. An attempt on her life had now been reduced to an act of negligence—an accident. Maximum jail sentence: two years.

Donna was now picking up on how the system worked. As a victim—one of the small people—she was an inconvenience, someone to be kept well away from court. The important thing seemed to be to keep the system running smoothly: neat pleas, quick sentences, efficiency for judges and lawyers.

Had she really come back from the grave, her face practically burnt off, her life wrecked, to be treated like this—for her would-be murderer to face, oh, two years in jail? Worse was to come: the solicitor told her the sentencing judge would have a number of options, ranging from jail, a fine or simply a good behaviour bond.

Donna was aghast. The man, still out on bail, might yet escape jail. "I want the judge to see me," Donna said. "I want him to look into my eyes and know about my life before he decides on this good behaviour bond."

She persisted, "What do I have to do to be able to take the stand so that the judge gets to see me?" She was informed she had to make a special request.

As she handed in her request to an official at the DPP office, she was warned she would be subjecting herself to cross-examination. "Is that worse than being set on fire?" Donna asked.

While Garry Clynes pleaded guilty to the lesser charge, there was a month's adjournment before sentencing—requested by the defendant. Was someone hoping that Donna would simply go away? On March 8, 1996, nearly two years after the attack, Donna finally got her day in court. There was silence as she made her way to the witness box. The judge stared at her—clearly stunned by what he saw. From the pile of paperwork in front of him, the wads of medical reports, the fat briefs of legalistic circumlocutions, Donna had at last become a real person. The judge said he needed time to rethink the case, and ordered that Clynes be remanded in custody.

> Donna finally got her day in court. There was silence as she made her way to the witness box.

A week later, unable to vary the charge that had been brought, Judge Terence Christie finally told the court, "The public is going to find it very hard to understand why I cannot give this man even the two years' maximum sentence." As the defence had rightly pointed out, as a first offender and because he had pleaded guilty, Clynes was entitled to a mandatory discount. The sentence: 15 months in prison and then nine months' parole.

Exhausting Feat

As Gabriella Mazzali's attacker, Stephen Rae, recovered enough from his injuries to face the judicial system, there seemed every indication that Gabriella might be treated in the same way Donna had been. Rae was doggedly denying responsibility for any part of the attack, and constantly changing his lawyers. With each change, the new lawyers had to be given yet more time to prepare his case.

Repeatedly, Donna warned Gabriella that she too might become another nameless, faceless victim—someone to be kept well away from court. She stressed, "Don't ever assume that the professionals, the so-called experts, will make sure you get a fair deal in court."

For the moment, however, Gabriella was still hardly able to rise from her bed. Her recovery had once again lurched down on one of its periodic dips. Despite 11 operations, doctors remained optimistic she would walk again, but it was becoming increasingly obvious to Gabriella it would be with extreme difficulty. But she refused to give up. She used visualization to picture herself walking out of hospital. If Donna could walk, so would she.

At last, Gabriella was able to be tilted up onto her feet and assisted into a chair. From there, she graduated to her first steps, leaning heavily on a special Zimmer frame with forearm support. But would she ever be able to walk again unassisted?

Saviour with a scalpel—plastic surgeon Dr Peter Haertsch performed several skin grafts on Gabriella's tortured body.

One afternoon, she was in a chair alone in her room. *Go for it, Gabriella. Go for it,* she told herself. Painfully, she levered herself upwards—and tottered forward a pace. *Go for it.* A few more paces—and she was out in the corridor.

Now she was lurching back to her room. She was burning up with the heat now that she could no longer perspire. Exhausted, exultant. It was a feat that she was not to repeat for weeks afterwards. But she had done it at least once. She had done it.

As Gabriella healed, Donna spoke about the other massive changes in her life. She warned against tormenting herself too much with the question: *Why me?* "It's not a feasible question to ask really. There's no point trying to make sense of the senseless. I wasted too much time on trying to work out how could I let this happen to me. Why didn't I see it coming? But four years on, I'm no nearer to the answer—because there is no answer.

"People have said to me, 'Why don't you go back to teaching?' But I can't. That person died in the back yard. I'm now physically unfit. Once it's been taken, you cannot go back and pretend everything is back to normal. But I've been given a second chance of life—I can still help others. You've got your nurse's training and now know things that can never be taught in any university. You've still got so much to give."

Finally, on July 7, 1998, Gabriella walked out of Concord Hospital—as she had always determined she would—for the start of her flight back to Britain.

There, she was to spend another seven months in hospitals in Leicester and London, shaking off the last of the infections that plagued her body and continuing with her slow rehabilitation. She kept in touch with Donna by mail and telephone.

Legal Ploys

Back in Australia, Stephen Rae was still refusing to admit blame for anything that he had done. In a series of police interviews and early court appearances, he insisted that Gabriella's injuries had been the result of a suicide pact that had gone wrong. Petrol had been spilt on the floor—and Gabriella had slipped on it. As he continued to change lawyers, the trial date was pushed further and further back.

Donna recognized the pattern only too well. Howard Brown of the Victims of Crime Assistance League (VOCAL) was also keeping track of these manoeuvres in the courts and sending out clear signals to the police and DPP's office that VOCAL was taking an interest in the case.

When Gabriella herself contacted the DPP's office, she was assured, "Don't worry about it. We'll take care of it. We'll let you know the outcome." There was no need for her to return to Australia. Perplexed, Gabriella phoned Donna. "I don't understand it. They're saying they don't need me now. It's as if I don't really have anything to do with the case. How can they do the case without me?"

"Believe me," Donna responded, "they would far rather do it without you. They're probably hoping you won't be there, Gabby. You tell them you're coming over. It's necessary. It's part of your healing process to see justice done. It's only then that you can move on with the next phase of your life." She was adamant. "You've got to be there," she insisted. "You've got to make sure that the judge and court and everyone gets to see you and know what you have been through. If you need me, I'll be in court with you."

Then, just when it appeared that she would be called into court as a witness, Rae changed his plea and his lawyers yet again and his trial was postponed. But Donna was reassuring. "Don't worry, Gabby. It's all part of the tactic of wearing you down, hoping that the victim will run out of the emotional stamina needed to turn up in court. Now what you do is you keep your case packed—and then just push it under your bed until the trial is definitely on."

Donna warned her that they would in all probability try to destroy her in the witness box. "They will argue that you provoked him. They will ask questions about your private life. They will try to paint you as a liar or a loose woman."

70

Hope and healing—Concord Repatriation General Hospital, situated on a peninsula on the Parramatta River, Sydney, was where Gabriella took her first painful steps to recovery.

Circle of Concern

Finally, in October 1999—18 months after the attack—Gabriella returned to Australia for the case in Parramatta District Court in which Stephen Rae was listed as pleading not guilty to the charge of attempted murder. She spent a couple of weeks at a secret, guarded address preparing her evidence for the trial. Just days before the trial, Rae once again sacked his lawyers. But after discussions with their replacements—his fifth set of lawyers—he decided to plead guilty to maliciously causing grievous bodily harm with intent to murder. It carried a maximum sentence of 25 years. Gabriella would no longer have to give evidence in a trial. *Had he been scared of confronting her in court? Had he brought her to Australia simply as a final gesture of control?*

Sentencing was deferred until December. But before then, with Gabriella back in Britain, Rae tried to retract his plea of guilty. He claimed that he had been given bad advice—that he had been coerced into pleading guilty. But when all his previous solicitors had been subpoenaed to give evidence on this, his application was turned down.

Finally, on December 23, 1999, Judge Angela Karpin sentenced Stephen Rae to 19 years and eight months' imprisonment and set a minimum term of 14 years, nine months.

By then, Gabriella was getting on as best she could with the rest of her life. She went back to Concord Hospital to thank the staff. Dr Peter Haertsch and Dr Peter Kennedy were awestruck at the progress she had made since they had last seen her. Before she left the burns unit, nursing manager Peter Campbell led her to the bedside of 22-year-old Thong Ma. The son of Vietnamese migrants, just five weeks earlier he had been hideously burned when his car crashed into a petrol station pump during a violent rainstorm.

For Gabriella, it was like going back into a time warp—completing the circle of concern begun by Donna. She sat beside the young man and touched his hand. Quietly, she told him, "There is light at the end of the tunnel. It's a long, long journey but you will get there."

Gabriella spent several days with Donna in Wingham. "There are some things," Donna

Staunch champion—Donna Carson's support saw Gabriella through the arduous process of healing and seeking justice.

advised, "that you've just got to accept. But we have a choice: we can either sit behind closed doors and complain of an unfair life—or get out and do things." Donna spoke of her work with other burns survivors and the support group she has set up to try to correct some of the inadequacies of the criminal justice system. Each Monday, she attends the court in nearby Taree to help victims of crime find their way through the court system: to tell them of their rights to attend court proceedings and have a support person with them. She explains to those suffering violence at the hands of a partner how to take out restraining orders.

Gabriella, meanwhile, struggles to regain some semblance of a normal life. She lives on her own in a small flat in London.

Since the attack, she has lost some ten kilos in weight. She can walk up to 400 metres and now goes swimming regularly. But she still tires easily. Able to perspire only in that small part of her body that has not been grafted, and with her new skin highly sensitive to the sun, she is unlikely to realize her dream of a permanent return to Australia.

However, with Donna's urging and example, she is trying to look past the pain and agony of her experience. She has completed a one-year course in counselling at London's Birkbeck College, and she now often visits other burns survivors in hospital or in their homes.

Stephen Rae's appeal against the severity of his sentence was dismissed in December 2001.

THE IMPOSTOR

Randy Fitzgerald

Gerald Barnes is an actor, but his most daring role was never on a stage. For more than 20 years he managed to fool both patients and physicians alike, treating thousands of people for everything from cuts to cancer. Too bad he was just a disgraced pharmacist with no medical training.

Sitting in a jail cell in Illinois, Gerald Barnes doesn't look much like a legend—he looks like a loser. A tiny man, no more than five foot five, in his prison-issue clothes he's the kind of jowly, aging, bespectacled guy most people would not look at twice. But that's often the way it is with con men: the best of them pass through the world unnoticed, quietly fleecing the unsuspecting.

And fleece Barnes did. From 1992 to 1996, the US attorney's office in Los Angeles reports that Barnes bilked businesses, insurance companies and Medicare of some $4.9 million. But money isn't what sets him apart from other fakers and phonies. It's the 20 years Barnes—a would-be actor and disgraced pharmacist—spent posing as a doctor, seeing thousands of people for everything from cuts to cancer.

Barnes made his con look easy, in part, because law enforcement and the medical-licensing system in California made it so. While practicing medicine without a license can be a felony, Barnes—arrested on at least five occasions—spent less than two years at any one time behind bars. After serving his term, he'd dust off his fake M.D. credentials, and again invite patients into his examining room.

In fact, in 1996, at the height of his masquerade, Barnes served as the director of a top Los Angeles medical clinic, treating corporate executives of Fortune 500 firms and FBI agents, the very people who could bust him.

It wasn't just patients he hoodwinked: Barnes married five times and had several children; typically they knew nothing of his real life until his arrest.

"He was the most brazen white-collar criminal I had ever seen," says Eddie Banks, a former investigator for Orange County, California, who arrested Barnes in 1980 for practicing medicine without a license. "He's a hell of an actor."

But Barnes, while confirming his love of the stage, denies his "practice" was an act. "I was a good doctor," he says.

Whether it's hubris or delusion, he genuinely believes he has the skills of a physician. Even after one man died under his care, he persisted in putting thousands of unsuspecting patients at risk.

Today he insists his days as Gerald Barnes, M.D., are over. Now he says he hopes only to live out his prison sentence so he can play ball with his son and grandkids. Yet in the next breath, he sounds ready to don a white lab coat, grab a stethoscope and go: "There are people out there who need me."

He was born Gerald Barnbaum in 1933, the only son of a blue-collar Chicago couple. His father, Sam, was a Russian immigrant who worked different jobs to support wife, Elsie, Gerald and daughter, Janice. The parents were forced to marry after Elsie became pregnant with Gerald. "It was a marriage made in hell," says Patti McGowen, a college sweetheart who became the first Mrs Barnes.

Gerald made up for his unhappy home life by seeking attention elsewhere. In school he was the class clown. He loved performing in plays, and singing in the temple choir. "He was a comedian," says McGowen, who met him in 1954. "His ability to mimic was extraordinary. He could pick up mannerisms easily."

Barnes's interest in medicine began as a boy. He recalls with awe an orthopedist who helped his mother. "He took time to explain to the son of a hysterical mother what was wrong with her back," he says. "I always wanted to be a physician. To be able to help people is a gift."

College charmer—Barnbaum had leading-man looks when he was at college. His smiling demeanour masked an unhappy home life.

But he never pursued a medical career. Instead he enrolled in the University of Illinois and its college of pharmacy. He and McGowen married in 1956. Two years later Barnes graduated from school, and a son, Steve, was born. Twin girls were adopted in 1964.

Acting, albeit on the amateur stage, continued to play an important role in Barnes's life. Even after college, he pursued the spotlight, performing in productions of *Man of La Mancha*, *Arsenic and Old Lace* and *You Can't Take It With You*.

Barnes's interest in medicine began as a boy. "I always wanted to be a physician. To be able to help people is a gift."

Other roles interested Barnes. McGowen recalls a night in the early 1960s when Barnes read her a passage from *The Great Impostor*. Published in 1959, it recounted the career of

Ferdinand Demara Jr, who posed as a member of any number of professions, including as a doctor. Barnes says he read the book several times. "It was fascinating that the guy could pull it off," he recalls. "I didn't base my whole career on him. I kind of melded into it."

A career like Demara's must have been escapist fare for Barnes, who spent his days working as a pharmacist in a South Side Chicago drugstore. There, he watched the medical profession up close, and he didn't much like the view. "I saw doctors prescribing drugs people didn't need," he says. As his opinion of doctors soured, his self-image became more grandiose. Physicians, he decided, were more interested in writing prescriptions and billing patients than caring for and about them. He believed he could do better. "I was going to do it right," he says.

But medical school wasn't an option with a family to feed. If he wanted to practice medicine, he'd have to find a short cut. Around 1974, Barnes met two doctors newly arrived in Chicago from India. Barnes says they agreed to let him work as their assistant. He asked them to teach him how to suture wounds. Buy a fresh chicken, make a slice on it and close it up, he was told. Barnes did so and won praise for his tight, tidy stitches.

A lead role—Barnbaum on stage. According to one of his ex-wives, he changed his name to Barnes because it looked better on a billboard.

During the next few months, Barnes sutured wounds and administered shots and EKG tests. He'd found his true calling. "I fell in love with the practice of medicine. I could not get enough." He read medical texts, studied EKGs. He took a course on X-rays. With this background, he felt sure he could be a good doctor.

Maybe good at medicine, but not at marriage. In 1973, McGowen filed for divorce, saying Barnes physically and psychologically abused her. (He admits that over the years there were times when he drank too much, which may have contributed to his various marital difficulties.)

Nevertheless, he soon married again, this time to an actress he'd met while appearing in a community play. With a new wife, alimony and child support to pay, he struggled to make ends meet. Things got worse in 1976, when

Barnes says he got caught up in a medical fraud scandal and lost his pharmacist's license for keeping shoddy prescription records.

He decided to make a clean break, moving his new wife to southern California, where his sister, Janice, lived. Besides, "you know everybody comes to LA to be a doctor—an actor," he says, laughing at his Freudian slip. Soon he was working as a pharmacist. He claims his employer never checked to see if he was licensed.

From there, it was a short leap to the obvious. If no one bothered to check his bona fides as a druggist, would they verify his credentials as a doctor? Barnes scanned the employment section of the *Los Angeles Times*; an ad for a doctor to work at the Hofgarden Medical Clinic in the suburb of Alhambra caught his eye. "I called up and they said, 'Oh, yeah, we'd like to interview you.' I made a résumé. I went in and showed it to [Dr Luther Hofgarden]. He hardly looked at it."

Despite no documentation or true experience, Barnes wasn't nervous about the work he'd be doing. Many of the patients he'd see were there for pre-employment physicals. "Nothing more than a quick eye, ear, nose and throat, chest [exam]. You're going to do heavy lifting? I gotta check for a hernia. Goodbye."

Plausible practitioner—with false credentials and a convincing persona, con man Barnes managed to fool physicians and patients alike.

Since Barnes was so successfully fooling his bosses and patients, it was probably no great feat for him to fool his family as well. He recalls a day when his second wife visited him in his clinic for lunch. He says she asked him how he'd become a doctor and he replied, "I told her I took a test and I passed it."

He knew, though, that if he was going to pass as a doctor he needed the right props: a medical degree and a state medical license, which would allow him to write prescriptions.

At Hofgarden Medical, he found a book listing all of California's doctors, and by coincidence there was a real physician named Gerald Barnes, an orthopedic surgeon in Stockton. So Gerald Barnes the con man phoned the Medical Board of California, identified himself as Gerald Barnes the physician, and told them his medical license had been destroyed in a fire. Barnes says the board sent him a copy of the real Dr Barnes's license. Using the same ploy, he got a copy of Barnes's med-school diploma from the University of Wisconsin.

It was that simple. Thereafter, any identity checks would confirm the existence of Dr Gerald Barnes of Los Angeles, who had an exemplary academic and professional record. During the span of 20 years, these were the primary documents needed to perpetrate his fraud.

Barnes did pick up as much real medical knowledge as he could. He'd taken basic science and medical courses for his pharmacology degree. Now he read medical books and journals, and took continuing-education courses for physicians at area med schools. He says that no one ever questioned his credentials. "You pay the fee for the seminar and they're glad to take the money. You could be a plumber or a butcher for all they care. They'll take your money."

Barnes took courses for physicians at area med schools. No one ever questioned his credentials.

The time Barnes put into burnishing his image as a physician paid off. In 1978 he joined the Pacific Southwest Medical Group, a clinic based in Orange County, at a salary of $70,000, plus bonuses. Once again, he says, his credentials were accepted. And by now Barnes had honed his bedside manner, which he considered key to his success. "I knew how I'd been treated in the doctors' offices and I admonished the front office, 'How can you let this man sit there for 45 minutes and not tell him why he's waiting? [You go explain that] I've got a man bleeding. I've got to take care of him.'"

On December 26, 1979, John McKenzie walked into Pacific Southwest Medical. The 29-year-old factory employee had lost 16 pounds in 10 days. He was wary of doctors, and perhaps Barnes, with his warm, confident manner, seemed like just what McKenzie wanted.

Barnes says the patient told him he was always thirsty and eating candy. Barnes suspected a diabetic condition and drew a blood sample. Then he did something he criticizes real doctors for: he prescribed medication for McKenzie's dizziness, and sent him home. Two days later McKenzie was dead from a diabetic seizure.

I blew it, Barnes thought, cursing himself.

More than the loss of life, the impostor understood the implications of his error: soon he would be unmasked.

Sure enough, a physician's assistant at Pacific Southwest grew suspicious. He had learned from a lawyer involved in a child-custody issue between Barnes and Patti McGowen that the "doctor" might be a pharmacist. The assistant called the references listed on Barnes's résumé. They didn't check out. Soon the Orange County District Attorney was investigating, then prosecuting Barnes.

A physician's assistant at Pacific Southwest grew suspicious. He called the references listed on Barnes's résumé.

Barnes pleaded guilty to involuntary manslaughter, and on May 29, 1981, a judge gave him three years in prison. As Barnes was sentenced, Orange County prosecutor James Enright, who says he sensed Barnes's love of the good life and the admiration the practice of medicine afforded him, turned to an investigator and said, "I have a feeling we'll see him again."

His second wife never wanted to see him again; she divorced him that same year.

Enright, though, had been correct. In 1984, he again saw Barnes busted for grand theft and forging prescriptions in the LA area. "He was a good actor and knew the medical language," says Enright of Barnes's desire to continue a medical career. "Money, the lifestyle and respect in the community were what motivated him."

Between December 1984 and March 1991, Barnes was imprisoned for posing as a doctor or pharmacist three times. After each conviction, he'd do his time, be released, and head back to LA to work again.

In that same period he was married twice. First, in 1987, to Nicolette Fleming, who died of cancer within months of their union. Then in 1988 he remarried yet again. Wife No. 4 divorced him in 1991, but not before Barnes was caught for posing as a licensed pharmacist. Despite his record as an impostor, he was sentenced to only three years in prison.

By December 1992, Barnes was again out of prison and working as a physician. He had his career; now all he needed was a wife.

Within months, he was dating Lisa Roberts, 32, a bank employee he'd met in choir practice at Adat Shalom Synagogue in west Los Angeles. There, Barnes was once again a star. At breaks he'd entertain the group with imitations of Marlon Brando and Dustin Hoffman.

Despite his winning personality, Lisa Roberts had reservations about her

59-year-old suitor. "I didn't think we should be dating because he was much older," she says. But Barnes wooed her ardently, taking her to restaurants and shows. Roberts says that, personality aside, she was impressed by his stories about medical school, and the patients he had treated over the years.

Just about everyone in Roberts's life—friends, her mother, even her dog, Starlight—loved Barnes. Gradually she fell for him too. In February 1994 they were married. She had no idea she was wife No. 5.

Barnes exhibits little remorse for his work as a medical impostor, and has few regrets for the damage he inflicted on those closest to him. Of the women he deceived, he says, "I love women. I enjoy taking care of them, I treat them like queens. I loved them all."

He says similar things about his kids: Steve, 43, and his adopted daughters, BJ and Ty, 37. Yet for weeks at a time in the 1980s his daughters were forced to live on the streets or sleep in cars, because their father was either in jail or failed to pay child support. According to BJ, her credit was destroyed around 1989 after Barnes—having applied for credit cards in her name—failed to pay the bills when he was sent off for another stretch in prison.

In 1995, Barnes applied for a physician's post with Executive Health Group in downtown LA, and soon became its medical director. The occupational-health clinic offered physicals to executives, including employees of the US Secret Service and the FBI. A background check of Dr Gerald Barnes verified no criminal record, no medical complaints and a valid medical license—although the credentials actually belonged to the real Dr Barnes in Stockton. His salary was $100,000 a year. "I was thrilled when I got the job," says Barnes. "I enjoyed every minute of it with the FBI. I'm proud I pulled that off."

His fun lasted about a year. In April 1996, during a routine check of previously convicted phony doctors, California Medical Board investigator Vaughn Cain tracked down Barnes using driver's-license records. When confronted, Barnes insisted he was a licensed physician. Barnes's acting ability, his appearance, his manner of speech impressed Cain. "He seemed so convincing that several times I felt like calling him 'Doctor.'" Facing

"He seemed so convincing that I felt like calling him 'Doctor,'" said California Medical Board investigator Vaughn Cain.

arrest, Cain recalls, Barnes put his acting talent to use again, faking a heart attack so convincingly that he was briefly hospitalized.

In 1996 a federal judge brought down the curtain on Barnes, sentencing him to twelve and a half years in prison.

Final curtain—officers lead Barnes away from court in 1996 after the phony doctor was sentenced to more than 12 years of imprisonment.

Even years after the fact, few of Barnes's colleagues or patients are willing to talk on the record about him: many say they are embarrassed that they were duped so thoroughly. One who will talk is Dr Richard Katz, who hired Barnes to work in his clinic in Beverly Hills. "He had a passion for medicine, and worked long hours," says Katz, who recalls his former associate spending much of his spare time reading medical journals. Others have been left with lesser opinions of Barnes's efforts. A lawsuit, involving some 500 people who Barnes examined, resulted in a settlement that was worth more than $9 million.

And Sharon Jarrett, Barnes's former office manager at Executive Health, says that she went to a dermatologist after her boss was arrested. Barnes had examined a spot on her wrist that turned out to be cancerous, and a small mole on her neck that was precancerous. She says Barnes assured her "they were fine."

Lisa Roberts, who had her marriage annulled in 1997, can barely bring herself to say Barnes's name. She calls him "Never Was" and rues the day she let him into her life. "I'm not the same person I was," she says. "I don't think I'm as good a person as I was before I met him."

Today Barnes sits in the Federal Correctional Institution in Waseca, Minnesota, where he was allowed to serve his sentence so he could be near his son, Steve, and four grandchildren.

Over time, Barnes says, he came to see himself above the law. "I was playing God a bit," he concedes. Yet Barnes remains convinced of his skill with the people he calls "patients"—people who were actually a con man's victims. "I put myself in that stranger's place. What do I want from the doctor? I want compassion. I want communication. 'I know it hurts you, but I can fix you. And if I can't, I'll send you to someone who can.' " He says this with such conviction that one almost believes he really is a physician.

But the spell doesn't last for long. At this point, would he do things differently? Sure, Barnes says. He wishes he'd gone to medical school. That's probably what the patients who trusted him enough to call him "Doctor" wish too.

In February 2003 federal prosecutors announced that Gerald Barnes had been indicted on 16 felony counts including mail fraud, identity theft and illegally dispensing controlled substances. If he is convicted of all charges, Barnes faces a maximum possible penalty of 104 years in federal prison.

THE POLICE CHIEF'S SECRET

Bernard Kerik

We saw Bernard Kerik standing firm at Ground Zero, mobilizing rescue forces after the September 11 attacks on the World Trade Center. But there's another story about this New York City police commissioner—a deep personal mystery that he was determined to solve. It began with a haunting dream.

L ight streams through the crack in the door. From the bed I hear voices on the other side, and I desperately want it to be my mother or father. Instead, it's the woman who lives in this house. I have no idea who she is.

Sometimes there are other children here. I play with them during the day, but when darkness sets in they disappear, and the feeling of loneliness is deeper. *Where is my mother, and why won't she come to get me?*

I cry myself to sleep believing that I will wake up in her arms. But in the morning I'm still alone. I drop out of bed and trudge into the kitchen. I see the woman and ask her, "When is Mommy coming to get me?"

She looks at me and smiles gently. Her voice is not unkind.

"Maybe today, dear."

But quickly it is night again and the fear comes over me like a fever. I don't want to go back to that room.

The woman reaches out with a dark, worn hand. She walks me to the room and guides me into bed. I don't want to be here! I lie there, staring at the column of light through the crack in the door.

"Where is Mommy?" I cry out, but no one answers.

Suddenly I sit up in bed, drenched. It's 5.45am, and I'm not four years old. I'm 45, lying in bed next to my wife. I've had the dream again.

I've had this dream for 40 years, and I know that it is tied to real memories. The parts of my life that I do remember—the poverty and crime, the years of struggle, the fights and hassles, the unlikely achievements, the tragedy—these feel like dreams themselves.

But this other dream is the one that haunts me—these vivid memories of an abandoned boy, of a lost son waiting for his mother to return. This is my deepest mystery, a hole in the center of myself.

I can't believe I've had my nightmare this day of all days. I shake my head as I climb out of bed and walk toward the shower.

It's August 19, 2000. In a few hours I will be in City Hall, reaching the pinnacle of my profession as a New York City cop. I'll be standing next to Mayor Rudolph Giuliani as he announces to the world that I am to become the 40th police commissioner of the city of New York.

The Coroner's Report

Nine months later, in May 2001, the private telephone in my office at One Police Plaza rings. It is Lenny Lemer, a sergeant assigned to the intelligence division and a long-time friend.

"I got some information on that thing you wanted," he says.

I grip the phone. "What've you got?"

"Looks like it's her," he says. "Maybe we shouldn't talk about it over the phone. Maybe I should come down there."

"It's OK," I say. "We're on a hard line. Just tell me."

I can hear papers shuffling in the background. "She had a pretty substantial criminal record," he says. Then he hesitates.

There must be something he doesn't want to tell me. "It's all right," I say. "Just read it." He sighs.

"She had 10 aliases: Joann Evaline Bailey. Patricia Joann Curtis. Joann Evaline. Patricia Joann Fletcher. Patricia J. Bailey . . ."

After he reads the 10th, he says, "And there are three arrests. Two for prostitution, one for escape."

Again, I push him to continue. But this time, he won't. "I really need to come down there," he says.

"OK."

I hang up the phone and sit back in my chair, waiting.

As New York City's police commissioner, I work 18-hour days, six days a week. All day long my office buzzes with meetings and phone calls and the lightning pace of decisions about tragedies and heroes, scandals and absurdities. But right now, time is standing still for me and I feel like I can't move.

Finally there's a knock at the door. Lenny walks into the office. I can tell by the look on his face that the news isn't good. "I have the coroner's report," he says.

"Is it worse than I thought?"

"Yes. Let me read the summary:

'This is the case of a female who apparently received multiple traumatic injuries, resulting in multiple bruises of the left eye, left buttocks, thighs and lower legs. The bruise to the eye resulted in a cerebral hemorrhage . . . causing her death.'"

I'm staring at the paper. I feel sick. "Anyone arrested?"

"No," he says. "That's the weird thing. I don't even see any sign of a homicide investigation."

"Why wasn't there an investigation?" I ask.

Lenny, not knowing what to say, just sits there, staring at me.

I hear stories like this 10 times a day. I hear about so many victims like this woman that it becomes hard to keep them all straight. But this one, this case from the past, I've got to investigate myself. And I won't rest until I find out why this woman was killed and who killed her.

My stomach is in a knot. I look down at the coroner's report again. It's dated December 14, 1964. Patricia Curtis, a white female, 34 years of age, died in Newark, Ohio. She was beaten to death.

She is buried under one of the 10 names listed on her arrest record. When I say it out loud, I nearly lose my breath. "Patricia J. Kerik."

Patricia was my mother.

Second Chances

Patricia Jo Bailey was a small, intense, dark-haired woman whose childhood did not prepare her for marriage or motherhood. Growing up in Cleveland, she was one of eight children—four boys and four girls. Her mother didn't have much use for the children, except for the housework they could do. Then one day her father simply walked off and abandoned the family.

Most of the kids became alcoholics, and two of Patricia's older sisters turned to prostitution as teenagers. One of my aunts told me that Patricia "was the smartest and the prettiest, but she was always in the wrong place with the wrong people."

It was Patricia's eyes that caught the attention of my father, Donald Kerik, the one good man in her life.

It was Patricia's eyes that caught the attention of my father, Donald Kerik, the one good man in her life. You don't have to look too deeply into old photos to see those eyes as round, dark pools of suffering and trouble.

To this day, my father looks pained when he describes Patricia: he says she was just "wild." When they met in Cleveland, she was 21, three years older than my father, and had already had two husbands.

My parents got married in 1952. From the beginning there were problems. My father couldn't keep my mother out of taverns and gin mills. And once she got inside those places, he couldn't keep her away from other men.

In the summer of 1955 the couple moved to northern New Jersey, where my father's sister, Betsy, was living. Pops got a job in a machine shop, and my aunt Betsy's family seemed to be a calming influence on the young Keriks.

That September, Patricia gave birth to a seven-pound, six-ounce baby boy, 19 inches long. They named me Bernard Bailey Kerik, after my mother's brother Bernard. And they called me Beezy, because of the two b's in my name. Unfortunately, having a baby didn't make my parents' life any more

A good heart—"How different her life might have been," says Kerik of his mother (above), "if someone had simply said to her, 'You can do it.'"

stable. They fell into an awful pattern: my mother would go off on some fling and then come back a few weeks later, begging my father to reconcile. Sometimes she'd take me with her to Ohio, to see her family or some man she didn't want to give up. But then she'd drag me back to New Jersey with her and ask my father for a second chance.

After several years of this, she finally ran out of second chances. In 1957 my parents separated, and soon after that they filed for divorce. Pops tried to get custody of me, but the lawyer told him that women almost always won custody battles like theirs.

"You can probably prove she's an unfit wife," the lawyer said to my dad, "but you can't prove she's an unfit mother."

In the end, that wouldn't be so hard to prove after all.

The Shadow of Abandonment

Back in Ohio, it didn't take long for Patricia to find herself in the same old life of booze and derelict men. On the nights she didn't come home, I stayed with a succession of relatives and friends. Sometime in late 1958, my mother married again. I know very little about that husband, Jack Dean, or about our life in Ohio. She met him at an AA meeting after being ordered by the courts to spend 12 weeks in a hospital or institution of some kind, in an attempt to control her alcoholism. I stayed with an aunt at least part of this time. The hospitalization didn't stop Patricia's drinking for long, if at all.

I also found out, from interviewing a family member, that Patricia was involved in a white slavery ring—young girls transported to New York to work as prostitutes.

Immediately I flash to my years as a policeman in New York, walking up and down West 42nd Street, and the women selling themselves there. I try to picture my own mother in those sad faces. How many dozens of women did I arrest, women like my mother?

"Your mother would do a good job raising you for a while," the family member tells me. "But then she'd always give up and run off. You were a sweet baby, a happy baby. She took care of you. She wanted to be a good mother. I don't think she knew how."

Somewhere in there, marriage No. 4 failed, too, and my mother began a relationship with Claude Curtis, a 23-year-old black man from Newark, Ohio. While she and this man were out drinking and running around town, I was left with Claude's mother in her tiny house near Columbus. I even lived with her for several months at a stretch.

It is this woman's hand that reaches out to me in the recurring dream I have, and it is her house that I see at night, the place in which I feel so alone.

Yet had it not been for this woman's kindness and gentle touch, the months I spent there would have been so much worse. During the day Claude's mother took in other children to baby-sit. When they were there, I played with them. But when night fell, the other kids always disappeared, which increased my feelings of loneliness.

As I went to sleep at night, two questions burned in my mind. *Where was my mother, and why didn't she come for me?* Each morning I was still alone, my questions unanswered.

Finally my uncle Bob Bailey had seen enough. He was one of my mother's older brothers and also my godfather. One day in 1959 he picked up the phone and called my father at work in New Jersey.

"Don," he said, "you'd better come back and get hold of Beezy. Pat's really f——— up. She ain't taking care of him. She's moved in with a black guy and is leaving the baby with this guy's mother while they run around drinking and carousing."

Pops was suspicious. Patricia's family had always taken her side in the past, and they were deeply attached to me. They ended up watching

Good connection—me with my uncle, Bob Bailey, one of my mother's brothers. "I always thought about you," he told me.

me much of the time. So why would Bob risk hurting his sister and losing contact with his young godson?

"Come on, Bob," my father said. "You and I both know blood's thicker than water."

"Maybe to the rest of the family," Bob replied. "But Don, I love that boy and I know you'll take care of him."

"If I come get him, that's it," my father said. "You ain't gonna get to see him anymore."

"I know that," Bob said. "But if you don't come now, he'll be lost forever."

It took my father about three months to get custody of me. When he followed the police to Claude's mother's house, he thought I seemed healthy and that the woman had treated me well; he says I called her Grandmother.

As they took me away from her house, she pleaded with my father and the police not to take anything out on her son. My father never did.

By early 1960 I was beginning a new life in New Jersey with my father, who soon married his second wife, Clara. At just about this time, 30-year-old Patricia Bailey was arrested in the small town of Mansfield, Ohio, charged with prostitution. I never saw or heard from her again.

When my father took me away, I have to imagine that it only accelerated the end for my mother. I've spent so many years being angry with her, wondering why she never came back for me, that I never really thought what it must have been like for her: to be so low and then to lose the only connection she had to a normal life.

It is hard now, looking at my mother's life reduced to a rap sheet and a coroner's report. And part of my life is in those pages too. I often wonder how much of a person's personality is forged by events and people in early childhood that we can't even remember. I wonder if the traits that have allowed me to be successful in life—a heightened sense of justice and duty, a need to protect people, an impatience with criminals and a deep personal drive—are nothing more than a child's tools of survival and defense.

Maybe what I've thought of as striving for a career and a life of honor is actually just chasing the shadow of my own abandonment.

Baby Album

In the tough neighborhoods of industrial New Jersey, I grew up watching "The Green Hornet" on TV and developed an interest in the martial arts. I didn't care much for school and ended up dropping out at age 16 and eventually entering the army.

By 1977 I had returned from a tour in Korea and was stationed at Fort Bragg. Approaching the end of my army career, I wasn't sure what else I could do. I knew I wanted to go into law enforcement, and even had a few applications in to various police departments, but I had no solid leads.

One day I walked into the barracks and a guy at the desk told me I had a phone call. "Beezy?" asked the voice on the other end. It was my Uncle Bob. My dad had told me a little about him, how he'd arranged to get me back to my father.

Uncle Bob asked how I was doing, and seemed genuinely pleased when he heard about my martial arts training and my tour in the army. Then he told me my mother had died, back in 1964.

Standing in the barracks listening to him on the phone, I looked around, maybe to see if anyone was standing nearby. But I was alone. "OK," I said. It was the only thing I could think to say. "OK."

Bob said he had some things for me. I told him to send them to my parents' house. He wished me well, and after a while we hung up.

Two months later I was home in New Jersey when Clara, my stepmom, handed me a small box addressed to me. Inside was a simple baby album.

On the cover of the book were the words "Diary of Baby." I turned to the first page: "Our priceless gem."

The next page had a picture of a baby boy, a dusting of dark hair on top of his head, his eyes closed peacefully. A woman's careful handwriting said, "This picture of you Bernard Bailey Kerik was taken right after you were delivered into the world."

There were several more pages, but I couldn't read them. I just couldn't. I closed my eyes and then closed the baby book. I put it back in the box, and slipped the box in a drawer.

Twenty-five years passed before I opened that baby book again. By then I had worked in corrections, managed the Passaic County jail in New Jersey, and done police and undercover work in New York City. I had also helped transform Rikers Island as deputy commissioner of corrections. After that I was promoted to commissioner of the department of corrections. Then came my appointment in August 2000 to New York City police commissioner.

And that's how I found myself sitting in my office at One Police Plaza in May 2001, wondering about my mother's death back in 1964. Even after all these years, her disappearance remained the deepest mystery of my life—a mystery I wanted very much to solve.

Likely Suspects

"This is him." Lenny Lemer drops a thick file on my desk. It is two months later, and he has just returned from Ohio, where he and another detective, Bobby Hom, were continuing to research my mother's murder. Thanks to our

On guard—in 1985, while I was working in corrections, I escorted the political extremist Susan Rosenberg to and from her trial.

enquiries, the police chief of Newark, Ohio, H. Darrel Pennington, agreed to reopen the case and assign some of his detectives to it.

I look down at the file on my desk. I open it and see the cold flat stare of Claude Curtis, the man who was with my mother in 1960. This picture is a mugshot from 1969, clipped to a list of the criminal charges and warrants filed against him during his lifetime.

The list covers two pages: vandalism, disorderly conduct, drunkenness and rape. But Claude Curtis's favorite crime was assault. Between 1960, when my mother lost custody of me, and 1964, when she died, Curtis was arrested four times for assault and battery.

I pay special attention to the assaults. Sometimes Curtis used a knife, but more often he punched people—usually on the left side of their faces. He was probably right-handed. My mother's killer was probably right-handed, since the bruises were mostly on the left side of her face and body, although this in itself doesn't tell me much. I set the file down and look up at Lenny. "So what do you think? Is it him?"

Lenny shrugs. "I don't know. Maybe."

I nod. Claude Curtis would be an obvious suspect. The crime is certainly consistent with his record. But Lenny and I have slowly been putting together a timeline of my mother's life from 1958, when she divorced my father, until her death in 1964, and Claude may have been out of the picture by then.

Sometime around March of 1960, when my father found me at Claude's mother's house, my mother was arrested for prostitution in Mansfield, Ohio, an hour north. I think Claude and my mother may have split up around that time, because in 1960 he was arrested twice for assault in Dayton, Ohio—halfway across the state.

With Claude gone and me in New Jersey, my mother drifted even further. She was arrested again for prostitution in 1961, and served two months of a year-long sentence. She escaped from a Columbus hospital—where she was getting alcohol treatment—then she was arrested again in Cleveland in December 1962.

She finally hit bottom in 1964, on the east side of Newark, Ohio. At the time it was a rough, mostly black section of taverns, brothels and ramshackle houses—a wild area known as Little Chicago. Men came from all over to drink, buy drugs and have sex with the hookers. Apparently the police just ignored Little Chicago and left the neighborhood to the pimps, bartenders and madams.

It was there my mother met up with a pimp and hustler named William E. Byes, who was—hard as it is to imagine—a step down from Claude Curtis. Byes hung out with an even tougher and more violent guy, an enforcer named Jay W. Allen. Byes and Allen ran a handful of apartments in Newark where they set up hookers for a buck or two each time. In one of those apartments, on a December morning in 1964, my mother's life ended.

Lenny slides a single piece of paper across my desk. It's a faded newspaper story from *The Advocate*, the Newark, Ohio, newspaper. The 1964 story mistakenly reports that my mother was married to Claude Curtis, who was, by some accounts, her common-law husband. The article says that a coroner's inquest "definitely will be held into the death of Mrs Patricia Curtis."

But there's no record of an inquest or police investigation. The cops apparently had no desire to probe into the murder of a white prostitute who slept with black men. So the case was buried, along with my mother.

> A rookie cop could have looked at the bruises and trauma to my mother's body and known that those injuries didn't occur while she was sleeping.

A rookie cop could have looked at the bruises and trauma to my mother's body and known that those injuries didn't occur while she was sleeping in William Byes's bed. No, Lenny and I are convinced there's only one explanation: my mother was brutally murdered.

The possibilities race through my mind: Byes is an obvious suspect. According to the news story, he claimed to have found her semiconscious in his bed at 9am. So where was he all night? Did he have an alibi? Did the cops even ask?

Maybe they believed Byes didn't kill her because he was the one who

Company of men—Rudolph Giuliani, left, with my son, Joe, and me at the St Patrick's Day Parade in New York, March 2001.

called for an ambulance. Maybe he beat her up routinely, but this time went too far. Or maybe it was his friend Jay W. Allen who killed her.

Then there is Claude Curtis. The news story says he and my mother were separated. But maybe he was angry that she was working for Byes and went to Newark looking for her.

I stare at the stacks of odd documents, police reports, death certificates. Lenny and I have said all along that coming up with anything after 37 years would be tough, that solving my mother's murder may be impossible. And yet I still have so many questions.

"I need to go there," I say suddenly to Lenny.

Lenny looks up at me. "What?"

"I need to go to Ohio."

Patricia's World

Lenny Lemer hates to fly. So when my airplane touches down in Columbus, Ohio, in August 2001, Lenny and Bobby Hom are already on the ground. They're waiting for me in the car they have driven from New York.

I climb into the back seat and stare out the window, losing myself in the flat Ohio landscape. Maybe somewhere inside of me, I've always known that one day I would have to come back.

We make our way east of Columbus until we hit the town of Newark, the last stop on my mother's descent. It's an old Midwestern rail town of almost 50,000 people, built along the slow-moving Licking River and the network of little streams and creeks that feeds it.

Newark is a company town now, home of the Longaberger Company, which sells handmade baskets and other home and lifestyle products. Longaberger owns the hotel where we're staying, The Place Off the Square.

As we stand in the parking lot of the hotel, preparing to retrace my mother's steps, I tell Lenny that I want to start at the end. I want to see 62 Brice Court, the apartment where—according to the news story and the death certificate—my mother was found murdered.

Lenny and Bobby shift their weight.

"What? What is it?" I ask.

"The house isn't there anymore," Lenny says.

"OK," I say. "Let's just go look at the street."

Lenny and Bobby catch each other's eyes.

"What?"

"You're standing on it," Lenny tells me.

The building at 62 Brice Court and whatever ramshackle buildings surrounded it have all been torn down to make way for this hotel and parking lot. I shiver as I realize we're standing on the very spot where my mother was killed. I look from one end of the parking lot to the other, trying to picture what it looked like then, what my mother would've seen as she staggered along this street.

Lenny has a street map of old downtown Newark that shows which houses and buildings have been razed since 1964. Almost every building has the word *gone* written on it. Brice Court isn't even on the old map. It may have been little more than an alley or a dark courtyard.

We do find Brice Court in the city directory, however, with only three addresses listed: 58 Brice Court, home of the enforcer and pimp Jay W. Allen; 60 Brice Court, which was vacant; and 62 Brice Court, the house where my mother died and where William E. Byes is listed as the sole resident.

The newspaper story said my mother's home was 194½ East Main Street, maybe half a mile from where she died. She probably walked back and forth between East Main and Brice. I can almost see her shuffling down Second to Easy Street—I wonder if she saw the irony in that name—and then across a bridge over the Licking River and into east Newark.

Standing on the street, I realize that this Newark is far different from the place my mother haunted 40 years ago. It's not just the people who are dead; her whole world is gone now.

A Memorable Visit

I decide it's time to take the next step, so we drive over to Plain City, a speck of a town on the other side of Columbus. Lenny, Bobby and I go to the office of Police Chief Steve Hilbert, tall and solidly built like the state trooper he once was.

One of the early mysteries of this case centered on where my mother was buried. Lenny and another NYPD detective checked every cemetery within a 25-mile radius of Columbus, but found nothing.

Eventually they tracked down Uncle Bob's wife, who remembered that my mother was buried in Plain City, under the name Patricia Bailey. But when they called Chief Hilbert, he couldn't find her registered there.

Then one day, after checking funeral-home records, Chief Hilbert walked into the cemetery. There, at a marker, he looked down and read the stone at his feet: *Patricia J. Kerik.*

Stunned, he called New York and said, "I found her."

It turned out that my Uncle Bob had registered my mother at the cemetery under Claude Curtis's last name, as Patricia Curtis. But my namesake Bernard Bailey, Bob's older brother, made a decision that would lead me here today.

He'd had the name Kerik placed on her gravestone, maybe because he believed that Donald Kerik, my father, was the best man in her life.

I think he must have had another reason. He must have known that one day the son Patricia lost would come looking for her.

Resting place—"Pieces of my mother still live in me," says Kerik.

I ride in Chief Hilbert's car to the cemetery, Lenny and Bobby behind us. From the highway, a dirt road leads toward the flat, austere graveyard. It's eerily quiet as I get out of the car and follow the chief a few steps off the path. He stops in front of two small stone markers set next to one another in the worn grass.

I step around Chief Hilbert, heart racing, stomach knotted. I read the name on the first stone. John Bailey. It's one of my mother's brothers, who was beaten to death in 1952. This is the family legacy—brutal childhood, drug and alcohol problems, premature death.

Next to him lies the other stone, and I know what it says before I even look at it: Patricia J. Kerik.

It takes my breath away, seeing her name etched in granite. And I can't believe I've finally found her.

Here I am at last, standing in the place where my mother rests. Here I am so close to the woman who gave me life. I can't bring her back; I can't change what happened to her. But at least I've found her.

Tears fill my eyes, hidden behind my sunglasses. A lost soul is buried here, forgotten in this small Ohio town. I'm sure I am her first visitor in decades, a son who has come to reclaim his past, to discover his own shadowed legacy, and maybe to give her—a battered woman, lost and forgotten—a voice.

I stand near her grave for a few minutes more, quiet and bewildered. And I know that I want to resurrect in whatever way I can—by my words or deeds—the goodness that must have once dwelt in her heart, the love she never knew.

Back at my hotel I pace around the room, peering out the window. I have never been one to look back at life. I've always been too busy clawing ahead, just trying to survive.

When I look back now, I think about my mother and how different her life might have been if someone, anyone, had had faith in her, had believed in her, had simply said to her, "You can do it." And I see that from the scraps of my mother's life I have built the man I am today. I've been lucky to find people in my life—Mayor Giuliani and others—who believed in me, provided me with opportunities, and catapulted me beyond my expectations.

I finally turn away from the window. And I'm at peace with myself.

Case Closed

The morning before my flight back to New York, I meet two Newark police officers for breakfast. They've worked hard searching for new information on the case, for anyone who might have known my mother. But the years, booze and drugs have left few witnesses. Most are long dead.

A few old prostitutes do remember Patricia, and some of the women recall her death. But they don't want to talk about it. "Why do you want to dig that up?" an old madam asks. "Bury it and let it go. Forget about it."

The two Newark detectives echo what Lenny and I have found on our own: William E. Byes, who claimed to have found my mother having convulsions in his apartment, was a vicious criminal. His partner, Jay W. Allen, may have been even worse. One woman said he was "as violent and mean as a rattlesnake." Both were pimps with long histories of brutalizing women. You could say the same about Claude Curtis.

As we tracked them down, we found that Claude Curtis lived the rest of his life in Dayton, Ohio, and died in 1992. J. W. Allen and William Byes are dead too. Byes had died in February 2000, just 18 months earlier.

And so the questions continue to haunt me. *What happened in the early morning of December 14, 1964? And who killed my mother?*

After looking back at her life and mine, I know that her death began before that day. It began with a brutal, lonely childhood and ended at the hands of violent men. Each of them beat the life out of her, bit by bit, until one of them struck the final blow. When I ask "Who killed my mother?" now I know the answer.

They all did. Her own desperate family, as well as the three men she was with near the end of her life.

What disturbs me is that none of them are alive to answer for her death. I've spent a life in the pursuit of justice, and in the case of my own mother, it will never come.

I thank the detectives for their time, dedication and perseverance. I get into the car and begin the hour-long ride to the Columbus airport.

My mind fades; I close my eyes.

Light streams through the crack in the door. I hear voices on the other side. I can see my mother's face. From an old photo I recognize her eyes. They are my eyes. I try to reach out to her. I want to talk to her. Just once.

I want to tell her I understand now why she wasn't there for me. Why she never came for me. I want to tell her it's all right. And I want her to look at me, to see the man I've become. I want her to be proud of me.

For 41 years I've been haunted by a dream of that four-year-old boy left alone in a room. I know where I was now. And I know why. And for the first time, I can say to my mother, "I understand. I forgive you."

Since publication of his book, The Lost Son, *from which this extract was taken, Bernard Kerik has retired as police commissioner in the New York City Police Department and now works with his friend Rudolph Giuliani, the former Mayor of New York, in a joint business venture. In June 2003 he was named senior policy adviser to the Iraqi interior ministry, with a brief to bring civil order to Iraq. Kerik has said he expects to serve at least six months.*

Declan Donnelly was just 13 years old when two children of almost the same age disappeared from their homes and were eventually found dead in Epping Forest on the outskirts of London. The legendary "Nipper" Read had investigated the "Babes in the Wood" case, but an inquest had recorded an open verdict. Now a policeman himself, Donnelly had a new lead, which suggested something sinister. But he needed Nipper's help.

He had never met Leonard "Nipper" Read, but Detective Chief Inspector Declan Donnelly well knew his reputation. Read, who'd gained his nickname because of his slight build and lack of height, was one of the few Scotland Yard officers to take on the Kray twins in the 1960s. The former police lightweight boxing champion had smashed their criminal empire and put them behind bars for 30 years.

Although Read had moved on from the Metropolitan Police before Donnelly had even joined, his exploits had inspired the younger man to pursue a career in CID. As Donnelly pulled up outside a neat house in Broxbourne, Hertfordshire, on a brilliant summer afternoon in 1996, the lean, balding 39-year-old knew that Nipper would be vital in assessing new information received in the past few weeks on an old case.

Back in 1970, Read had reluctantly consigned case 231/70/15 to Scotland Yard's General Registry, where old investigations are filed. Now, suddenly, Donnelly's new lead, if true, meant the Babes in the Wood had been murdered. But, because the case was 26 years old and never classified as a homicide, much of the evidence had been destroyed.

Donnelly knew that not only did Read have a good memory of the most perplexing case in his long career, he had kept his own paperwork. The fit and cheerful 71-year-old showed Donnelly through to his garden, where, on a table, he had placed a pile of well-thumbed documents.

As the two men sat down Read began: "You see, Declan, I always insisted it was murder."

Children's Games

"Susan's come round, Mum. Is it all right if we play outside?" Twelve-year-old Gary Hanlon was standing at the back door, a football in his hands. Through the kitchen window Beryl Hanlon could see 11-year-old Susan Blatchford, Gary's new school friend, standing in the garden.

"All right, but don't go further than the front," Beryl told him. "Your tea's nearly ready." It was 4.30pm on Tuesday, March 31, 1970, and his mother didn't want him roaming the suburban streets of Enfield, north-east London.

Fresh eyes—Detective Chief Inspector Declan Donnelly's new lead reopened the murder inquiry.

As Beryl Hanlon closed the back door, she heard Gary's football bouncing outside. Then silence.

After a few moments, she went to the front-room window and looked outside. First she checked the front garden, then the street.

There was no sign of either child.

March 31 was Detective Chief Superintendent Nipper Read's 45th birthday. The celebrations would have to wait: he was on duty until late that night. As the head of Y Division CID, it was his responsibility to make a nightly call at the various police stations on his patch, an unglamorous sprawl of terraced houses and light industry in north-east London.

At Ponders End police station, WPC Josie Lowbridge had some news for Read. Two local children had gone missing. After a fruitless search the parents had reported it around 8pm. Police had contacted Gary and Susan's friends, teachers, relations and drawn a blank.

"There's something that's not right," Lowbridge said. Neither child had quarrelled with anyone. Both were expected home for tea. Gary had never missed a meal in his life. There was no reason for them not to go home.

103

Read trusted Josie Lowbridge's judgment. "Keep doing what you're doing," he told her. "If they haven't turned up by tomorrow morning, I'll take charge myself."

When the next day Gary and Susan had still not turned up, Read visited the parents. To stand any chance of finding the children he had to learn all he could about them.

Of the two, Susan was the dominant character. Though a year younger than Gary, she was considerably bigger and would easily pass for 15. Like many adolescent girls, she had two apparently contradictory sides to her personality. On the one hand she liked wearing make-up and telling her mates that she had "boyfriends"; on the other, she preferred trousers to dresses and enjoyed climbing trees and playing with a train set.

Susan got on well with her parents and three older sisters, and had no health problems other than a history of pneumonia. She was excited about being bridesmaid at her sister Linda's wedding. She had also left behind her beloved terrier Blackie.

First attempt—back in 1970, Detective Chief Inspector "Nipper" Read had reluctantly consigned the case to Scotland Yard's General Registry.

Like Susan, Gary was from a settled working-class home. Slightly built and shy compared to extrovert Susan, his great love was football. It was typical that he would ask his mother's permission to play outside.

"There seem three possible explanations for these kids going missing," Read told his assembled team at Ponders End. "One, they've run away. Two, they've had an accident. Three, they've been abducted."

He was almost ready to discount the first. The children had taken no money, no food and, despite the cold weather, little warm clothing. An accident was more likely. The area was fraught with hazards. The River Lea was less than half a mile from the children's homes and had recently burst its banks. The area also contained gravel pits, sewage farms and two enormous reservoirs. There was extensive woodland and open countryside, together with miles of streets, houses and factories.

Harnessing all the expertise accumulated in his 23-year career, Read launched the most extensive search ever mounted by the Metropolitan Police. Thousands of houses, sheds, cars and even boats were marked systematically with indelible ink as they were eliminated from the hunt. Dog teams combed the woods and fields either side of the busy Sewardstone Road, which ran near the children's homes. Read hired a helicopter to sweep the area.

Every police force in the country searched all known travelling fairs in an effort to find out whether the children had followed the one Susan visited on the Sunday before she disappeared.

Nothing.

Speaking to a reporter, Read was frank: "We haven't been able to turn up a single fragment of evidence between the lot of us. It's torture for the parents, hanging on to the slender thread that somehow, sometime, somewhere, their children will be restored to them like magic."

Unfinished business—26 years after his initial enquiries, Read still believed that the Babes in the Wood had been murdered.

Nearly three decades later, Declan Donnelly watched Nipper Read pause and then look straight at him with clear eyes.

"I'm still amazed," Read said, "that at 4.30 in the afternoon, two children could walk off and simply vanish."

Forest of Clues

Eleven weeks after the children disappeared, farm labourer Leonard Cook was out shooting in woods on Barn Hill at the edge of Epping Forest—about half a mile from the children's homes—when his Labrador disappeared into a copse and refused to come out. Cook found the dog in what appeared to be a small birdwatchers' hide fashioned out of branches and twigs. Peering inside, he saw a child's foot.

When Read arrived at the scene at dawn on June 18, pathologist James Cameron was already there. Read crawled into the hide. Two bodies lay side by side, partially covered with leaves. Susan's arm was round Gary.

Read drove first to the Blatchfords' to break the news. He watched helpless as both sets of parents disintegrated before his eyes, all hopes that their children would be restored to them suddenly extinguished.

Back at Ponders End, Read checked the maps covering the wall of the operations room. Barn Hill had been shaded—meaning it had been searched by dog teams. *Why hadn't they found the bodies?*

As he sat gloomily in his office, there was a knock on the door. It was one of the dog handlers. "Guv'nor, those kids weren't in that wood when we searched. There were no bodies there."

Read exploded: "If you're telling me they were put in there after you searched, you can forget it! I don't want excuses, I want reasons."

Later that day, he discovered that most of the police dogs had never even seen a human corpse. It was quite possible that one of them had found the children's bodies, but the handler had failed to recognize the dog's behaviour.

There was more bad news from James Cameron. Both bodies were so badly decomposed they could only be identified by their clothing and dental records and, in Susan's case, by the fingerprints of her right hand, which had been scrunched up inside her coat sleeve. Frustratingly, the standard tests to establish cause of death could not be done. All the internal organs, and many of the bones, had disintegrated. Signs of minor internal bleeding in Susan's chest cavity could almost certainly be explained by her pneumonia.

Concluded Cameron: the children had got lost and as night fell and temperatures dropped below freezing, they had crept into the hide to keep warm. In all probability, Gary and Susan had died from hypothermia.

"How did you react to that?" Donnelly now asked Read.

"It went against all my instincts," Read replied, "not only as a policeman, but also as the father of a young daughter. I just could not believe that those kids—or any kid—would just curl up and wait to die."

To Read, the hypothermia theory just didn't stack up. "Gary was a plucky lad," his father Frank told him, "but he was afraid of the dark. Nothing would have induced him to enter that copse even when the sun was shining, let alone at dusk."

Not only that, Barn Hill was within sight of

Susan Blatchford—as a tall 11-year-old she could have passed for an adolescent.

Gary Hanlon—the shy, polite 12-year-old asked his mother's permission to play outside.

Sewardstone Road, less than a quarter of a mile away. The lights of a pub, the Royal Oak, would have been clearly visible across the fields.

Surely, Nipper surmised, *every instinct would tell the two children to go where there were lights and people.*

Other findings increased his suspicions. When Susan's body was found she was still wearing her blouse and raincoat, but her torn corduroy trousers had been thrown over her body and her shoes, socks, underwear and tights were missing. Read had much of the wood chopped down and raked, but the search turned up just one of her shoes, found next to a ditch that surrounded the wood.

One detail above all convinced Read that the deaths were no accident. Susan's green cords had been torn completely along each seam. He was convinced this could only have been done by a third party. But how?

Read obtained a dozen identical pairs of trousers in an adult size and summoned a young male officer.

"Right," said Read cheerfully, "get your trousers off."

What followed would have looked farcical to an observer, as the young policeman put on pair after pair and Read tried to reproduce the pattern of tearing on Susan's trousers. There was only one way it could be done. With the officer lying on his stomach, Read grasped the back of the waistband with both hands and yanked. It was possible to rip the garment completely along the seam. Had an attacker done the same?

The scientists didn't think so. In mid-September an inquest recorded an open verdict on the deaths of Susan and Gary. The coroner said that the missing and torn clothing could have been the work of animals.

Summoned by senior officers at Scotland Yard,

Read seized the chance to convince his superiors of his version of events.

"Gary and Susan are walking innocently in the fields by the copse," he began. "They're met by someone who threatens them, or forces them to go into the wood. Susan loses her shoe as she negotiates the ditch.

"Once in the wood the man strangles Gary. He rips off Susan's trousers, sexually assaults her and strangles her. He places the bodies in the hide, throws Susan's trousers over her body and takes her underwear and other shoe with him." Read paused. "It's the only theory that fits the known facts."

Theories were all very well, they said, but Read could no longer spend time and public money on a murder which he couldn't prove had been committed.

Heavy-hearted, Read made a last visit to the

Gateway to hell—a path leads towards the woods on Barn Hill where the bodies of Gary Hanlon and Susan Blatchford were eventually discovered.

Shreds of evidence—how had Susan's green cord trousers got ripped along both side seams?

children's parents to tell them that the investigation was being wound down. He had spent many hours with them and of all the cases he had worked on, this was the one in which he had become most personally involved. In his final report Read was pessimistic. "Unless somebody surrenders himself or comes into custody and admits this offence, it is most unlikely that it will ever be resolved."

Third-Party Claims

Now, in June 1996, a copy of the same report lay on Nipper's garden table in the sunshine. "Not a single birthday has passed without my thinking of Gary and Susan and their families," he told his younger visitor.

"There's been a potentially startling development," Donnelly now revealed to Nipper. Earlier that month, a warder at Wakefield Prison had been approached by a 58-year-old prisoner called Ronald Jebson, who was serving a life sentence for an unrelated murder. He told the officer: "I've got some information about the murder of two children in Enfield, about 1970. The people behind it were a couple I was staying with at the time. I helped dispose of the bodies."

The information was passed to the Area Major Investigation Squad for north-east London. Detective Chief Inspector Donnelly was given the job of looking into Jebson's claim. He was bolstered by Read's briefing, but solving the riddle of the Babes in the Wood would take more than a prison confession. Yet, as Read had graphically described, the case had been stymied from the outset by a lack of hard evidence and reliable witnesses.

Pure Evil

Declan Donnelly had plenty of experience of interviewing murderers, rapists and paedophiles. The articulate and steely detective took it in his stride, but when he met Ronald Jebson he was surprised to find he was afraid of him.

Sitting opposite him in an interview room at Wakefield Prison, Jebson was a big man, well over six feet tall. But the air of menace was more than physical. Calm and quietly spoken, his receding grey-white hair scraped into an unlikely ponytail, he exuded an aura of pure evil.

Even by the standards of career paedophiles, Jebson had racked up an appalling catalogue of crimes against children dating back more than 40 years. In all, he had 11 convictions for offences ranging from petty theft to rape and eventually murder.

Less than a month before Gary and Susan went missing, Jebson had been released from a two-year sentence for indecently assaulting a six-year-old girl. Returning to his home town of Hatfield in Hertfordshire he had run into Robert Papper, an old school friend. From then on, he alternated between his rented flat in Enfield and the house in Hatfield where the Pappers lived with their four children.

On April 4, 1970, five days after Gary and Susan disappeared, Jebson enticed an 11-year-old boy into his car and sexually assaulted him in woods near Nottingham. Jailed for five years, freed after three, he returned to live with the Pappers. In June 1974 the couple ordered him out of the house when he flew into a drink- and drug-fuelled rage. Jebson vowed: "I'll do something you will regret."

He was as good as his word. Shortly afterwards, he collected the Pappers' four-year-old daughter Rosemary from school. Driving her to a wood, he raped her and strangled her with baling twine. He was sentenced to life for murder. It was now 1996, and he had been in jail all that time.

Like scores of other known sex offenders in north-east London, Jebson had been interviewed by Nipper Read's officers in 1970, shortly after his arrest in Nottingham. He had given a full account of his movements.

On March 31, the day Gary and Susan disappeared, Jebson and the Pappers had gone to the local labour exchange. From there, Jebson was sent for a job interview in Ordnance Road only a few minutes' walk from Gary Hanlon's home in Marrilyne Avenue. According to Jebson's 1970 statement, he'd then driven back to Hatfield and spent the afternoon watching television alone.

Had his involvement gone beyond disposing of the bodies? Donnelly marked a route with his finger on the whitewashed prison wall. "This is you going down Ordnance Road. Here are Susan and Gary going down Marrilyne Avenue. Your paths crossed. *You* abducted those children, didn't you?"

Jebson stared fixedly at Donnelly for perhaps 15 seconds.

"You're right," he said finally.

For a split second, Donnelly was jubilant. *He's confessed!*

But Jebson went on: "Yes, we were there. Robert was there. Maureen was there. We were in a car, saw the kids. Robert and Maureen enticed them inside. We drove them back to Hatfield."

There, alleged Jebson, the Pappers imprisoned the children in a cellar and abused them for several days before killing them. According to Jebson, he accompanied them as they drove the bodies back to Enfield and hid them in the wood on Barn Hill.

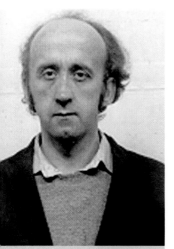

Cold stare—calm and quietly spoken, Ronald Jebson exuded an aura of pure evil.

False Trail

Robert and Maureen Papper proved surprisingly easy to trace. When Donnelly questioned them under caution, they denied all knowledge of the deaths of Susan and Gary. As he interviewed their three surviving children and their former lodgers and neighbours, Donnelly became increasingly convinced that the Pappers were telling the truth.

Their council house in Hatfield had been like Piccadilly Circus, with a constant stream of friends and relatives calling in at all hours of the day and night. Jebson's claim that Gary and Susan had been secreted there, tortured and murdered without anyone noticing a thing, beggared belief.

"Jebson is a particularly sadistic paedophile who gets pleasure out of recounting his crimes," clinical psychologist Dr Adrian West warned Donnelly before his next interview with Jebson.

It was also clear that Jebson was trying to edit out key details that would cause him pain or guilt. When they met next at Enfield police station Donnelly encouraged Jebson to talk freely. *Maybe he'll spin enough rope to hang himself.*

In the earlier interviews Jebson was keen to emphasize his normality. He had talked about his Jewish upbringing and his marriage to a girl called Wendy.

"Tell me more about Wendy."

Jebson described their wedding, on a Saturday in 1960.

"Are you sure that's the right date?" Donnelly asked.

"Of course I'm sure."

Donnelly put a wedding photograph on the table.

"Who's in this photograph?"

"Me at my wedding reception."

"No it's not, Ron," Donnelly snapped. "That's your *brother's* wedding reception. You didn't get married that day, he did." Jebson's arms were folded defensively, his face taut. "You're wrong."

Donnelly switched plays. "You're Jewish, aren't you, Ron?"

"Of course. I'm circumcised."

"Your brother tells us you were circumcised for medical reasons."

"He's lying."

"Really? Tell me Ron, if you're a practising Jew, how come you got married on a Saturday morning?"

Jebson was silent.

"There's no record of your *ever* having been married. You never even met Wendy! She was someone who wrote to you in prison."

As Donnelly dismantled Jebson's fantasy world piece by piece, the expression of the man in front of him changed to one of barely contained fury. However, Jebson was unwavering about Gary and Susan. He would admit only that he had been present when they were abducted, and he had helped dispose of their bodies, but nothing more.

Like Read, Donnelly hoped to win a conviction for the sake of the families. But there was still not enough evidence and after five days' questioning, Jebson returned to prison without charge.

Behind bars—while an inmate of Wakefield Prison (above), Ronald Jebson telephoned police to confess.

Sickening Justification

It was nearly two years later, in August 1998, when Ronald Jebson, calling from prison, rang the incident room at Enfield police station. Donnelly and his boss were both out. "OK. You can pass on this message," Jebson told a detective constable. "I killed those two children."

When he arrived at Enfield police station, Jebson described to Donnelly that winter afternoon, 28 years earlier. After visiting the labour exchange with Papper, he had driven alone to the job interview in his tiny Standard Ten. Afterwards, he saw Susan and Gary, whom, he said, he knew by sight. He arranged to meet them later to go for a drive. He then went home and got high on brandy and cannabis.

As planned, he picked up the children in the late afternoon and drove along Sewardstone Road, turning on to a narrow track leading to Barn Hill. The children laughed as the car jolted along the unmade road. He recalled a gateway, fields and finally the wood.

Jebson alleged that Susan and Gary had smoked cannabis with him. "When we got out of the car, none of us was what you might call steady on our feet," he smiled.

Donnelly recognized the sinister doublethink of the sex offender. Not only had Jebson used drink and drugs to reduce his own inhibitions to commit murder but, by suggesting that the children had shared the drugs, he was trying to convince himself that they were somehow culpable.

"They didn't want to play," Jebson shrugged. It was the paedophile's euphemism. *The children wouldn't let me abuse them.*

The scene then exploded in violence. Jebson grabbed Susan and tore at her trousers. Gary cried, "I want to go home."

Jebson turned on the little boy: "You're not going anywhere."

Jebson described to Donnelly how he raped, beat and strangled Susan Blatchford and Gary Hanlon and put their bodies together in the hide.

In the same tone of voice, he remembered how when he got back to Hatfield, Robert Papper joked innocently that Jebson's car was caked with mud and grass.

As the father of three children Donnelly was sickened by the confession.

Backtracking

The knowledge that Jebson's confession was not in itself enough to secure a murder conviction nagged at Donnelly's mind. Under English law, his statements would have to be corroborated with independent evidence. Since there were no other witnesses, the only option was to re-examine the forensic evidence with the help of modern techniques, in the hope that it would back up Jebson's testimony.

Gary had been cremated, but Susan's body had been buried at St James's Church, not far from her home. Donnelly was in the churchyard as the child's coffin was removed from the family grave.

Later, at the mortuary, he noticed a poignant detail: Susan's hair was still in an elastic band. On the last day of her life she had tied up her hair and breezed out of the house. To meet, of all people, Ronald Jebson.

This second post mortem was carried out by two eminent pathologists. They concluded that the internal bleeding in Susan's chest was almost certainly not due to pneumonia, but was consistent with someone kneeling on, or striking, her—both of which Jebson had said he'd done. The absence of Susan's underwear, and the way in which her right arm was drawn up inside her sleeve, meant only one thing. "This child has been re-dressed," they told Donnelly.

The Babes in the Wood had been murdered and almost certainly sexually assaulted, the pathologists agreed. Gary and Susan had been positioned by their killer to look as if they had died in each other's arms. It was a typical example of what the FBI now terms "staging", in which bodies are placed in a particular pattern or state of undress.

Susan's missing clothes could also be explained. Jebson had probably taken them as trophies. *After nearly three decades,* Donnelly reflected, *Nipper Read has finally been proved right.*

But he was still worried about winning a conviction. Three years had passed since his first interviews with Jebson. For the 1974 murder of Rosemary Papper, Jebson had been ordered to serve a minimum 25 years. "Now he can be considered for parole," Donnelly warned Crown Prosecution Service lawyers who would present the new evidence that Jebson had killed the Babes in the Wood. "We've got to pursue this case to the end," Donnelly insisted. "If Jebson gets out I believe he will kill again within a month."

"How do you plead?"

Ronald Jebson, you are charged with two counts of murder," the court official announced. The atmosphere inside the windowless courtroom at the Old Bailey on May 9, 2000, was humid and tense.

"Count one, that on a day between March 1, 1970, and June 30, 1970, you murdered Susan Blatchford. How do you plead?"

A few feet in front of Jebson, Nipper Read scribbled in his notebook. Declan Donnelly looked on from the back of the court, sick with worry that if Jebson pleaded not guilty it would mean a full trial before a jury, which, after such a lapse of time, could well lead to an acquittal.

For a few seconds time ceased, then Jebson answered calmly. "Guilty."

"Count two," continued the official, "that on a day between March 31, 1970, and June 17, 1970, you murdered Gary Hanlon. How do you plead?"

"Guilty."

Donnelly felt the tension inside him suddenly evaporate. Ronald Jebson was sentenced to two further life terms.

Outside, in the spring sunshine, the children's mothers congratulated Nipper Read.

"You were the only one who kept faith," Muriel Blatchford said to him.

Read was quick to praise his successor, Declan Donnelly.

"If it hadn't been for his persistence, the case would never have been solved," he said.

During the long hours spent questioning Jebson, Donnelly's initial reaction had not changed. *If I find this 60-year-old man frightening, how much more terrifying must he have seemed to Susan and Gary?*

Then he remembered Susan's hair, the way she had tied it up in a ponytail and breezed out of the house. To meet, of all people, Ronald Jebson.

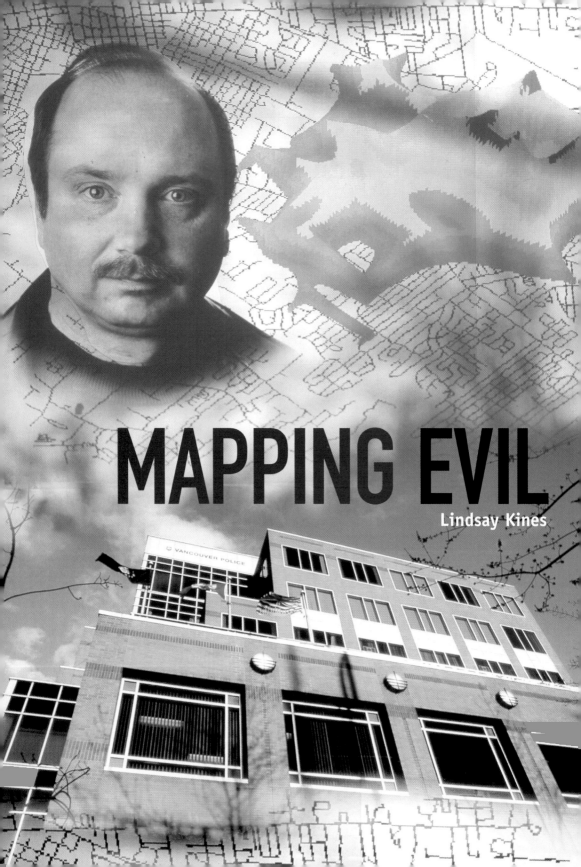

MAPPING EVIL

Lindsay Kines

Geographic profiler Detective Inspector Kim Rossmo targets serial criminals with his own unique weapon. A former mathematics major, this Canadian cop has developed an extraordinary computer program to home in on crime. And it's all based upon a universal character trait: laziness.

The eyes give him away. Red-rimmed and slightly bloodshot, they hint at the crushing workload that has become routine for Detective Inspector Kim Rossmo.

The previous night, he was up until 2am writing a textbook. Six hours later he was at CBC Radio studios in Vancouver to talk about the new novel in which Rossmo, appearing as himself, saves the day. Then it was back to Vancouver police headquarters to meet a reporter, lecture a group of students, and make last-minute preparations for a trip to South Africa and Germany, where he would join another manhunt. This time it's . . . a serial killer? A rapist? Rossmo won't say. But if a police agency has asked for his help, it has to be horrific.

In June 1984 a masked man broke into a house in Lafayette, Louisiana, and raped a woman at gunpoint. A number of similar rapes occurred in the years that followed; but partly because of the turnover among detectives, police never twigged to the idea that they were the work of the same person.

It might have stayed that way if Detective Mac Gallien had not overheard a colleague discussing a case in August 1995 that sounded strikingly similar to one of Gallien's own unsolved files. After DNA evidence confirmed the link, Gallien went searching through old cases and eventually found 14 or 15 unsolved files that fitted the pattern. Of those, DNA evidence confirmed a definite link among six, and police realized a serial rapist had been at work in their city for the past 10 years. Investigators went public with the discovery, and the rapes suddenly stopped.

In the ensuing years, two task forces were created and disbanded, and hundreds of leads and tips failed to catch the rapist. Gallien was still searching for answers in late 1997 when he read about a Vancouver cop who had developed a new technique for tracking serial predators. The cop's name was Kim Rossmo, and he called his new technique geographic profiling.

Everyone is lazy. You need a litre of milk, you walk to the corner store. You want to go to the gym, you use the local fitness centre. This is known as the nearness or "least effort" principle. If you were to plot it on a map, there would be a bunch

117

of dots around your house and office to indicate the places you stop in a day or week. The farther from home and work, the fewer the stops. It's as if people rely on a geographic template in their heads, an inner logic that guides their movements.

Police headquarters—the building in Vancouver where Rossmo's innovatory geographic profiling was developed.

Petty crooks are no different, neither are serial killers. Rossmo learned this while studying criminology at Simon Fraser University, and he decided to make it the basis of his doctoral research. The question central to his idea was this: if you knew where a series of crimes took place, could you apply the nearness principle and the laws of probability and logic to develop a formula that would accurately predict where the criminal was most likely to be living?

The question would consume Rossmo for years. Already a full-time cop, in the 1990s he would finish his shift on Vancouver's downtown east side at 2am, then drive to Simon Fraser and work in the lab until morning.

A former mathematics major, he developed a complex formula to answer his question and then wrote his own computer program to handle the myriad calculations. The first time he tested geographic profiling was on a serial-arson case that had already been solved using more conventional means.

Rossmo entered the fire locations into his database, and the computer spat out a map showing the most likely area where the arsonist lived. The map also highlighted specific zones in the overall area where the police should begin looking. Since the firebug was already in custody, Rossmo could check the hot zones against the arsonist's known address.

He was ecstatic. The computer had zeroed in on exactly the right area. If investigators had been able to use geographic profiling, they would have searched just one per cent of the total area before knocking on the culprit's door. The real tests, though, were still to come.

It was a stifling evening when Rossmo and his understudy—Detective Sergeant Brad Moore of the Ontario Provincial Police—landed in Louisiana in late May 1998. Together with Gallien, they retraced the steps of the South Side Rapist, reviewing files, visiting crime scenes, flying over the neighbourhoods in an airplane. They checked traffic flow at different times of the day and considered the routes the rapist might have taken.

On the fourth day, Rossmo and Moore flew back to Canada, where they analysed the data and entered it into the computer. As in the arson case, the computer spat out a profile. But this time, Rossmo had no way of knowing immediately if it was right. All he could do was mail off the results and wait for an answer.

The computer spat out a profile. Rossmo had no way of knowing if it was right. All he could do was mail off the results and wait.

From the beginning, geographic profiling was a hit. Even before he received his doctorate, Rossmo was giving lectures to the FBI, Scotland Yard and the Royal Canadian Mounted Police. The FBI and five major universities offered him jobs. But the Vancouver police chief at the time, Ray Canuel, in an unprecedented move, promoted his coveted officer from constable to the newly created rank of detective inspector.

Then the grumbling began as Rossmo faced resentment at his rapid rise through the ranks and skepticism of geographic profiling. To combat the skepticism, he began giving lectures around the world, agreed to dozens of media interviews and started work on a textbook for a prestigious science publisher.

119

But his best marketing tool may prove to be his appearance as a character in *Burnt Bones*, a psycho-thriller by Vancouver writer Michael Slade. Slade's books have developed a strong following among police officers because of their strict adherence to proper police procedure. Rossmo hopes the novel will do for geographic profiling what *Silence of the Lambs* did for its psychological counterpart. "I know it works, this invention of yours," Slade's hero, Chief Superintendent Robert DeClercq, tells Rossmo in the novel. The difficulty is in convincing real cops.

Psycho-thriller—Rossmo appeared as a character in Michael Slade's *Burnt Bones*.

Lafayette is a long way from Vancouver, physically and figuratively. Gallien wondered how anyone could possibly hope to say where the South Side Rapist was after spending just three days in the city. "I mean, the man doesn't live here," Gallien says. "This is bayou country."

So Gallien was amazed when the profile highlighted one particular neighbourhood, covering just over one square kilometre of Lafayette. Investigators, of course, had already considered the area, since it was close to a number of the crime scenes. "But we looked in a lot of places," Gallien says. "There was nothing to distinguish that area from any other until Kim came in."

In just three years, Lafayette police had cleared more than 100 suspects using DNA and had compiled boxes of tips, leads and other pieces of information on the case. They also had a composite drawing of a suspect and a psychological profile suggesting the rapist might have links to law enforcement.

Investigators were looking at a number of suspects, but one, it turned out, lived within jogging distance of the area suggested by Rossmo's profile and had once resided right in the middle of it. He also fitted aspects of the psychological profile and bore a resemblance to the composite. In the end, says Gallien, Rossmo's geographic profile, along with the other clues, "helped us make a decision to place this guy at the top of our list of suspects."

It was enough to convince police to surreptitiously obtain DNA from his discarded cigarette butt. The saliva matched DNA evidence obtained at the crime scenes and, in January 1999, police arrested the suspect, a long-time investigator

in the juvenile division of the Lafayette Parish Sheriff's Office. Ernest Randal Comeaux, 39, was indicted on six counts of aggravated

Vancouver skyline—from the sixth floor of the Vancouver police headquarters (centre), Rossmo could see Cambie Bridge and the tangled web of streets that triggered his unique method of criminal profiling.

rape, pleaded guilty and received multiple life sentences. Looking back on it now, Gallien admits his amazement at the accuracy of Rossmo's profile.

"I bombarded him with a whole pile of information," Gallien says. "Now, what's the chance of him narrowing it down? That's almost unbelievable."

Rossmo is sitting in his office on the sixth floor of Vancouver police headquarters, overlooking Cambie Bridge and the Vancouver skyline. When he was signed to his original contract, Rossmo promised that, in addition to working cases around the world, he would write a book, train other profilers and generally raise the image of geographic profiling. In the years since, he's done all of that and more.

Since completing his contract at the Vancouver Police Department in January 2001, Kim Rossmo has become research director for the American Police Foundation in Washington DC, where he has used geographic profiling in more than 150 criminal investigations. He has also worked on cases in Africa, Australia, the Middle East and Europe and has seen several thousand crime sites.

FIRE LOVER

Joseph Wambaugh

In the 1980s a series of suspicious blazes hit southern California, killing four people. The arsonist grew ever more bold, seeming to taunt his pursuers. Then John Orr stepped to the forefront of the hunt. Now, surely, it was only a matter of time before the case was solved—because no one knew arson better than Orr.

I t had been a long shift for Jim Obdam. The young clerk was working all day at Ole's Home Center in South Pasadena, California. Just after 8pm he headed for the front of the store, an 18,000-square-foot hardware emporium. He was astonished to see a column of dark smoke rising from a display rack.

Obdam hurried through the store, looking for customers. In the paint department he ran into a woman who worked there. He told her about the smoke. "Are there any more people in your section?" he asked.

"I'll check," she said, and left in search of stragglers. Nobody was unduly alarmed, having seen no fire, just the column of smoke. Obdam found two people looking at tools, and told them to leave.

Then he encountered a middle-aged woman with a small child in a shopping cart. Ada Deal and her husband, Billy, had brought their grandson Matthew to Ole's about a half-hour earlier. Knowing the store was about to close, Ada and Billy had decided to split up and shop separately to save time.

"Don't be alarmed," Obdam told Ada, "but there's a fire and we've got to leave." He set off down the aisle, but when he looked around, the woman hadn't started to follow, so he went back.

"Leave the cart here," he said more forcefully. "Take the child and let's go!" He headed toward the front of the store, with Ada Deal and her grandson following behind him. Then he looked over toward the column of smoke.

It was no longer a cloud—it was a wall of flame, bright orange and raging. Obdam noticed that the steel fire door in the back of the store, a safety feature designed to compartmentalize the building and contain the blaze, had dropped down. When he turned to look for the woman and child, he heard a popping noise and the lights went out.

In the darkness he battled panic. Obdam knew there was an emergency exit in the far north-west corner at the rear of the store. He staggered back there and duck-walked his way along, feeling the wall, groping for merchandise, anything to guide him. Holding his breath, he dropped low to the floor, and then even lower, desperate for the same oxygen the fire craved.

Obdam was about to give up, when he realised he was just a few feet from the emergency exit. He felt an energy rush and lunged, pushing the bars, activating the alarm.

And he was out. The hungry flames couldn't reach him, but the trailing heat did. His arms, neck and ears were still hot and burning. Covered head to toe with soot, Obdam ran around to the front of the store, eager to call his parents to tell them he was all right. As he touched his hand to his burning wrist, flesh fell off onto the pavement.

The Big Picture

Billy deal spotted Obdam running in front of the store toward other employees huddled in the parking lot. They shouted to him, overjoyed to see him alive. Billy thought, *Well, he got out, didn't he? Maybe Ada and Matthew did too.* Maybe.

Billy ran to the fire captain, who had just arrived with his men. He cried out that his wife and grandson were trapped, maybe only 10 feet inside the front door. Captain William Eisele felt confident that if people were only 10 feet inside, he could rescue them. He said to Billy, "Don't worry, we'll take care of that!"

But when the captain and his men entered the building, they looked into a blinding orange inferno. There were no aisles, no people, nothing but fire. Then came an eerie sound co-mingled with the noise of the conflagration: the display smoke detectors were going off, one after another. The fire-fighters could hear the devices' high-pitched squeals within the flames, like animals burning alive.

Where in the hell was Engine 41? Captain Eisele wondered, yelling into the radio. *And why did he hear an engine being radio-dispatched in the wrong direction?* What Captain Eisele didn't know was that there was another fire at nearby Von's supermarket. It was unheard-of: two fires in such close proximity, in retail establishments, during business hours.

That evening of October 10, 1984, was indeed bizarre for fire-fighters in the San Gabriel Valley. Prior to the Ole's fire, and the one at Von's Market, there had also been a fire in Pasadena, at Albertson's Market, about seven miles from Ole's.

Arson investigator Scott McClure had arrived at Albertson's at 6.45pm. He found the fire's point of origin easily enough, in the grocery racks piled high with bags of potato chips. At 7.45pm McClure called dispatch and requested that they send arson investigator John Orr, from the Glendale Fire Department. McClure considered him an accomplished arson sleuth.

John Orr showed up quickly. People described him as an "average-looking" guy—not tall, five foot nine, maybe 20 pounds overweight, most of it around the middle. He sported a mustache, while his slate-blue eyes were a bit narrow and almost lashless, and he had straight dark hair just starting to recede.

Orr knew about the volatility of potato chips, that the oils in the chips and the bag material are highly combustible, basically making them a sack of solid fuel. He would later conclude that the Albertson's fire was set deliberately, as is usually the case with fires in retail stores when customers are present.

After McClure finished his investigation and returned to his car, he heard radio reports of the disaster that was unfolding seven miles away at Ole's Home Center. McClure sped toward the scene, and when he arrived, John Orr was already there, taking pictures with his 35-millimeter camera.

While fire-fighters awaited the arrival of reinforcements, while Jim Obdam was being led to an ambulance, and while Billy Deal stood in front of Ole's Home Center where he would remain for the next 22 hours, John Orr shot film of the roof caving in and a geyser of flame and sparks exploding high into the night.

The Wannabe

In 1971 John Orr, newly discharged from the military, had applied to the LA Police Department, the LA County Sheriff's Department, the City of LA Fire Department and the LA County Fire Department. The LAPD sent Orr a letter inviting him to test. He passed the written exam, the physical-agility test, the oral interview and the medical. He was given a date when he'd be starting the police academy, and he was ecstatic. There was only one more hurdle—the medical exam had a second part: psychological testing.

Orr's psychological file noted both marital and job-related problems. It pegged him as "irresponsible and immature," with an "emotionally unstable personality." Some weeks later Orr received a rejection letter from the LAPD. But the letter said only that he was "unsuitable." Orr was shattered, then outraged. He would have been a good cop, he thought.

He next applied and was accepted by the Los Angeles Fire Department. He was a fire-fighter now—almost. He still had to get through the academy. Having served as a fire-fighter in the services, Orr felt that he was prepared. But the academy was more rigorous than he'd thought. The LAFD used heavy wooden ladders instead of the lightweight aluminum ones Orr had been accustomed to in the military. Lots of the other recruits had practised ladder carries on their off-duty days, but not Orr. As a result, he flunked the physical test and was released from the department. He went home and wept. Later he described his rejection as "paralysing."

In desperation, he applied in January 1974 to the Glendale Fire Department, which was near the bottom of the pay scale for the 55 fire agencies in Los Angeles County. But Orr would gladly settle, if Glendale would take him. And it did. Now no one could say he was unsuitable. He was a real fire-fighter.

On his off-duty days he took a part-time job as a security employee at a department store. In his first few months there, he arrested 30 people, including a husband-and-wife shoplifting team, which led to the recovery of $30,000-worth of property. Impressed, the police chief's administrative assistant, who also worked off-duty at the store, helped the new employee get a concealed-weapon permit.

Now Orr could legally carry a gun, and he began hanging out at bars where cops gathered, entering into all the cop talk with a notable swagger. And soon, around the fire department and the police department, Orr became known as a "cop wannabe."

During the late 1970s a series of arsons occurred in Glendale. It was rumored that the Glendale Fire Department intended to hire a full-time arson investigator. Orr wanted the job badly, and he got it. The fire chief told him the new position had peace-officer authority, which meant that Orr could carry a firearm full-time. Now no one could call him a wannabe.

By the early '80s Orr had a departmental car and all the overtime pay he wanted. He had also begun a sideline career as a writer, contributing articles to *American Fire Journal*. All things considered, his life was pretty good— except in one area. In 1983 his third marriage ended. A self-described "eccentric" and well-known womanizer, Orr had trouble sustaining long-term intimate relationships.

His job left him little time to brood over this latest marital failure, however. The city of Glendale was having far more than its share of arsons, although Orr maintained that it only seemed that way because he worked harder at identifying them. He was building a reputation, and soon began conducting training sessions for other arson investigators.

Then in October 1984, Orr attended the most monumental fire of his career, the blaze at Ole's Home Center that left four people dead: two clerks, customer Ada Deal and her grandson Matthew. Orr did not take part in the investigation, conducted by Sergeant Jack Palmer, a 25-year veteran assigned to the arson-explosives detail of the Los Angeles County Sheriff's Department.

Sergeant Palmer concluded that the fire had probably been started by an electrical short in the attic space. Lawyers retained by the families of the victims settled out-of-court for $4 million. John Orr told the Glendale Fire Department he was disappointed the fire had been called accidental. He said that if investigators knew what to look for, they would probably have found an incendiary device.

Four months after the Ole's calamity in South Pasadena, the Ole's Home Center in Pasadena barely escaped a similar fate. Some wondered if the fire setter was graduating from potato chips to bigger targets. Another possibility would not be considered for some time to come: by attacking the second Ole's store, perhaps an arsonist was making a statement to investigators—that they had got it wrong the first time.

Strange Ideas

In January 1987, the city of Fresno was swarming with men and women whose lives were dedicated to fire prevention and suppression. John Orr was one of 242 investigators, prosecutors, cops and fire-fighters who had come from all over the state. They were attending a three-day seminar hosted by the California Conference of Arson Investigators.

The conference might have come and gone and passed from memory except that on the night before it started, at about 8.30, an employee at Payless Drug Store in Fresno spotted smoke rising from a display of sleeping-bags. Helped by the overhead sprinklers, the store manager contained the fire with a handheld fire extinguisher.

Two days later at Hancock Fabrics, across the street from Payless, a shopper glanced up from examining some fabric in the center of the store to see smoke in the corner of the building. Suddenly the smoke cloud erupted in a ball of flame. She watched slack-jawed as the fireball divided into fingers of fire that danced up the walls and along the ceiling. It all happened unbelievably fast.

She watched slack-jawed as the fireball divided into fingers of fire that danced up the walls and along the ceiling.

The blaze was so intense that the fire department did not dare enter the building. Even though the store was destroyed, everyone was relieved that customers and employees had escaped without injury.

At House of Fabrics, just a block away from the other two stores, an employee saw smoke rising from a bin stacked with pillows. It had scorched the wall, but had not ignited into a full-blown blaze.

The day the seminar ended, in the town of Tulare an hour south of Fresno, there was a fire at Surplus City, followed by another attempt at Family Bargain Center. After a customer saw smoke in a display bin, the manager pulled the pillows out and extinguished the flames. At the bottom of the bin he found a partially burned incendiary device. Arson investigators called it a "signature device"—a cigarette with three paper matches attached by a rubber band. Such a device could provide up to 15 minutes for an arsonist to get away before the burning cigarette ignited the matches, which in turn would ignite the flammable material around them. A similar fire starter had been found at an arson that had occurred in the LA area in the late 1970s. The presence of the device was known only to investigators, who hadn't made it public, which ruled out the possibility of a copycat.

Time bomb—the arsonist used a signature device like this one—paper matches rubber-banded to a burning cigarette—to give him the opportunity to leave the scene before all hell broke loose.

Later that day in Bakersfield, an hour south of Tulare on the way to Los Angeles, an employee of CraftMart spotted a column of smoke coming from a display of materials used in making dry floral arrangements. The manager put out the fire with a dry-powder extinguisher while the engine company was en route.

The fire captain called for an investigator, and Captain Marvin Casey of the Bakersfield Fire Department responded at once. With nearly 20 years of experience, Casey had investigated hundreds of fires. The former Texan had thinning gray hair, a blue-eyed panhandle squint, and a face creased from years in the dust and wind of the San Joaquin Valley.

Casey looked inside the bin where the fire had broken out. There he found an incendiary device composed of a cigarette and three matches, two made of paper, one of wood, and a scorched sheet of yellow lined notebook paper. He carefully placed these items in evidence containers.

It was destined to be a busy day for Casey. At 2pm that same afternoon, another fire broke out in a bin containing foam rubber in a fabric store in Bakersfield. Fortunately, employees and fire-fighters were able to extinguish the blaze.

The next day Casey met with investigators from Fresno and learned of the suspicious fires there over the past few days—ironically while the conference of arson investigators was underway. All the fires took place in retail stores during business hours. All began in displays of highly flammable materials. And then there was the incendiary device that Casey had found.

That was when Casey began to get some strange but exciting ideas. All the fires took place close to Highway 99, as though the fire setter had been in Fresno, then had driven down the road to Tulare on Friday morning for two fires, and then on to Bakersfield where he'd struck twice. After that he seemed to vanish from the San Joaquin Valley.

Casey sent the evidence he'd collected to a nearby laboratory operated by the Bureau of Alcohol, Tobacco and Firearms (ATF), where a fingerprint analyst obtained a readable print from the yellow notebook paper. This fingerprint was sent to state and national databases, but whoever the print belonged to had no criminal record.

Marvin Casey's next step was to obtain the Fresno arson conference roster of 242 names. He determined from their places of employment who would have driven home south from the meeting. His list had 55 names on it.

Though Casey could have guessed at the response he'd get, he had to turn to the feds for help on something multijurisdictional like this. As he expected, ATF Special Agent Chuck Galyan in the Fresno office was more than skeptical.

"I certainly didn't think that Marv Casey's intuition was worth a wholesale inquiry into travel records and so forth," Galyan later recalled.

Another Outbreak

And so matters rested until March 1989, when an arson conference was held in the town of Pacific Grove, near Monterey. On March 3, the day before the conference was to begin, business was brisk at Cornet Variety Store in Morro Bay, two-and-a-half hours south of Pacific Grove. Suddenly a clerk heard a woman yell "Fire!"

The clerk grabbed the fire extinguisher and ran toward the screaming voice. He saw flames licking out from a pile of foam pillows stored in aisle displays. The fire was put out quickly.

The next day a second fire broke out in Salinas, just 19 miles north-east of Pacific Grove. In all, six fires were set in retail establishments on the Central Coast at the time the arson symposium was being conducted in Pacific Grove. When Marvin Casey learned of this, he was energized: it had happened again!

Casey once more obtained a roster of participants and pared down the suspect list to those from southern California who had attended both conferences. There were only 10 people who'd been in Fresno *and* Pacific Grove. The names on the list were respected arson investigators. One of them, John Orr from the Glendale Fire Department, was familiar to Casey. Two years earlier he had taken a class from Orr in order to get his state certification.

Once again Casey phoned ATF Special Agent Chuck Galyan. This time Galyan agreed to submit a photo Casey had obtained of the print, along with the 10 names culled from the roster of both conferences, to a Department of Justice laboratory in Fresno.

After the fingerprint cards of the 10 arson investigators were retrieved from the state database of people who hold public safety jobs, they were analyzed by a veteran Department of Justice fingerprint expert. His report stated that there was no match between Casey's image and the inked fingerprints of the 10 men in question.

Marvin Casey thought that everyone would probably have a good laugh at the Bakersfield hick. The not-so-mighty Casey had struck out.

Meanwhile, two months after he returned from the Pacific Grove conference, John Orr was promoted to fire captain.

Pool of Fire

There was another Fresno symposium in June 1990, but this time John Orr decided his subordinate should go. Orr would stay behind and tend to duties in Glendale.

On Wednesday, June 27, temperatures were topping 100 degrees, and Santa Ana winds were blowing into the Los Angeles basin from the desert. This was the season to fear. This was the time of fire. Every summer there were brush fires in the foothills of Glendale. Orr told the local news media that all of them were probably set by the same person. But the arson unit never had much luck in locating likely firebugs.

Winds were blowing into the Los Angeles basin from the desert. This was the season to fear. This was the time of fire.

Orr was out of the office when a call came into the Glendale Fire Department around 3pm, reporting a brush fire sweeping up a hillside in the College Hills area. A dispatcher activated the first alarm.

Arriving on the scene, Captain Greg Jones of Engine 29 saw John Orr standing by his white Chevy Blazer near the area of the fire's origin. Orr approached Captain Jones and asked if he needed help. Jones told the arson investigator to grab a line and hose down the adjacent house to keep the fire from spreading. Jones then began working on a house where the roof was on fire.

A few minutes later, when he returned to the street, Jones saw Orr dragging a tarp from the fire engine into the house that Jones was hosing down. This was puzzling behavior; protecting the contents of a house was a low priority when the attic was on fire and the whole damned neighborhood was threatened.

But Orr simply covered a living-room couch with the tarp as embers fell around him. Then he walked outside and drove away, without hosing down the house next door. Jones later said that Orr was acting very strangely.

There were outbreaks everywhere in College Hills. The land was smothered by smoke and ash, and the skies swarmed with police, fire and news aircraft.

John Orr later described the scene: "Water-dropping helicopters dove at the hottest flanks of the fire, unleashing over 350 gallons of water each time they swooped down. The big Hueys looked like dragonflies in slow motion, skittering over a pool of fire."

Late that afternoon, Moses Gomez of the California State Fire Marshal's Office called Glendale, offered assistance, and was asked to respond to a command post that had been set up in the 1100 block on North Verdugo Road. Before reaching the command post, Gomez saw a white Chevy Blazer parked on the street. He recognized John Orr standing behind the Blazer removing his coveralls.

Gomez waved to Orr, offered his help and was asked to join him. Orr pointed to a nearby area marked by crime-scene tape and said to Gomez, "That's the area of origin. I found a delay device."

He showed Gomez an evidence vial with a disposable lighter inside, and said that the cap was jammed open, allowing the butane to flow. Later Gomez was shocked when Orr told reporters everything—the point of origin, the butane lighter—all of it. These are things arson investigators never reveal, things only the arsonist would know about.

Orr joined Gomez and a Glendale police officer when they went to interview a woman who reported that before she'd noticed the fire, she'd seen a man standing across the street at the edge of the brush. He was about five feet ten inches, had dark hair and a mustache, and wore khaki pants. He had been standing with his back to her. The man drove a white or tan car, she said.

John Orr didn't open his mouth during the interview. In fact, he showed no interest at all in what the woman was saying. Moses Gomez later became the second person to report that the behavior of the Glendale arson investigator seemed very peculiar.

By the time the College Hills fires were over, more than 60 homes had been damaged or destroyed. Miraculously, nobody had been killed or seriously injured. For the Glendale Fire Department, one good thing had come out of the disaster. The budget cuts they'd been facing were called off. The fire setter, if there was one, had made their argument for them.

No More Doubt

Beginning in December 1990, and continuing through March 1991, the Los Angeles area was blitzed by an arson series of a kind never seen before. Nineteen fires were set in retail stores in the Los Angeles area. On March 27 alone, five fires occurred in retail stores within a two-and-a-half-hour period.

One of the arson investigators, Glen Lucero of the Los Angeles Fire Department, recalled a similar series of fires up in the San Fernando Valley the previous December—set, like these, in piles of pillows and bedding. The LAFD asked for assistance from the ATF. Special Agents Ken Croke and April Carroll joined Lucero in an investigation, supervised by ATF Special Agent Michael Matassa. The new team was dubbed the Pillow Pyro Task Force, after the pyromaniac who liked to set bins of pillows on fire.

A flier was printed to spread the word about the modus operandi of the Pillow Pyro and to solicit leads. At the Glendale Fire Department, John Orr and his partner received a copy.

It came to Mike Matassa's attention that after a series of arsons in the Central Valley back in 1989, Marv Casey of the Bakersfield Fire Department had developed a theory that a fire-fighter might be involved. Matassa also found out that Casey had a good fingerprint from one of the fires.

The Pillow Pyro Task Force was sent to Bakersfield to meet Captain Casey. They came away with the fingerprint photo. "Let's run it through again," Mike Matassa said. "Maybe he got busted in the last couple of years for stealing pillows or whatever else he does to get his kicks."

Matassa took the photo of Marvin Casey's fingerprint to the LA County Sheriff's Department laboratory. There it was put on a scanner that gave a numerical score indicating how well the computer "liked" the print as a match to something already existing in its files.

This time, the print was run through the Los Angeles Hall of Justice computer. That database contained, in addition to criminal fingerprint cards and the prints of all county law enforcement officers, the fingerprint cards of everyone who had ever applied for a law enforcement job. When the computer read the prints of an applicant who had tried to join the Los Angeles Police Department 20 years earlier, it "liked" that applicant very much indeed.

There was no doubt: the fingerprint was John Orr's.

_____

Diary of a Psychopath

Captain Marvin Casey was suspicious when the three investigators and Special Agent Chuck Galyan arrived back at his office. "Two visits from the feds in one month?" he said. "To a country boy in Bakersfield?"

All they would tell him was that his latent print was "promising" and that they had a few suspects in mind. They wanted to establish the chain of evidence, they said. By the time Lucero, Croke, Carroll and Galyan left, they were satisfied that no outsider could have touched that evidence in any way. Because the investigation was classified, however, they did not tell Casey that his hunch was correct. It would be months before he would learn of his vindication.

The Pillow Pyro Task Force next held a confidential meeting with Glendale battalion chief Christopher Gray, John Orr's immediate superior. The three investigators informed Gray they would need call-out sheets as well as fire department phone records. In the course of their meeting, the battalion chief mentioned that Orr was writing a novel about arson investigation. Chief Gray said that Orr had given him the first couple of chapters to read, but all Gray could remember was that it was full of filthy dialogue. None of the task force members could think of how Orr's literary efforts could assist them, but they thanked the chief for the information.

During the next months, the investigators lined up witnesses and reviewed Glendale fire department call-out sheets. The records showed that John Orr's whereabouts were unaccounted for when every arson had occurred.

By September 1991 they felt they had accumulated nearly enough evidence to arrest Orr. Mike Matassa called Marvin Casey, at long last giving Casey credit for what he had done. ATF agents had scoffed at the Bakersfield fire captain's theory for years. Now an ATF agent had phoned to say that Casey had been right all along. In fact, it later came out at trial that the Department of Justice expert who had tested the 10 fingerprints after the Pacific Grove conference had simply made a mistake, failing to make the match with Orr's print.

In early October the task force was reminded of something that Chief Gray of Glendale had told them back in April: John Orr was writing a novel about arson called *Points of Origin*. Maybe it would shed some light upon the case. But how to get a copy?

The task force enlisted a retired LAFD arson investigator, A. J. Jackubowski, himself a writer. Jackubowski called the Glendale arson captain and said he'd heard that Orr was writing a novel and wondered if there was anything he could do to help a fellow fire-fighter get published. Jackubowski suggested they exchange and compare manuscripts.

Orr sent out a copy of his manuscript by overnight mail. The next day *Points of Origin* was being copied at task force headquarters in Los Angeles. It was immediately obvious that Orr had written in detail about the very fires the task force was investigating. In a matter of minutes everyone was ganging up on the machine operator, grabbing at copies.

In chapter six the villain, Aaron, a fire-fighter turned arsonist, set fire to a hardware business in a "small community south of Pasadena." A chilling passage described how a grandmother, "Madeline Paulson," was caught in the fire with her three-year-old grandson, "Matthew": *She felt herself losing her grip on Matthew. The contents of the annex exploded into flames. Their last breaths were of 800-degree heat that seared their throats closed.*

When Madeline's body was found, she was on her back with Matthew clinging to her ankles. The fire was ineptly termed accidental. Aaron was so furious that he set a nearly identical fire at another hardware store. Aaron wanted the fire to be called arson. He hated it when he wasn't properly recognized.

Prisoner For Life

On December 4, 1991, when John Orr came out of his front door at 7.10am, a team of about 15 agents and arson investigators from the ATF, LAFD and LA Sheriff's Department was waiting for him. Partially concealed in the bushes near his house, they all had their guns drawn.

Larry Cornelison, supervisor of the ATF's Los Angeles arson division, approached Orr and said, "You're under arrest, John."

"For what?" Orr asked.

"Arson."

A shocked Orr protested his innocence as they handcuffed him and took him away for interrogation. But a search of his black canvas bag, car and office turned up some incriminating objects: a pack of Camel cigarettes, two books of matches, rubber bands, a steno pad of yellow lined paper, and videos and photographs of fire.

In 1992 Orr was tried in a United States district court on five counts of arson: two in Fresno, one in Tulare and two in Bakersfield. He was convicted on three counts and sentenced to 30 years. But he would be eligible for parole after serving just 10 years.

Orr then faced another federal trial on eight counts of arson for the Central Coast fires and others in the Los Angeles area. On the advice of his lawyer, Orr pleaded guilty to three arson counts that had no significant damage involved and thus would carry no civil liability for restitution. Pleading guilty to these crimes would not increase his sentence. So John Orr could still seek parole in 2002.

But the criminal justice system was not finished with him. On June 27,

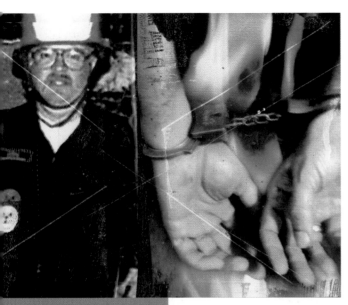

Burning passion—for John Orr (left), only one thing could provide the irresistible thrill, the indescribable reward— the fire, *his* fire.

1995, Deputy D.A. Michael J. Cabral presented a 25-count indictment before a Los Angeles grand jury. Among the charges were four counts of murder for the Ole's Home Center fire in South Pasadena and 17 counts of arson for the College Hills fires. The trial took place in 1998. When it was over, John Orr had been convicted of 24 out of the 25 counts, and was also found guilty of multiple murder. He was sentenced to life in prison without possibility of parole.

Although Orr steadfastly maintained his innocence, after his arrest there was a 75 per cent drop in brush-fire activity in and around Glendale. And there were no more suspicious fires in Los Angeles retail stores.

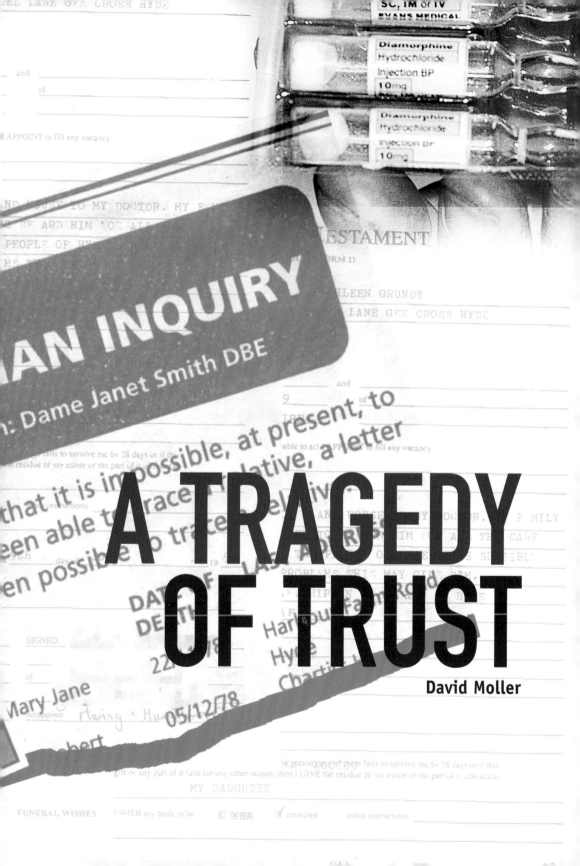

"It was comforting to know you were with her during her final moments. We couldn't ask for a finer, more caring doctor," wrote the grieving son of one of Dr Harold Shipman's older patients. Those who were treated by the GP thought the world of him. But why had so many of his patients died without warning?

H is maroon Renault Espace people carrier crested Mottram Old Road on that sunny summer morning, giving Dr Harold "Fred" Shipman a fine view of Greater Manchester down below. A few tall chimneys and six-storey cotton mills stood out from the city sprawl on the skyline—a reminder of its past days of glory.

Caring GP—the benign, grey-haired Harold "Fred" Shipman was well-known for his willingness to make home visits.

Shipman, 52, was on his way to see a patient in Hyde, the quiet, pleasant town where the GP maintained his practice. Hyde, mainly a home for the elderly, as well as a dormitory town for those who worked elsewhere, had its share of imposing structures, including Hyde Chapel with its soaring spire. That was where the doctor turned left, up narrow Joel Lane.

Parking partly on the pavement, Shipman grabbed his black leather case and pushed his way through the white wooden gate of No. 79. Of short, slim build and with a beard already showing grey, he strode across rough Yorkstone paving to the front door of the stone-built, two-storey cottage. He'd known Kathleen Grundy for almost two decades; they served together on the Community Health Council. So it was not surprising that he should offer to come along to her house, saving the 81-year-old woman a two-mile trip into town.

It was 8am when Mrs Grundy, trim and auburn-haired, greeted Shipman at the door, then led him to her elegant living room. The visit wouldn't take long.

As she rolled up the left sleeve of her blouse, Shipman put a dab of antiseptic on cotton wool, then cleaned the skin on her upper arm. Taking a hypodermic syringe from his bag, he guided the needle to a vein and gently gave her an injection.

Mrs Grundy relaxed, leaning back on the settee. Shipman, meanwhile, packed up his bag, returned to the car and drove back to his surgery on Market Street.

Later that morning—Wednesday, June 24, 1998—a letter with Kathleen Grundy's return address arrived at Hamilton Ward & Co, a firm of solicitors, also on Market Street, just up the road from the doctor's surgery.

"You've got to go to the police"

Angela Woodruff kept breaking down in tears; the idea of her mother, Kathleen Grundy, no longer being there was overwhelming. She tried to focus on what Dr Shipman was saying.

He was explaining to her and Phil, her husband, how he had visited her mother the previous morning. She had complained of feeling unwell during a recent consultation, he said.

A few hours later, however, a couple of her friends discovered Angela's mother curled up on the settee, fully dressed. She had passed away.

They summoned Shipman and he returned to the cottage. There he examined the body, later filling in the certificate showing the cause of death. Angela Woodruff looked at the certificate in her hand. Shipman had simply written down "old age". She still couldn't quite understand.

"Quite often, the old complain of not feeling well a few days before they die," Shipman said. "She might have had chest pains or something masked as indigestion." Angela was relieved to hear the doctor add that there was no need for a post-mortem.

Later that day, as they drove the 80 miles back to their home in Warwickshire, Angela couldn't get over her mother's sudden passing. Just a few weeks earlier, she had been to stay with Angela, Phil and their two sons, accompanying them on several long walks and helping out with the household chores.

Phil gently reminded her that what had happened to Kathleen wasn't so unusual. "It was almost exactly the same pattern of events with your aunt," he said. Two years earlier, Elsie Platt had also died suddenly of a heart attack. She too had been a patient of Dr Shipman's.

Angela buried her mother at Hyde Chapel on July 1. Some two weeks later, at her offices in Warwickshire where she practised as a solicitor, she took a call from Hamilton Ward & Co. They said that they'd received a will in the name of Mrs Kathleen Grundy, leaving her entire £386,000 estate to Dr Fred

```
                              KATHLEEN GRUNDY
                                 LOUGHRIGG COTTAGE
                                    79 JOEL LANE
                                       HYDE
                                         CHESHIRE
                                           SKI4 5JZ
```

RECEIVED 2 4 JUN 1998

```
                                           22.6.98
Dear Sir,
        I enclose a copy of my will. I think it is clear in intent. I
wish Dr. shipman to benefit by having my estate but if he dies or
cannot accept it ,then the estate goes to my daughter.
        I would like you to be the executor of the will, I intend to
make an appointment  to discuss this and my will in the near future.
        Yours sincerely

                    K. Grundy.
```

Doubtful legacy—Angela Woodruff (above) was suspicious of the will supposedly left by her mother, Kathleen Grundy (left).

Shipman. The firm was puzzled, as it had never before acted on Mrs Grundy's behalf.

Woodruff was astounded, for as she explained, she had represented her mother in legal matters, including her estate. When a copy of the new will was faxed to her, Angela received a second shock—nothing about it seemed right. The language was cold, unfeeling. Messily typed—on a typewriter with a defective shift key—it would have appalled her proud, meticulous mother. Angela knew her signature well. This one looked far too big.

Convinced that the will was a fake, and a crude one at that, Angela discussed the situation that evening with Phil, a physics professor at the University of Warwick. He wondered: *Could someone be trying to discredit Dr Shipman?*

He suggested approaching the doctor. "Maybe he can throw some light on what is going on," he said.

"No," said Angela, her lawyer's caution taking over. "I think we should do some more research first."

The will had been signed by two witnesses, neither of whom were known to Angela and Phil. They returned to Hyde to visit both.

When the first witness, a young mother, was shown the document, she said, "That must be my signature," adding, "That was done in Dr Shipman's surgery." The Woodruffs looked at each other open-mouthed.

She hadn't actually seen the will itself, which, she'd been told, was that of an elderly woman sitting in the doctor's surgery at the time. She didn't know her name, and couldn't identify Kathleen Grundy when Phil showed her a snapshot.

The reaction from the second witness, a burly local shopkeeper, was much the same. He remembered being asked to witness a document, but wasn't shown what it was. Instead, he put his signature on a folded piece of paper. Scrutinising the will, he wondered if it was his actual signature or just a copy.

Over the next few days the Woodruffs visited several of Angela's mother's old friends. All of them were amazed at her sudden death—and all mentioned how fit and active she had appeared in her last few days.

Once back in Warwick, Angela Woodruff tried to collect her thoughts, writing down all that was giving her cause for concern. Then she showed the paper to one of her partners, a man well versed in criminal law.

"You've got to go to the police," he said.

"There's only one way to clear this up"
Detective Superintendent Bernard Postles, 45, sat quietly in Stalybridge police station, listening to his colleague tell him about Kathleen Grundy and the suspect will.

"Maybe a case of sour grapes?" he asked. "A child being left out of her mother's will?"

"No, boss," said Detective Inspector Stan Egerton, 55, shaking his head. He'd interviewed Angela and Phil Woodruff with another detective for some three hours. "This one's solid gold."

Both men had spent the bulk of their service as detectives and had worked on dozens of cases together. Still, Postles had to ask the obvious.

Egerton looked across the desk. "There's a certain amount of history on this one," he said, waving a beefy hand at a stack of files. It was not the first time that the doctor had come under suspicion.

Debbie Bambroffe tried to rationalize the uncanny similarities. After all, Dr Shipman, like other doctors in Hyde, had a great deal of elderly patients; and as such a caring doctor, it was known how often he might drop in on patients just to see how they were getting along. Still, so many single elderly women, living on their own and with no recent illnesses, were dying—during or just after a visit from Dr Shipman.

Bambroffe worked in her family's firm of undertakers. Although she was young, she already had enough experience to know that sudden heart attack or stroke victims who lived on their own were often found on the floor, not usually sitting peacefully in a chair like many of the deceased she had recently seen.

Eventually she conveyed her suspicions to a local doctor.

"There is something I wish to discuss with you," Bambroffe said, as Dr Susan Booth appeared in the undertaker's offices one day in early 1998. Before a cremation, a doctor from a separate practice must examine the body. In Shipman's case, this second doctor was usually enlisted from the nearby Brooke practice, of which Susan Booth was a partner.

Task force—Detective Superintendent Bernard Postles led the Harold Shipman investigation.

The two women began to talk. Shipman was one of the most respected members of their close-knit community. Still, wasn't it unusual how often women of a certain age were dying?

Booth spoke to her colleagues, who all voiced concerns over how often they'd been asked to cosign Shipman cremation certificates for patients who'd passed away while the doctor was present or had just left. In March 1998, Dr Linda Reynolds, one of Booth's partners, approached the local coroner John Pollard.

Pleasant facade—Shipman's surgery in Hyde. Like other doctors in the town, he had many elderly patients.

"I feel concerned about a colleague in Hyde," she said, "and so do other people." Then she outlined the odd pattern of events over the last year.

Reynolds stressed the delicacy of her position; she didn't want to do or say anything that might affect any future working relationship with Shipman, or that could be construed as defamatory. Pollard understood.

"As far as I am concerned," he said, "if nothing comes of this, it will be as if we have never spoken." He contacted the Greater Manchester Police—but urged absolute discretion. An investigation was opened.

Detectives were told that Dr Shipman had signed 19 death certificates in the previous six months; in fact, as they would only learn later, the real figure was 30. In any event, the medical records of only 14 of the 19 deaths were located by public health authorities, and they contained only sketchy details of the circumstances surrounding the deaths.

There didn't seem to be any disturbing pattern; and in any case, most of the dead had been cremated. After several weeks, the inquiry fizzled out in April 1998.

———

"From a police point of view," Stan Egerton said to Postles, "it was always going nowhere, given that the detectives couldn't interview the doctor himself, couldn't look at all of his medical records and couldn't interview the relatives of any patients who had died."

Postles picked up a photocopy of the Grundy will, noting that the box indicating a desire for cremation had been filled in. However, in the event, this did not happen. *Thank goodness she was buried*, thought Postles. *Cremation would have neatly destroyed much of the evidence.*

As if reading his mind, Egerton cut in. "There's only one way we're going to clear this matter up," he said, "and that's with an exhumation of Mrs Grundy's body."

"I believe this is what you're looking for . . ."

The rain was descending in an almost continuous sheet when the generator rumbled to life and the unnaturally bright arc lights were turned on. Through the blackness, Egerton witnessed eerie shadows thrown on to the ancient graveyard by the tall spire of Hyde Chapel looming above.

It was 2am on Saturday, August 1, and Egerton, wearing gumboots and anorak, had taken shelter under a golf umbrella. Around him was huddled a gathering of police officers, undertakers and workers from the specialist exhumations company.

They watched the mechanical digger churning up great swathes of the sodden lawn as it went towards Kathleen Grundy's grave. Several hours later, hidden under a white tent, the coffin was eased from the dank earth and slipped into the back of a van.

The post-mortem began at 8.30am. Police teams later searched Shipman's surgery and home. It was nothing dramatic; two detectives simply waited in an unmarked car until the doctor had dealt with the last of his Saturday morning patients and was about to lock up.

Shipman registered no surprise at seeing them—just a gentle smile as they read out the search warrant. Back inside the surgery, he walked to a cupboard and produced a small manual typewriter.

"I believe this is what you are looking for," he said. Then, as if reading their minds, said, "Mrs Grundy borrows it from time to time." It was the typewriter used for her last will.

Five miles away, in the garage of Shipman's house, police found boxes and carrier bags stuffed with the medical records of patients who had died. West Pennine Health Authority was aware that Shipman was storing them, but presumed that they had been filed in his surgery.

Postles thought about the violent, blood-splattered deaths he had investigated—so unlike the immaculately dressed old woman, laying peacefully on a settee in the comfort of her living room. If this was a murder case, it was unlike any he'd worked on before. *Maybe there's nothing there at all*, he thought.

The forensic examination of Kathleen Grundy's remains would tell. But that would take several weeks to complete. In the meantime, they had better learn all they could about Dr Fred Shipman.

Key to the case—a manual typewriter kept in a cupboard in Shipman's surgery proved to be what the police were looking for.

"You will have to trust me"

In the summer of 1963, Vera Shipman was dying of lung cancer. Her middle child Fred would sit beside her in their Nottingham home, and watch the doctor administer the morphine injections which helped ease the pain that wracked her emaciated body.

After her death, Fred wore a black armband to school for a few days. But he never spoke of his loss. He never misbehaved and never joined in the raucous crudity of his contemporaries. Nor did he seem to have a girlfriend. He just worked and worked with an icy, relentless concentration.

He began studying medicine at the University of Leeds, an immature and raw 19-year-old, when he met Primrose Oxtoby, a 16-year-old window dresser. She became pregnant a few months later, marrying the young medical student three months before the birth of their first child, Sarah. They went on to have three more.

Shipman became a GP in a practice in Todmorden, West Yorkshire, in March 1974. He was aloof and reserved—yet he appeared to have encyclopedic medical knowledge, and his energy was boundless. Then he began having blackouts.

Shipman said he had epilepsy, but the real reason was uncovered by chance. One day a receptionist from the medical practice was in the chemist's shop across the road from the surgery, chatting with friends. She noticed the book detailing the prescription of dangerous drugs was open.

Dr Shipman had been prescribing prodigious quantities of a narcotic drug called pethidine.

Shipman admitted his addiction, and was dismissed from the practice and disciplined by the General Medical Council. It ruled that he could continue to work as a doctor—as long as he carried on being monitored by a psychiatrist. Shipman also appeared in the local magistrates' court and was fined £600 for dishonestly obtaining and unlawfully possessing a controlled drug.

In 1977 Shipman applied for a vacancy in the Donneybrook Medical Centre in Hyde. He was candid about his past problems with pethidine and his conviction, assuring those interviewing him that all of that was now well behind him.

Constant support—Shipman's wife, Primrose, photographed here next to her son, David, stood loyally by her husband.

"I'm off the drug," he said. "I don't use it. You will have to trust me."

Certainly, he impressed his new colleagues with his energy, quickly establishing himself not simply as a good doctor, but about the best in Hyde. He was particularly attentive to his elderly female patients. But colleagues noted that Shipman could be rude with subordinates and those who disagreed with him.

Shipman also pitched into a wide range of community activities, rising to be area commissioner for the St John Ambulance. He was also active in the Parent-Teacher Association at his children's school.

But he stunned his colleagues when, after some 14 years, he decided to set up in practice on his own.

The departure was not pleasant; spotting a chink in his partnership agreement, Shipman set up a surgery close to the Donneybrook practice and took with him his 2,300-strong list of patients.

His former partners were hit financially with his refusal to pay his share of the tax bill that was levied on the practice. They seethed but were powerless to do anything.

Shipman soon built his patient list to new heights.

"You've got the wrong man"

In mid-August 1998, news of the police inquiry leaked to the newspapers. The result was uproar and an outpouring of community support.

As growing numbers of journalists and photographers descended on Hyde, they were sometimes accosted by enraged patients. "Dr Shipman is a marvellous doctor," one said. "Why don't you leave him alone?"

Even Detective Inspector Egerton was confronted. "You've got the wrong man, copper," one woman said, spitting in the gutter.

Peter Wagstaff, 49, was one of Shipman's defenders. The operations director of a home furnishings company in Oldham, Wagstaff remembered vividly one occasion when the doctor turned out on a Bank Holiday Monday to see his unwell daughter. Another time, when his second daughter was born—and his wife had just lost her father—Shipman arrived at their home totally unheralded.

So, when Wagstaff lost his mother Kathleen in December 1997, the family raised £325 for Shipman's fund for buying equipment for the surgery, asking mourners for donations rather than flowers. With the cheque, Wagstaff enclosed a note.

"It was comforting to know you were with her during her final moments. We couldn't ask for a finer, more caring doctor."

"The morphine levels are consistent with overdose"

Towards the end of August, Postles took a phone call from Julie Evans, a toxicologist at the Forensic Science Service Laboratory in Chorley, Lancashire. "The levels of morphine found in Kathleen Grundy's body," she said, "are consistent with that found in cases of overdose."

Postles had already suspected poison; nevertheless he was surprised. He thought that morphine, unlike insulin, potassium or some other hard-to-detect substance, was among the least likely of poisons to be used in a killing. Even he knew that it left traces that can last almost indefinitely; and if he knew, Shipman surely did. The time had come to interview their suspect.

The police station at Ashton-under-Lyne is a modern, three-storey, glass-fronted building. But Interview Room Number One is a stark affair. There are no windows and the fluorescent lighting is protected by a grill. The only furniture is a wooden table and four plastic chairs in the middle of the room.

As Shipman took his seat on the afternoon of September 7, 1998, he betrayed no hint of nervousness or fear. Next to him was Anne Ball, his solicitor; across the table were Detective Sergeant John Walker and Detective Constable Mark Denham. They turned on a tape recorder and began the questioning.

Could Dr Shipman account for the presence of morphine in Kathleen Grundy's body? Perhaps, he responded, she might have become an illicit user.

Shipman was happy to take the officers through his medical notes. "'Pupils small, dry mouth, possible drug abuse again,'" he read; "the patient 'denies taking any drug other than for irritable bowel syndrome'."

Warming to this task, Shipman said, "I'm sure you're well aware that drugs like morphine, heroin, pethidine all cause constipation, all cause small pupils."

Turning back to his medical notes of November 26, 1996, he continued, "'Irritable bowel syndrome again, shall I do blood tests and check the urine? Really difficult as she denies everything and is not really at risk.'"

The detectives weren't impressed. Many of Shipman's notes had been squeezed on to the ends of paragraphs and in the margins of Mrs Grundy's records. Postles's team had already suspected they might have been placed there later.

Shipman said that details of her case were in his computer. Rather pompously he said, "I'm a firm believer that the concept of GP and computerization is being held back by finance, underdevelopment and political decisions by government. That doesn't stop me computerizing my practice."

But what the good doctor apparently never realized was that the exact time and date of his computer entries were on his hard drive. And while Shipman was being interviewed, a police specialist team was copying that hard drive.

It didn't take long to establish that many of Kathleen Grundy's records— some ostensibly made during consultations months and years earlier—had actually been entered into the computer on the day of her death.

Later that day, Shipman appeared before Detective Inspector Stan Egerton. "Harold Frederick Shipman, you are charged that on 24th June, 1998, you murdered Kathleen Grundy at her home, at 79 Joel Lane, Hyde, contrary to common law."

"I can't remember doing it"

After the initial shock reverberated through the community, other people were now coming forward, many of them relatives of elderly women, all Shipman's patients, and all of whom—so their families said—had died under circumstances alarmingly similar to those of Kathleen Grundy. Postles's team grew—reaching up to 60 officers, typists and indexers.

Stan Egerton was having a drink one evening at the Hyde Club when taxi driver John Shaw approached him and asked for a quiet word. The story he related was a strange one.

148

Shaw told Egerton he had an extensive list of elderly female customers—often widowed or living on their own—whom he chauffeured round the town on a regular basis. Many became friends rather than just customers. He would fix a gate, change a fuse, do the odd DIY chore.

He was therefore hit hard when he heard of the death of one of his customers, a 73-year-old woman. She had always seemed so fit and well. As she suffered from arthritis, he used to carry her shopping into her kitchen after her regular Wednesday morning trip to the shops.

But then there were other regular clients who had also seemed active and healthy and who suddenly died.

At some time in 1996, Shaw remarked to his wife Kath, "You'll never guess what?" And she finished the sentence for him, "Another Shipman patient."

He had been keeping a list of all the customers he had lost, who had also been patients of Dr Shipman—a man he had never met.

Like many other people in Hyde, however, he found it almost impossible to suspect this most-trusted member of the community of any wrongdoing. He tried to block the matter from his mind.

> **John Shaw had been keeping a list of all the customers he had lost, who had also been patients of Dr Shipman.**

But now the death of Mrs Kathleen Grundy—another one of his customers—was being investigated, he could remain silent no longer.

"How many have you got on the list?" Egerton asked him.

"How many do you want?" Shaw said. "I've got a list of about 20."

"Bloody hell!" Egerton exclaimed.

From observations made by his team, Postles surmised that Shipman's arrogant and condescending manner became even more pronounced in the presence of women. And so, as he was led into the same interview room for his second interrogation on October 5, the doctor found himself facing Detective Constable Marie Snitynski and Detective Sergeant Mark Wareing.

They began questioning him about Mrs Winifred Mellor, who had died on May 11, 1998. According to Shipman's records, she had a history of angina.

Wareing: "Can you indicate to me how severe the angina was?"

Shipman: "She had no signs of congestive heart failure and she only got the pain if she rushed. But it was lasting two to three minutes."

Wareing: "But from the progression you've noted on your records, this was not something that was going to be unexpected."

Skilfully and exhaustively, the detectives walked the doctor through his diagnosis of the condition and the various dates on which its progression had been noted by him on his surgery's computer system. Finally, they ambushed.

Wareing: "Detective Sergeant John Ashley works in the field of computers . . . and he has gone into this computer of yours in some depth, and what he's found is that there are a number of entries that have been incorrectly placed on this record to falsely mislead and to indicate this woman had a history of angina and chest pains. What have you got to say about that, Doctor?"

Shipman: "Nothing."

Wareing: "I'll just remind you of the date of this lady's death [Mrs Winifred Mellor], May 11th, 1998. Perhaps you can explain to me then why at three minutes and 39 seconds after three o'clock that afternoon you have endorsed the computer with a date of October 1st, 1997, which is ten months prior, with 'chest pains'?"

Shipman: "I've no recollection of me putting that on the machine."

Wareing: "It's your pass code, it's your name."

Shipman: "It doesn't alter the fact that I can't remember doing it."

It was becoming increasingly clear that the doctor was now faltering, nearing breaking point. His solicitor Anne Ball broke in. "Can we have a consultation at this stage, please?"

"Certainly," Wareing said, switching off the tape.

As the two officers left, Shipman fell to his knees sobbing. Soon after, a doctor pronounced him unfit for further interview.

"BT has no record of any calls"

Driving to work in October 1998, Peter Wagstaff noticed the newspaper billboards: "Dr Shipman—Three More Bodies To Be Exhumed". Now he began to wonder: *Could the police really have got it so wrong?*

Wagstaff went back over the circumstances of his own mother's death. They were so traumatic, so bizarre, that he had no trouble recalling every detail of that afternoon of December 9, 1997.

It began with a call from the Dowson Primary School in Hyde, where his wife taught. Shipman had just been there with the tragic news that her mother, Ann Royle, had suddenly died. His wife had already rushed off to her mother's home. Wagstaff was on his way to meet her there when his mobile rang. It was his wife, in near-hysterics.

"My mother is OK. She's fine." Then she added, "Maybe it's your mother who has died."

Wagstaff pulled over to the side of the road and called his mother. Shipman answered, apologizing for the appalling mistake. It was Peter's mother who had died. Kathleen Wagstaff, Shipman explained, had rung his surgery, then had a heart attack. When Peter Wagstaff reached her home, he found his mother still slumped in her favourite armchair.

The next day Shipman explained how, after being summoned by Kathleen, he found her grey and sweaty, and slightly blue round the lips. "I took her pulse and found it erratic," he said. "I realized then that there was something seriously wrong, so I rang for an ambulance."

He went outside to get something from his car. But by the time he returned she was dead, "so I cancelled the ambulance."

At the time, Peter Wagstaff had not questioned anything that Shipman said. But now, for peace of mind, he rang the local ambulance service to ask if theirs was the number a doctor would call in an emergency. It was.

Wagstaff then asked, "Do you have any record of a call from 14 Rock Gardens, Gee Cross, on December 9th, 1997?" After searching their files, they could find none. "There's only one way we can clear this whole thing up," Wagstaff told his wife. "Ring the telephone company."

BT agreed to supply a complete list of all the calls made from his mother's telephone on December 9—but warned that it might take a while. A couple of weeks later, Wagstaff was on his way to work when his mobile rang; it was his wife, who had opened that morning's post.

"He's done it," she said bluntly. "BT has no record of any calls made from your mother's home to Dr Shipman's surgery or to the ambulance service that day."

In a specially designated incident room at Ashton-under-Lyne police station, a special plastic film was put on the windows. It allowed Postles's investigating team inside to see out—but no one on the outside to see in. Meanwhile, large whiteboards on the walls were filling up with details on the new cases.

Nagging doubt—Peter Wagstaff turned detective after his mother, Kathleen Wagstaff (inset), died.

151

In the case of Pamela Hillier, Dr Shipman had added six new entries to her computerized medical records in the space of six minutes, just two hours after her death. This was to build a picture of her suffering the sky-high blood pressure that would have led to the stroke that ostensibly claimed her life in February 1998.

Chillingly, with 57-year-old Maureen Ward, all the details consistent with a later death from a brain tumour—"headache comes and goes, dull, nauseous, legs not steady"—were inserted on the computer just 45 minutes before she was to die.

In the meanwhile, Shipman's story about Kathleen Grundy had been unravelled. Forensic evidence proved that Grundy could not have been taking drugs on her own. A sample of her hair showed that she was morphine "naïve"—that is to say she had no history of taking the drug.

No one felt comfortable with the ghoulish procedure, but 11 more bodies were exhumed. In every case the proximate cause of death was morphine toxicity.

By the beginning of October 1998, Postles felt they had enough evidence to charge Shipman with the murders of Winifred Mellor, Joan Melia and Bianka Pomfret; and then later in the year with the murders of Marie Quinn, Ivy Lomas, Jean Lilley and Irene Turner.

Even when the suspected victims had been cremated, it was still possible to bring a "similar fact" charge. This is where the circumstances of an offence are so close to the methods of a suspect in other cases as to justify a charge. One of the advantages of this approach was that Postles's team would not be limited by time—as with an exhumation. Marie West, for example, had died nearly four years earlier and so her remains would have deteriorated considerably.

And the drugs? Police found four ampoules of diamorphine in a back bedroom of Shipman's house. It was later established that these had belonged to a former patient who had died over three years before. Shipman was unable to explain why he had not disposed of them.

Through assiduous sleuthing, the police eventually located many more patients, 28 in all, from whom Shipman had managed to get the drug.

One was 54-year-old James King. The local hospital diagnosed him with cancer of the urethra in 1996, and King alleges that Shipman then prescribed him so much morphine that he became addicted to the drug.

In January 1997, King insisted on being referred to a different hospital for a second opinion. Tests there showed that not only was he clear of the cancer—he had never had it.

King says that yet another six months passed before Shipman chose to

Victims—Shipman faced 15 counts of murder at his trial in October 1999. Pictured above are 10 of his deceased patients: From left, top row: Norah Nuttall, Jean Lilley, Marie West, Irene Turner and Lizzie Adams; bottom row: Winifred Mellor, Joan Melia, Bianka Pomfret, Maureen Ward and Pamela Hillier.

pass on this news, meanwhile collecting King's prescription and keeping some of the drugs for himself. By that time, King had become impotent and lost his job.

"There is simply no explanation, save for your guilt"

Pale and thin-looking, his grey suit hanging loosely off his shoulders, Shipman seemed a diminished man as he climbed the steps from a holding cell to emerge in the dock of Number One court in Sessions House, Preston. Behind the oak railing in centre court, the dock's spacious, red leather benches seemed to swallow up the solitary figure. The walls of the courtroom were dark green tiles, topped by oak panelling alternating with full-length portraits of judicial notables from the past. Above was a delicately illuminated white, corniced ceiling with a central splash of stained glass.

Behind the dock was the public gallery in which Primrose Shipman would sit, every day of the trial, with at least one of her four children. And outside the court, she ran a gauntlet of some 300 journalists from around the world—to whom, at times, she smiled, but never uttered a word.

All stood as Mr Justice Forbes strode into court on October 5, 1999. Shipman faced 15 counts of murder and a further charge of forging the will of Mrs Kathleen Grundy.

Prosecutor Richard Henriques QC laid out the case. "None of those buried nor indeed cremated," he said, "were prescribed morphine or diamorphine, all of them died unexpectedly, all of them had seen Dr Shipman on the day of their death."

Henriques continued, "There is no question of euthanasia or what is sometimes called mercy killing. None of the deceased were terminally ill. The defendant killed those 15 patients because he enjoyed doing so. He was exercising the ultimate power of controlling life and death and repeated it so often that he must have found the drama of taking life to his taste."

Once the trial got under way, Shipman recovered much of his old aplomb. As many of the witnesses were being cross-examined, he took copious notes on a foolscap pad as if attending a conference on a patient.

Though Angela Woodruff was herself a solicitor, her time in the witness box was unsettling. Occasionally, overcome by the detail of some memory of her mother, she would murmur, "Just a minute, please." Fighting for control, she

154

would drink from the glass of water on the oak witness stand.

Shipman's defence counsel, Miss Nicola Davies, attempted to plant in the jury the idea that there had been some kind of rift between Angela Woodruff and her mother.

Woodruff was adamant: there had been no falling out. Intending to buy a new car, Kathleen Grundy had been planning to give her old one to one of Angela's two sons. "She loved my sons to pieces and they loved her to pieces too."

Shipman's testimony was, in the main, polished. Questioned about the presence of morphine in Mrs Grundy's body, he opined: "She was taking an opiate: codeine, pethidine, perhaps morphine." Then he added smugly, "Abuse of drugs in the elderly is becoming recognized."

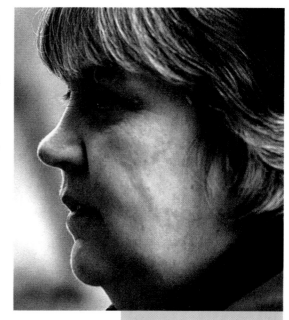

In the gallery—Primrose Shipman attended every day of her husband's trial.

Why had he backdated his computer records? In order to bring his files up-to-date when the patient told him when they'd first noticed the symptoms.

It was just coincidence, Shipman said, that he was making an unrequested call to the home of Norah Nuttall, minutes away from her death. As it was with Marie West, Lizzie Adams, Marie Quinn and Kathleen Wagstaff.

As the trial ploughed on, coincidence piled on coincidence, similarity on similarity. But his defence finally seemed to run into the sand during cross-examination on the death of Mrs Ivy Lomas.

She had lost consciousness while lying in his surgery treatment room, and Shipman said that he carried out heart massage and mouth-to-mouth resuscitation for 15 minutes. He couldn't revive her. But he left her there, lying dead, without telling his receptionist, "because", he testified to the court, "to tell her in front of three other patients I thought was inappropriate."

Questioned by Henriques, Shipman agreed that the morphine level in Mrs Lomas's body was so high that death would have taken effect within five minutes.

Henriques: "If this lady died at 4.10pm she must have been administered or administered to herself the drug between 4pm and 4.10pm, mustn't she?"

Shipman: "You can put the evidence that way, and yes I'd agree."

Henriques asked, and Shipman said he agreed, that he had not seen the patient administer the drug to herself, he hadn't left her alone in the surgery and nobody else had been present.

Henriques: "How did she get the diamorphine in her body?"

Shipman: "I have no knowledge."

Henriques: "Dr Shipman, there is simply no explanation, is there?"

Shipman: "I do not know of any explanation."

Henriques: "Save for your guilt?"

A time to grieve—as the verdict on each victim was announced, relatives cried out or sobbed in anguish.

"That's what you're saying," Shipman said, "and I disagree with it strongly. I didn't administer anything to this lady and I have no idea how it got into her body."

But as he stood in the witness box, it seemed to those in court, his eyes had the look of a broken man.

In her closing speech, defence counsel Nicola Davies did her best to depict her client as a man who went that extra mile for patients, often calling on them unexpectedly. Keeping records was not Shipman's strong point, Davies said, as he was "more interested in the patients than the paperwork".

After 57 days of evidence and the testimony of more than 120 prosecution witnesses, the jury took a week to render their verdict. On January 31, 2000, they found the accused guilty of all 15 charges of murder and the forgery of the will.

As the verdict on each victim was announced, relatives cried out or sobbed in anguish.

Shipman barely reacted.

Mr Justice Forbes did not mince his words. "You murdered each and every one of your victims by a calculated and cold-blooded perversion of your medical skills," he said. "I have little doubt that each of your victims thanked you as she submitted to your deadly ministrations. . . The sheer wickedness of what you have done defies description."

After passing 15 life sentences and a four-year sentence for the forgery, the judge said, "My recommendation will be that you spend the remainder of your days in prison."

Lingering Mysteries

Why did Fred Shipman murder Kathleen Grundy—and so many others? "We considered all the possibilities," says Bernard Postles, "greed, revenge, sex. Money appeared to be the motive only in the Kathleen Grundy case."

From Frankland Prison, near Durham, Shipman will not say. He has refused all interview requests, including one from Reader's Digest.

Says Angela Woodruff: "Maybe in some part of his mind he still feels in control of others: in never revealing how many he killed—or why."

Like so many others in the town of Hyde, Peter Wagstaff keeps coming back to the theme of trust. "The doctor is the last person in the community who you would suspect—particularly one who could seem so committed, so kind. It was the ultimate betrayal."

In June 2001, a public inquiry into Shipman's 28-year medical career was opened at Manchester Town Hall. On July 19, 2002, High Court judge Dame Janet Smith delivered decisions in 494 cases, concluding that the Hyde GP killed at least 215 people. In an audit by the Department of Health, conducted by Professor Richard Baker of Leicester University, it was determined that the real minimum number of Shipman's victims was probably 236. Despite all the evidence, Shipman himself continues to plead his innocence from his cell at HMP Frankland in County Durham.

SECRETS OF
THE MUMMY

Tim Bouquet

This man has been dead for 2,000 years, so what could he possibly have to tell us? The last people to see the high-born Egyptian in the flesh were the embalmers who mummified his body. As the hospital scanner peers through the thick layer of outer bandages, something very unusual shows up . . .

t is an early evening in October and security is tight as a white van backs into the rear loading bay of London's Royal National Throat, Nose and Ear Hospital near King's Cross station. On board is an exotic young man in his early twenties who must be moved with more secrecy than Michael Jackson.

Top ear surgeon Ghassan Alusi waits anxiously for his patient. His worries intensify when he sees that it takes six people to manoeuvre the man into the room housing the scanner.

This CT scan is far from routine. The patient's name is Artemidorus and he has been dead since the 2nd century AD. The last people to see the high-born Egyptian in the flesh were the embalmers who mummified his body in oils, salts and spices, wrapped it in half a mile of linen bandages and then sealed him inside the exquisite red casing that is now being lifted gingerly out of a large, foam-lined wooden crate.

Once it is on the scanner's conveyor, Alusi can see that the casing is decorated neck to foot in six ornate bands of gold leaf, depicting the triumph of cosmic order over chaos and Egyptian gods engaged in funerary rites. Now he understands why Artemidorus is one of the British Museum's most priceless objects and why the mummy galleries are the most popular attraction for its annual 5.6 million visitors.

By booking Artemidorus and 13 other gallery residents into London hospitals, the museum hopes that modern medical technology will reveal their centuries-old secrets.

Artemidorus's travelling companion is Joyce Filer, the museum's special assistant for human and animal remains and coordinator of this high-tech post-mortem.

"I deal with the dead," says raven-haired Filer. A cheerful northerner, she once worked with deaf people as an audiologist before requalifying as an Egyptologist and an enthusiastic hunter of clues to ancient diseases in very old bones.

It is time to delve behind the outer casing of Artemidorus. Alusi nods to the radiographer and the five-foot-seven-inch-long gilded mummy slides silently into the scanner.

Artemidorus was unearthed in 1888 by the father of modern scientific archaeology, an Englishman called Sir William Matthew Flinders Petrie, at Hawara, some 60 miles south-west of Cairo. He found hundreds of mummies piled up in large stone-lined pits, as though they were being stored.

Three caught his eye. "A procession . . . coming across the mounds, glittering in the sun," he wrote in his diary. "They are so fine and in such good condition. I must bring [them] away intact."

Each mummy's name was inscribed across its casing in Greek—the language of Alexander the Great, who conquered Egypt in 332 BC. One read: "Farewell Artemidorus". A member of the elite, he was among the last Egyptians to be mummified as the spread of Christianity put an end to the elaborate 3,000-year-old practice of preserving the dead for passage to immortality in paradise.

While Flinders Petrie sent the other two mummies—believed to be Artemidorus's parents—to museums in Cairo and Manchester, Artemidorus found his way not to paradise but to London. Which is where he has remained ever since, serene and horizontal in the subdued lighting of Room 62 of the British Museum's Egyptian wing, gazing up at the millions peering at him through the glass of Case 22.

"You can see the nose quite clearly," says Ghassan Alusi excitedly as the scanner starts to reveal Artemidorus on screen, the first proper glimpse of him in 1,897 years.

Unlike a standard X-ray which just shows the bones, the CT scan produces two-dimensional photographic cross-sections or "slices" of body tissue. For maximum detail, Alusi has set the scanner so the mummy will stop to be snapped every two millimetres on his way through the machine.

Just above the nose, Joyce Filer and Alusi see a hole punctured into the skull. This is where the embalmers would usually have started the mummification—a task that could take up to 70 days—by inserting a long metal hook into Artemidorus's nose. This they would have pushed up the sinuses and into the skull.

Catching his grey matter, they would have drawn it out piece by piece through his nostrils and then thrown it away. The brain was of no importance to ancient Egyptians, who believed that the heart controlled the body's physical and mental processes.

"Unlike the other mummies we've looked at, there's no packing in the skull," Filer remarks as she examines the scans.

Once they had taken the brain out, embalmers usually poured hot resin into the skull as a preservative and often filled the cavity with linen.

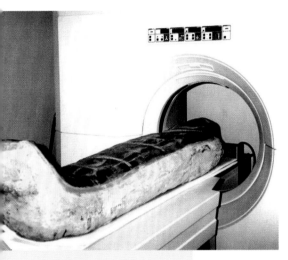

Into the deep—Artemidorus found his way not to paradise, but to a hospital CT scanner.

But as the scanner peers through the thick layers of outer bandages, something far more unusual shows up. Alusi points out eight straight linear fractures fanning out across the back of the skull.

"Completely different from the wavy sutures you would find in a normal skull," he explains, peering closer.

"There's no sign of healing; they seem to be almost fresh," Filer adds. "What do you think?"

Alusi is adamant: "If these didn't cause his death, then they happened very close to it. Someone or something has given him a brutal blow."

For a moment, neither of them says a word. Have they uncovered an ancient murder?

After six hours in the machine, Artemidorus returns to the museum under cover of darkness, as intact as when he left.

Others of his kind were not always so lucky. Nineteenth-century adventurers liked to goose-pimple their guests by having a mummy unwrapped after dinner. One American entrepreneur, responding to a shortage of rags, bought mummies at less than three cents a pound, selling their bandages on to make meat-wrapping paper for butchers. Mark Twain said he saw stokers shovelling mummies into the furnaces of a steam engine.

Back at the Throat, Nose and Ear, the scans of Artemidorus have been digitized and loaded into an £800,000 supercomputer. Using a special program they have written, Alusi and his colleagues begin to reconstruct on screen the 700 scanned slices of the mummy, stacking them from toe to head. The software also turns a two-dimensional image 3-D.

After three days, Joyce Filer is staring at a virtual Artemidorus. Now they can spin him round and study him from all angles. They can peel away the bandages and take him apart bone by bone. Filer can see that his pelvis is not fully mature and his wisdom teeth are not fully developed, suggesting that Artemidorus was only in his early twenties when he died.

But how did he die? She cannot hide her amazement when, easy as pushing open swing doors, the skull of the mummy opens on screen to reveal the shocking secret of the dark empty space within.

"Those fractures go right through to the inside," Alusi says, as they study each one in minute detail.

"It looks like a bang on the back of the head with the proverbial blunt instrument!" Filer suggests. None of the other British Museum mummies has suffered such severe head injuries. But is it enough to prove that the young man was murdered?

A macabre revelation—fractures spread deep inside the skull. Was the young man murdered?

Joyce Filer talks through her findings with John Taylor, the mummies' curator and a world-leading expert on mummification.

"Maybe it was just a bad day at the embalmers," says Filer. She knows that mummies, especially the later ones like Artemidorus, were not always treated with much skill or reverence. "Even so, they must have slammed his head down on to an alabaster embalming table with incredible force. And the injuries must have happened before they wrapped him, otherwise the thick bandages would have cushioned the blow."

Then there is the riddle of his feet. Most mummies are wrapped with feet ankle to ankle, side by side. The soles of Artemidorus's feet are facing each other but his knees are tight together, a physical impossibility without binding or breaking bones. Yet, perplexingly, the scans reveal no signs of either.

Given the lack of flesh on his body, Filer reckons that the young man was in a severe state of decomposition when the embalmers finally got to him. Could his body have been trussed while waiting in line? John Taylor smiles. It's a theory too far. Like detectives, Egyptologists prefer to work with fact.

While proof of how he died remains elusive, Artemidorus is helping Ghassan Alusi benefit the living from beyond the grave. Unlike a live patient,

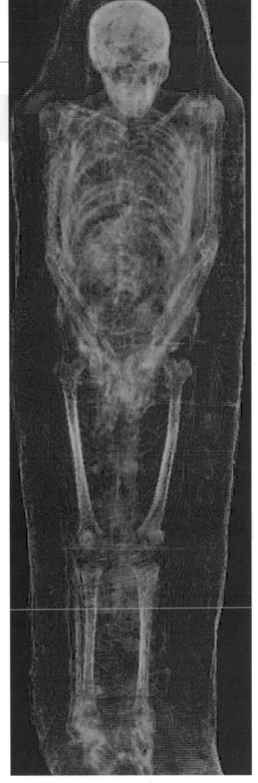

a mummy can be exposed without harm to large amounts of radiation, providing higher resolution images. This allows Alusi time to experiment with scanning techniques that could lead to earlier and more detailed diagnosis of ear problems. He can also try out several surgical techniques in virtual reality, thereby minimizing the risk to patients and reducing operating time.

"The ear is one of the most difficult environments in which to operate," Alusi explains. "In an area no bigger than a plum you have the carotid artery, cochlea, semicircular canals, the facial nerves and a sinus, and all completely enclosed in bone."

Mummies are now contributing to medical science as never before. A major project at Manchester Museum is using tissue from mummified remains to find out more about the common Egyptian parasitic disease, schistosomiasis. With samples collected from mummies all round the world, it is hoped that the research may give doctors a better idea of how to treat the condition today.

Scientists in the US are also using DNA from mummies to study the evolution of tuberculosis, work that could provide insights into how to control the disease.

More vital detective work still needs to be done. The other odd thing about Artemidorus's mummy case is the portrait of him painted in oil and wax on limewood and placed over his face.

Staring at us through big brown eyes and in three-quarter profile is the face of a beautiful young man with a long nose and large, pale pink lips. He looks more like one of the Romans, who by then were running his country, than an Egyptian. His dark brown hair, in which he wears a gold-leaf wreath of leaves and berries, is brushed forward. His white tunic contrasts with his tanned skin.

Unlike mummies from earlier periods, the artist has used light, shade and perspective. This portrait looks so fresh it could have been painted yesterday and yet it is among the oldest known to man.

"But is this what he really looked like?" Joyce Filer asks the medics. "Can a computer give us a better idea of the man inside?"

The face fits—Joao Campos's eerie recreation of Artemidorus's 3-D image shows us the man.

Brazilian bioengineer Joao Campos, whose PhD was on the analysis and measuring of faces, is the ideal man for the job. But as he stares into the screen he can see that most of the flesh has disappeared from the mummy's skull.

Fortunately, he can draw down data for the standard bone structure of a young man of Mediterranean origin and then add flesh to the mysterious face by adding 52 recognized landmark points. A bit like the contours on a map, these are used in facial reconstruction to show the depth and density of tissue round the eyes, nose, lower jaw and so on.

It is not long before the skull of Artemidorus is covered in computerized "flesh", but he still looks lifeless. Campos turns to the portrait. As he scans it into the computer, Artemidorus's face is reduced to millions of digits and then translated back into a full-colour portrait on screen. Now Campos begins to map the painting on to the blank face, stretching and pulling it like a rubber mask until it is moulded to the contours.

Where the portrait is oval and small-chinned, the skull of Artemidorus is squat and square-jawed. Where the portrait is side-on and painterly, the scans are face-on and scientific. After a few hours juggling and merging the two, Campos shows the results to John Taylor and Joyce Filer. It is a revelation. Staring back at them is the real Artemidorus.

By the time the mummies are back on display at the British Museum, they have told us a great deal about themselves. The scanners have revealed that, just like us, Ancient Egyptians suffered from arthritis and osteoporosis. Unlike us they had horrendous dental problems. Teeth ground down to stumps and abscesses were the result of eating bread fouled with grit and sand. Their temples might be breathtaking, but lung and other respiratory diseases were common killers lurking in their smoke-filled dwellings.

In front of Case 22, ranks of children are pressed to the glass. "It's spooky!" shudders one.

Right by Artemidorus's case is his computer reconstruction and an explanation of how he came by his new face. His features are stronger and heavier than his burial portrait.

Joyce Filer is convinced that he was from a Greek-Egyptian family, which would account for his robust Mediterranean looks and the inscription on his mummy case.

But what the scans reveal beyond all doubt is that the artist was a lot kinder to young Artemidorus than the embalmers or his ancient and unknown assassin.

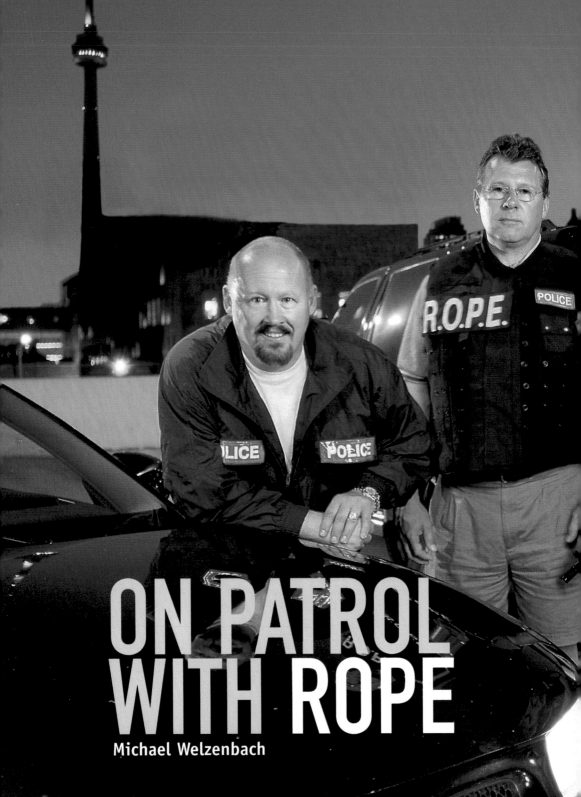

ON PATROL
WITH ROPE

Michael Welzenbach

Brainchild of police veteran Stephen McAteer, the Toronto Police Services' ROPE squad—the Repeat Offender Program Enforcement unit—is dedicated to the Canada-wide apprehension of parole-breakers. The squad has become an inspiration to other regional forces. Join members of this elite undercover police unit as they track repeat offenders on the lam.

We wait, binoculars glued to our eyes, on a bitterly cold day in December 2000. The target of our interest is a large beige house about 100 metres away, where we're hoping habitual bank robber Donald Turriff, 57, who recently skipped day parole, will appear. We have a tip that his former jailmate might be living here, and the pair may be planning another heist.

I'm with 30-year police veteran Stephen McAteer of the Toronto Police Services' ROPE squad—the Repeat Offender Program Enforcement unit—in an unmarked SUV in a bleak industrial area of Mississauga. We're cold; we've turned the engine off since exhaust might alert the fugitive. There are automatic weapons in the front passenger seat and bulletproof vests in the back, and an array of radios and cellphones bark and blink under the dash. Surveillance is tedious work; on a stakeout, patience is the greatest virtue.

Stocky, sandy-haired McAteer and his men must be prepared to move in at any time, never knowing what they might encounter. Just the week before, an escapee rammed into the team's vehicles with a stolen car as they tried to box him in. But woe betide anyone being pursued by this undercover tactical team. "They'll never see the hammer until it strikes," says McAteer, 52.

We've been watching for about five hours, McAteer manning the radios to stay in touch with four other ROPE officers parked nearby. People have been coming and going, but none matching the fugitive's description. Time to call it a day.

In the mid-1990s, McAteer realized Canada needed a squad to apprehend high-risk offenders who are unlawfully at large before they could offend again. The fact that some 40 per cent of criminals in Canada's federal system are reoffenders is bad enough. But of those offenders released and ordered to stay under supervision, almost 30 per cent are sent back to prison either for committing another offence, slipping away from halfway houses, failing to check in with parole officers or violating parole conditions. Nearly

900 are unlawfully at large nationally, about a quarter of them in Ontario. At the time McAteer was too busy with the Fugitive Squad, which he'd helped create in 1993 primarily to find foreign criminals hiding in Canada, to pursue anything else.

He was finally prompted to take action one February day in 1997. Opening up his *Toronto Sun*, he read that Michael Hector, a 32-year-old armed robber released on parole, had shot three people to death during two incidents in Thunder Bay. Sheet-metal workers Robert McCollum, 29, and Kevin Solomon, 29, were murdered inside McCollum's home, and 22-year-old Blair Aitken was murdered at the local Can-Op gas station Hector was robbing. Apprehended, he pleaded guilty to three counts of first-degree murder.

McAteer shook his head as he continued reading. *A federal offender gets released into the community, violates his parole, then goes and kills three people. Where was the funding to stop these guys before they had a chance to commit a violent crime?*

He discussed it with his partner, Doug Ducharme, a surveillance expert, and they came up with the ROPE concept: a Toronto Police Services squad dedicated to the Canada-wide apprehension of convicted pedophiles, robbers and murderers unlawfully at large.

Pioneer—ROPE founder Stephen McAteer of the Toronto Police set up the first ROPE squad with a handpicked team of experts. Pictured with him on pages 166–7 are, from left: SWAT specialist Greg Higgins, telecommunications expert Wayne Ward, surveillance pro Doug Ducharme and Hold Up squad-trained Eddie Pink.

Working with Correctional Service Canada, they'd know the moment a dangerous offender left a halfway house or violated his parole conditions. They'd also need funding for surveillance equipment, weapons and vehicles—and to hire elite officers. Indeed, Correctional Service Canada was already giving the John Howard Society more than $400,000 a year to supervise criminals like Michael Hector.

McAteer and Ducharme got to work. But over the next year, all appeals for funds were met with "Sorry, there's no money."

Frustrated, McAteer appealed to Toronto MP Dennis Mills. Mills loved their idea and got McAteer and other members of the squad 15 minutes with then solicitor general Andy Scott. Scott promised to help them, and by November 1998 he had got them $150,000 for a pilot project. "It's a start," McAteer told his boss, unit commander Mike Federico, at Toronto headquarters the next day.

Federico handpicked the best-trained investigators from his force and from the nearby York force. Along with McAteer, Ducharme and Federico, the first ROPE team consisted of telecommunications expert Wayne Ward, Hold Up squad-trained Eddie Pink and SWAT specialist Greg Higgins. All six had decades of law-enforcement experience and special FBI training; all were on call 24 hours a day.

ROPE on the range in 2002—one of an increasing number of regional ROPE police teams, pictured together on a training-camp exercise.

Despite limited resources, ROPE has reapprehended more than 320 fugitives since its inception. Among them is Turriff, the target of the parking-lot stakeout; investigators soon traced him to a downtown Toronto hotel, where he quietly surrendered. Here are just a few more:

Dean Duhamel. After serving almost five years for manslaughter for the beating to death of his stepmother in 1986, this violent cocaine addict was given statutory release and later robbed four banks. Rearrested and sentenced to almost five years, he was again given statutory release in 2000 and sent to an Ottawa halfway house. He walked away from it, robbed two banks in Ottawa, then fled to Toronto and held up six more banks. ROPE alerted Durham Regional Police, which by January 2001 had traced Duhamel to an ex-girlfriend's home in Port Perry, Ontario. There, Duhamel surrendered. He's back in prison now and has received a 12-year sentence for the bank robberies he committed while on release.

Scott Hardy. In September 1997 armed robber Hardy fled the minimum-security prison he'd been sent to in Ontario after serving 12 years of a 20-year prison sentence. ROPE traced Hardy, 31, to British Columbia, and after a joint ROPE–Vancouver Police probe, he was rearrested in a New Westminster hotel room.

Donovan McEwan. A violent offender with a history of assault and operating in Ottawa-Hull's prostitution trade, McEwan had been convicted of two sexual assaults and was serving eight and a half years at the maximum-security Kingston Penitentiary in Ontario. In November 2000, soon after being released to a Hamilton halfway house, he bolted. Thanks to a tip, ROPE and the Kingston Police traced McEwan to a local residence, where he gave himself up.

Brian Martin. In 1988 Martin robbed an Etobicoke, Ontario, cab driver and then shot him in the back. He received a life sentence for second-degree murder but escaped in August 2000 from a minimum-security institution outside Kingston. Ducharme and Higgins caught up with Martin in Mississauga, where they followed him and a woman as they drove to a Brampton business. Soon after, the couple came out of the business and were arrested in a high-risk takedown at a local intersection.

Successful outcome—Toronto Police Chief, Julian Fantino, is seen here at the podium on the occasion of the opening of the new ROPE office in Toronto in November 2002, together with Toronto Police Detective Joe Tomei—ROPE Unit Commander.

ROPE's efforts have enlisted further support from Ottawa. In October 2000, solicitor general Lawrence MacAulay announced that the federal government would increase its contribution to $500,000 in funding to allow for additional staff. But Toronto Police Chief, Julian Fantino, says more is needed if ROPE is to be effective nationally. "This is a significant public-safety issue," he says. "We need to be going after these people as soon as they violate their conditions."

It's noon on Friday, October 6, 2000, when a Crime Stoppers tip from a Halifax informant is relayed to ROPE "headquarters" in downtown Toronto. Richard Joseph Tremblay, 53, is a vicious murderer who walked away from a Vancouver halfway house in early September. The tip indicates that Tremblay, someone McAteer suspects is a hit man, has gone to Montreal—and that he's preparing to carry out some contract murders.

I remember this guy, McAteer thinks as he fishes out the Tremblay folder from the colour-coded pile on the round table in the centre of his office.

Plastered on the walls are photographs of criminals; those crossed with an X have been caught.

McAteer studies the file. In 1975, Tremblay shot dead a 77-year-old man and tied up his wife during a home invasion. He received a life sentence for second-degree murder. Released to a federal halfway house in October 1983, he absconded, and a warrant was issued for his arrest. He was again on parole by 1988.

An image of strength—badges of the 12 municipal police forces that are now supporting ROPE.

In May 1992 he was rearrested in Windsor with a loaded .45-calibre semiautomatic handgun. Police sources say that all signs pointed to murder for hire. Tremblay was reincarcerated, but granted day parole and released again to a federal halfway house by late 1998.

Working with Montreal police, the ROPE unit locates Tremblay's likely hide-out: a shabby four-storey brick tenement in north Montreal. McAteer orders undercover surveillance. Meanwhile, calls to and from the apartment are to be monitored.

At 1am on Saturday, October 7, McAteer, Federico and Pink assemble their gear into an unmarked SUV, and drive to Montreal. Arriving at 5am, tired and anxious, Federico touches base with Montreal's six-man SWAT team. They agree it's safer to grab Tremblay on the street. But by noon, after six hours of surveillance, the suspect hasn't shown. They'll have to go get him.

> **By noon, after six hours of surveillance, the suspect hasn't shown. They'll have to go get him.**

Swiftly and quietly, the SWAT team, with McAteer and Pink behind, swarms up the stairwell, guns ready. Men are stationed at both ends of the hallway to protect innocent residents who may appear; the others approach the apartment's door. On a silent signal, SWAT smashes it open with a battering ram, and shortly after, McAteer and Pink assist in the arrest of the burly, middle-aged man in the apartment's bathroom. Tattoos identify Tremblay, whose money-belt contains $20,000 in crisp $100 bills.

The United States has its Marshals Service to deal with dangerous criminals at large. Operating under the Department of Justice, the service consists of about 3,200 law-enforcement personnel for a population of 285 million. The Ontario-based ROPE team however, as of the end of August 2001, had just six men serving more than 30 million people. McAteer visualized a force similar to the Marshals Service. "With so many potential reoffenders walking our streets unlawfully, it's clear we need a national mechanism to nab them."

MP Dennis Mills agreed. "I'm passionate in my support for the ROPE squad. It can only do good in every community in Canada."

Steve McAteer's vision of expanding ROPE throughout the province of Ontario was achieved just months before his untimely death from cancer in May 2002. ROPE now includes members from 12 municipal police forces and is fully funded by the provincial government.

THE JUDGE
WHO CRACKED
AL QAEDA

Kenneth R. Timmerman

Judge Jean-Louis Bruguière has faced down some of the most dangerous terrorists in the world, and emerged victorious. But there is one particular case that lingers on his mind. It was a case which he says only hinted at the evil that was to come.

Ahmed Ressam has mixed the explosives many times before under the watchful gaze of his Al Qaeda trainers. Now he's on his own and he's nervous. It is December 13, 1999, and Ressam is staying at the 2400 Motel in Vancouver, British Columbia. The kitchenette in his small room will be his laboratory. He reaches first for a white powder, a volatile explosive called RDX that he had prepared earlier, and taps it into an empty Tylenol bottle. Next, he picks up small round tablets of hexamine, the booster for his bomb. After grinding them into powder, he pours it into an empty lozenge container.

Now comes the step he fears most: mixing the liquids. He has both nitric and sulfuric acids, stolen from a local chemical supply house. The measures must be precise. Sitting at the kitchenette table, he pours the sulfuric acid into a glass container that sits in an ice bath. He can't be too careful with the nitro; some have lost their manhood handling it.

He must watch the temperature too. Ressam has placed a thermometer in the container and as he adds the nitric acid, drop by drop, the red mercury leaps upward. Then he adds the glycol he brought from Afghanistan. Gently he stirs the brew. Finally he pours the viscous fluid into two empty olive jars he bought at a local grocery store. But a bit spills onto the table, burning the Formica. Some of it drips onto his leg. Despite the searing pain, Ressam remains focused on the task at hand. He seals the jars, and then washes the ugly burn. Later, he will package the acid compounds with the urea and aluminum sulfate powder—crushed fertilizer, really—which sits nearby packed in plastic trash bags.

The finished bomb should be small enough to fit in a suitcase. Yet it will kill many. Tomorrow Ressam will begin his trip to Los Angeles, and there at its airport, he will leave the suitcase in a luggage cart. All will go as planned, for he knows Allah is with him and all the soldiers of Al Qaeda.

Their victories were ordained: the slaughter of American soldiers in Somalia in 1993; the bombing of the World Trade Center that same year; the destruction in 1998 of two American embassies in Africa. And now his mission. He will give the American infidels a millennium they will never forget. But Ressam has not counted on the mission of another man: a French judge with the power and tenacity to bring him down. A man who has been on his trail for years.

———

Sitting in his tiny garret office high above the streets of Paris, chewing slowly on his pipe, Jean-Louis Bruguière could be mistaken for just another judge in the Palais de Justice. He is anything but that. Like a brain surgeon, Bruguière is a specialist who never handles routine cases. He does only one thing: he tracks terrorists. And the French government has armed him with extraordinary powers to direct criminal investigations and prosecutions wherever they lead. At his disposal is a worldwide brotherhood of intelligence and counterespionage agencies, including France's own Direction de la Surveillance du Territoire (DST).

It was early April 1996 when Bruguière got the break that would lead him to Ressam. He sat at his desk contemplating a small black instrument deposited there by a police officer. The electronic pocket organizer was the kind sold in airports and department stores around the world for under $50, but Bruguière suspected it was worth much more than that to him. With luck, it held clues to a case he had been laboring over for more than a year: cracking what he called the "Afghan Network," Al Qaeda.

With luck, the pocket organizer held clues to a case Bruguière had been laboring over: cracking what he called the "Afghan Network," Al Qaeda.

The organizer had been taken several days before from the corpse of a French Muslim killed in a gun battle with police. When the judge pressed the power button and watched the cursor start to blink, he thought for an instant it might be a bomb.

Bruguière had reason to worry: during the past few days France had been under terrorist attack. On March 25 Islamic extremists blasted a Brink's armored car with a military rocket. On the 28th, a car bomb exploded near the central police station in Lille. The police tracked those responsible for both attacks to a house at 59 rue Carrette, in an immigrant neighborhood in the town of Roubaix, 140 miles north of Paris.

At 6.15 the next morning, an elite police unit stormed the house, but intense automatic-weapons fire knocked them backward, wounding the first two officers who'd entered. There was more machine-gun fire, peppered with insults hurled in French from the terrorists. The battle lasted more than an hour. Then the building burst into flame, perhaps from a police-launched incendiary grenade or at the hands of the gunmen themselves, attempting to create a diversion to shield their escape. The house burned to the ground.

In the cinders where No. 59 once stood, four charred corpses were recovered. Within hours, two gang members who were not in the building during the firefight were stopped at the Belgian border, where they got into their own gun battle with police. One man was arrested carrying fake Canadian, Turkish and Belgian passports. The other man died from two bullets to the head.

The day's events were reported in clipped prose in the police file on Bruguière's desk, along with the organizer found on the dead man's body. The judge scanned the document. His instincts told him what the report could not. He knew that men like these Algerians and Moroccans were no ordinary criminals. They were Islamic fanatics who preferred death to surrender. He felt certain they were members of the Afghan Network.

As Bruguière fiddled with the organizer, he saw that all the entries were password-protected. No matter. French intelligence would make it a priority to crack the code. After a day or two, he could go to work.

Bruguière's office is a warren of rooms with the feel of a fortress. Thick bulletproof glass has replaced old mullioned windows; instead of suits of armor, bodyguards stand ready, and high-tech security devices monitor the rooms. In the early days, Bruguière himself carried a gun—a .357 Magnum he selected for its deadly power. Whenever he left his office, he strapped it beneath his often-mismatched suits. Now his bodyguards carry the weapons.

Bruguière takes danger in his stride. He believes a good meal and a fine bottle of Bordeaux, enjoyed with friends, is the best antidote to the strains of his job. But he is streetwise. His eyes are constantly alert, always scanning a room for any irregularity. He knows he is a target.

He still recalls with a shudder the evening in February 1987 when he was waiting for his wife to return home. By chance, a policeman making his rounds discovered a grenade hidden near Bruguière's front door, attached to a nylon thread that would set it off instantly when the door opened. In minutes the street was blocked off and 30 specialists from the antiterror unit were on the scene. Other men might have run, taken their families to a hotel. Not Bruguière. Once the coast was clear, he broke out champagne for his wife and the cops.

He never planned to become the "terrorism judge." But Bruguière knew he was destined for the bench. It was in his genes. Ten generations of Bruguières, going back to Louis XIII, had served in the court. During the French Revolution in 1789, a Bruguière ancestor in the southern city of Toulouse sat on a court that kept the reign of terror gripping Paris from descending on his region.

Bruguière was eight when his father took him for the first time up the broad marble steps of the Palais de Justice and let him watch as he donned the red robe of an appellate court judge. The boy never doubted he would wear the robe himself.

After completing university studies in literature, Bruguière attended a school to gain training as a judge, and in 1972 he graduated from the Ecole Nationale de la Magistrature. At first, the novice judge took the cases he was assigned: drugs, prostitution, murder, organized crime.

But Bruguière's path as a judge swerved sharply from that of his father in 1982, when a murderous attack on the rue des Rosiers—the heart of the Jewish quarter of Paris—killed a half-dozen innocent people, injuring many more. The case landed on Bruguière's desk.

Fiery end—French police nearly met their match when terrorists in a Roubaix neighborhood let loose their arsenal.

As he looked at pictures of the twisted bodies and interviewed survivors, he realized that this was fundamentally different from an ordinary crime. It was an attack on civilization. Standard legal procedures would not deliver justice. Bruguière lobbied the French government to create a special court to deal only with the shadowy world of terror. Once it was created, Bruguière was awarded vast powers far beyond those of American judges.

When a French jumbo jet exploded over the desert of Niger in 1989, killing all 170 aboard, terrorism was suspected and Bruguière was called in. He requisitioned a French government plane to tour the crash site himself. He brought back 15 tons of debris, and reconstructed the aircraft fuselage to determine where the explosion took place.

Forensics are like a jigsaw puzzle, and Bruguière loved this challenge most of all. As the pieces came together, he learned the identity of the individual who had carried the bomb onto the plane, and then he traced a computer circuit board, which had been used in the timing device, to a Taiwanese company that had produced it for Libya. Bruguière then drew up a list of top Libyan officials he wanted to interrogate under oath, but predictably, Colonel Muammar Qaddafi refused to hand them over for questioning. Bruguière interpreted the snub as Qaddafi's way of saying: "You and whose army?"

Bruguière turned to friends in the military, who put him on a frigate with a contingent of French marines. Steaming off the Libyan coast, he posed for photos as he gazed sternly toward Qaddafi, the barrels of the big guns clearly visible behind him. It was his answer to the question, and his appearance off the shores of Tripoli sent a clear message: *I know who you are, I know where you live, and I will follow you to the ends of the earth.*

Ressam waits until dark to prepare the car. Popping open the trunk of the rented Chrysler, he pulls up the carpet of the trunk, lifts the wheel-well cover and removes the spare tire and the jack stored there. Everything he needs will fit in the recessed space.

First Ressam places the plastic garbage bags filled with fertilizer along the outer wall and the base of the wheel well. Then he tucks in the two olive jars filled with nitro glycol, using the fertilizer as cushioning. One hard knock could explode the fluid. Next, the two powders in the small bottles. It all fits snugly in the space. Ressam replaces the cover, straightens the carpet and gently closes the trunk. He's done for now.

Ressam had heard and seen the *fatwas*—the decrees—of Osama bin Laden. *Kill the infidels wherever and whenever you may find them. Attack the enemy's economic centers. Put all places of amusement to the sword. For every infidel you kill, your reward will be great. Dark-eyed virgins await the holy martyr in paradise.*

It was time to put words into action.

Bruguière's confidence in French intelligence was well placed. Within days of receiving the organizer, the encryption code had been cracked. *It's amazing how much information these little things hold,* Bruguière thought, as he studied the piles of paper with names, addresses, phone numbers, dates, times, contact information.

There are numbers in Germany, Belgium, France, Turkey. His trained eye began searching for patterns, connections. New phone numbers had been entered on certain dates as well as reminders to call those numbers. Another name, another number, another strand to the web.

Bruguière was certain all the names, all the numbers, in Asia, Europe, the Middle East, were linked to one country. One organization.

He had never given a thought to Afghanistan before Christmas 1994. Before

Rescue on the tarmac—a French SWAT team storms a plane in Marseilles after Algerian hijackers opened fire on negotiators.

then, terrorism was Iran or Syria; it was Libya or the PLO. Then an Air France flight from Algiers to Paris was hijacked and flown to the southern French city of Marseilles.

After it landed, a SWAT team stormed the plane, overwhelming the hijackers. They were Algerians—Islamic militants from a group founded by men who'd fought the Soviets in Afghanistan. One of them had a slip of paper on which he had scrawled an address in London.

Armed with that address, Bruguière picked up the black secure phone on his desk and called a friend at MI5, the British counterespionage service. Together, they visited the London apartment.

The place was littered with documents, mostly in Arabic. Among them was a letter ordering the hijackers to seize the Air France flight, and a drawing that showed the Eiffel Tower exploding.

The French judge was stunned. The hijackers planned to crash into his country's most celebrated landmark, a tourist destination where hundreds of innocent people would be killed. He thought back to February 1993, and the bombing of New York's World Trade Center. Standing in that seedy apartment, Bruguière felt as though the paper in his hand were whispering in his ear: *No more negotiation, no more demands. Our goals are bigger, our targets have changed.* These zealots were unlike anything he'd confronted. They were attacking the West with a vengeance, seeking to destroy its monuments, its symbols. Somehow he had to get into their minds, probe their madness.

A few months later, the head of French counterintelligence plopped a thick white binder on the judge's desk. The report, ordered by Bruguière, identified a new breed of terrorist emerging from so-called Afghan Networks. It zeroed in on a loose confederation of radical Islamic fundamentalist groups, some of whom were trained by a charismatic Saudi who had fought in Afghanistan, Osama bin Laden.

An informer inside a bin Laden cell provided training manuals. French operatives on the ground took dozens of pictures of safe houses in Pakistan used by bin Laden as way stations for new recruits. Before graduating to the Afghan training camps, the report said the recruits were screened by bin Laden lieutenants in Peshawar, Pakistan.

Successful recruits spent six months in camps, where they learned to use automatic weapons and rocket launchers, to infiltrate Western countries, to target facilities like electric plants, airports, railroads and large corporations, to make explosives that would obliterate targets.

The growing terrorist network assigned and transported operatives to key locations around the world. They were at once soldiers and recruiters, inviting others into their cells who wished to join their *jihad*. This network had been operating for years.

In the months following the report, Bruguière seized on any tidbit, any clue that could unmask the workings of the Afghan Network. Now, studying the data pulled from the organizer, the judge realised he was peering at the vast matrix itself. He had the key—but what would it unlock?

Then Bruguière's gaze fell on one entry: "Ahmed in Montreal." *Montreal?* Bruguière sat back. For some reason, he hadn't expected to find the cells reaching deep into North America. The spider was spinning its web faster than he imagined. But Bruguière had a name now. Ahmed.

Ahmed Ressam eases out of the motel parking lot. He leaves behind a room that only hints at what has been going on there: the scarred kitchenette table, the acrid smell of all the chemicals, the damaged plumbing from the acids he disposed of in the sink.

Ressam isn't concerned. He is in a rush to get on with his mission. He will take two different ferries from Vancouver to Seattle, a roundabout way to be sure. But he's carrying a Canadian passport under the name Benni Noris. This should ease his way through Customs.

Bruguière had spent nearly a year since receiving the pocket organizer compiling names, interviewing sources, tracking intelligence reports from all over the world. It was a slow, painstaking business. But he couldn't move too quickly or he'd risk missing important strands of the web.

In spring 1997, the judge felt he had enough to start calling in some chits with colleagues in Britain, Belgium, Italy, Turkey, even Bosnia. He got them to pull the billing records of every telephone number that appeared on the organizer's list, and entered the information into a computer database. Bit by bit he began to put names and faces to the telephone numbers. More pieces of the puzzle fell into place.

He identified numbers in Hamburg, Germany. Bruguière requested that German police search an Islamic humanitarian organization that bin Laden's soldiers were using as cover. They found phone records that confirmed that members of Al Qaeda cells in Germany and France were calling the same telephone number in Istanbul, so in May 1997, Bruguière flew to Turkey.

In Istanbul, a Turkish police colleague traced the number to another aid agency used by bin Laden. Its employees, faced with deportation or worse—time in a Turkish prison—claimed to work with men based in Bosnia, a center for bin Laden's operations.

Bruguière compared the Turkish phone numbers with those in the organizer. They matched. So on June 18, 1997, he headed straight to war-battered Bosnia.

Two Arab men suspected of being involved in an extremist Muslim group were sitting in a jail in the countryside outside of Sarajevo. Bruguière recognized the names. Both were on the list of men wanted for questioning in the Roubaix shoot-out. He called the local NATO office and arranged a ride with peacekeepers to the jail.

He met with the suspects one-on-one. He was at his best this way, cool and methodical. Thanks to the organizer, he had names, numbers and addresses. Occasionally he glanced up from the papers and looked the men in the eye as he read out the chronicle of their lives over the previous two years: who they called, when, the number. "Is that correct?" he asked. It was the Bruguière method. Slowly, confronted with his overwhelming knowledge of their guilt, they broke.

The network from Afghanistan passes through London, they told him. There, a bin Laden contact supplies recruits with fake passports. Where does he get the passports? From Montreal. Two Algerians are part of the operation, Kamel Fateh and Ahmed Ressam.

When Bruguière heard the name, he suppressed a smile. *Hello, Ahmed*, he thought. *I'm coming for you.*

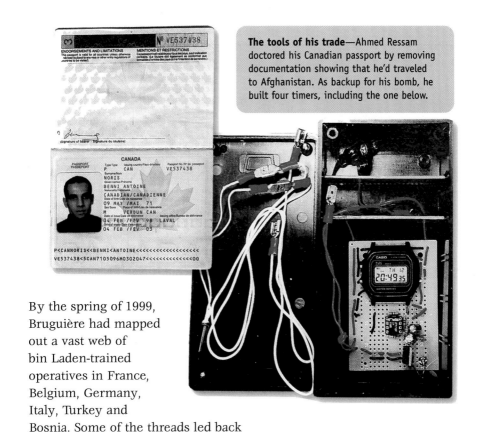

The tools of his trade—Ahmed Ressam doctored his Canadian passport by removing documentation showing that he'd traveled to Afghanistan. As backup for his bomb, he built four timers, including the one below.

By the spring of 1999, Bruguière had mapped out a vast web of bin Laden-trained operatives in France, Belgium, Germany, Italy, Turkey and Bosnia. Some of the threads led back to North America. Now it was time to pounce.

On April 7, 1999, he sent a 40-page, single-spaced rogatory letter—an international version of an arrest warrant—officially requesting that the Canadian Ministry of Justice open an investigation of Ahmed Ressam and members of his Al Qaeda cell. It spelled out their training in Afghanistan, their travels and the terrorist acts committed by their accomplices. But the Canadians didn't budge. Bruguière was thought to be imperious, a judge who saw terrorists in every dark corner.

Then a call came in to Bruguière: one of the men in Montreal, Kamel Fateh, was in Saudi Arabia to meet other Al Qaeda members. From there Fateh would travel to Europe.

Bruguière called a confidant of King Abdullah in Amman, and had Fateh picked up as he drove across the Jordanian border. The judge flew to Amman, carrying a thick file. Fateh wouldn't crack. But he didn't have to. His actions spoke volumes: the travel to Saudi Arabia, the meetings, the phone calls to Europe and Montreal. It all pointed to planning, to a plot. The unanswered question was where. Bruguière suspected Canada held the key.

In October, Bruguière and the head of the French counterespionage service, the DST, flew to Ottawa to make a personal appeal to the Canadian Ministry of Justice. Bruguière laid out his case against Ressam and his network in Montreal and warned that they were plotting an attack. He was certain of it. The Canadians brushed him off. There were procedures of investigation, civil-liberties concerns. What could they do? *The fools*, Bruguière thought.

Yet the Canadians did agree to send police to search an apartment in Montreal used by Ressam's cell. Bruguière waited while Canadian authorities combed through the apartment. One of the pieces of evidence seized was a small day planner. Bruguière took possession of it, and had the DST examine it.

A ferry from British Columbia chugs up to its slip at Port Angeles, Washington. It is just past dusk on December 14, 1999, and US Customs inspector Diana Dean is ready for her day to end. Already her mind is on fixing dinner for her teenage kids and tending to her menagerie of pets: two dogs, two cats, two llamas, two tortoises, fifteen chickens. Funny how, after dreams of becoming a veterinarian, she had wound up here at Port Angeles, standing alongside a scrap wood table, waiting for passengers to pull up in their cars.

Last line of defense—after Bruguière's warning fell on deaf ears, Ressam had just one more hurdle to clear: Customs officer Diana Dean.

Everything seems routine as the vehicles, about 20 in all, pass through inspection. At last, the final car—a green Chrysler. The driver rolls down the window.

"Where are you going?" Dean asks.

"Sattal," he replies. Seattle, he means. She notices the accent.

"Where do you live?"

"Montreal."

Ah, must be French Canadian. But something's odd. The man seems agitated, and he begins fumbling around in the console. Now Dean is nervous too. She gives him a declaration form to fill out, something to occupy his hands. He signs a name: Benni Noris. Then she has him pop the trunk and step from the car.

By now Dean's three colleagues—Mark Johnson, Mike Chapman and Dan Clem—have walked over to help. Johnson takes the driver to one side to search him; Clem and Chapman lift the wheel-well cover in the trunk. Garbage bags of white powder. Drugs, they assume.

As Dean goes to telephone the port director, she hears shouting. The man has broken from Johnson's grip and is sprinting off. Johnson, momentarily stunned, tears off after him, along with Chapman. The chase goes for blocks until, after turning a corner, the man seems to disappear.

Then Chapman spots movement beneath a parked pickup. He draws his gun, orders the man to come out with hands up. Noris bolts again, and heads for a car idling at a traffic light. He tries to yank open the door. The terrified driver zooms off and Noris is knocked off-balance.

Chapman catches up, wrestles the man to the ground and holds him, until Johnson manages to cuff him. They take Noris back to the Customs trailer, where Dean is behind the counter. He stares directly at her, and she feels a chill. His eyes are dead, she thinks. Not a spark of light in them.

He stares directly at Dean and she feels a chill. His eyes are dead, she thinks. Not a spark of light.

It will be days before she learns the man before her, "Benni Noris," is Ahmed Ressam.

When Bruguière hears of Ressam's arrest, he shakes his head. If it hadn't been for an alert US Customs officer, perhaps hundreds of Americans would be dead. He gets in touch with a friend at the Department of Justice in Washington and sketches out what he knows of Ressam. The Americans quickly realize what a mother lode of information the Frenchman has compiled. He offers to send them some of the files he has put together in his five-year investigation.

He realizes American authorities are under the gun. They don't know about Ressam's links to Al Qaeda and have little evidence besides the explosives found in his car.

But Bruguière is certain he has enough to put Ressam behind bars for life. His forensic experts have the day planner seized in Montreal, showing contacts with the global network of Al Qaeda, even a list of purchases for the bomb. They also found Ressam's fingerprint on one page of the planner. Bruguière sends it off to Washington.

The FBI confirms the print, helping to persuade a jury to convict Ressam on charges of conspiring to destroy or damage structures, evading immigration laws, transporting explosives and smuggling. The threat of spending the rest of his life in prison convinces Ressam to become a government witness against bin Laden and his Al Qaeda network.

To Bruguière, Ressam's conviction in April 2001 is but one victory in a much larger war. The rest of the world soon learns this truth. On September 11, after both towers of the World Trade Center have fallen, Bruguière picks up the phone at his desk. A senior aide to Attorney General John Ashcroft is on the line. Can Bruguière help? Certainly. When the planes are back in the air, he flies to Washington.

Because Bruguière is one of the few officials who understand the vast reach of bin Laden's network, he becomes a de facto tutor to American law enforcement. For almost every terrorist incident that takes place, he has something in his file. For almost every detainee, he can confirm or deny ties to the network.

Within weeks of the attacks in New York and Washington, Bruguière's information helps authorities in France, Germany and Spain round up suspected Al Qaeda operatives.

In mid-December, Zacarias Moussaoui, a French Muslim of Moroccan descent, is charged in the United States for his suspected involvement in the September 11 attacks. In the indictment, with the help of Bruguière's files, prosecutors reconstruct Moussaoui's trail from Afghanistan to England to Pakistan to America.

Just before Christmas, a British Muslim named Richard Reid is taken into custody in the US after allegedly trying to ignite explosives in his shoes during a flight from Paris to Miami. Investigators are tracing his movements from England, France, Belgium, Israel and Afghanistan.

Connecting strands of the web is a task Bruguière is still tackling daily. Along the way, the prosecutor has become the professor, teaching America and the West all he has learned. Sitting in his office, the blue smoke of his pipe wafting to the ceiling, Judge Jean-Louis Bruguière smiles grimly when asked about his future. He plans, he says, to be busy for a long time to come.

THE
FIGHT
TO FREE
MY SON

Joyce Milgaard with Peter Edwards

In 1969 David Milgaard, like many teenagers of the era, was a free spirit, experimenting with soft drugs and free love. Unfortunately, his youthful rovings put him in the wrong spot at the wrong time, and his name became inextricably linked, it seemed, to a grisly crime. Joyce Milgaard never doubted her son was innocent. But it took her 28 years to convince the justice system it had made a tragic mistake.

O n a late afternoon in May 1969, two police detectives from Saskatoon knocked on my door and asked, "Are you David Milgaard's mother?"

I was puzzled but not overly concerned. I led a simple, happy life looking after my husband, Lorne, a foreman in a potash mine, and our three youngest children in the tiny prairie farming community of Langenburg, Saskatchewan. Our first-born, David, was in Prince George, British Columbia, selling magazine subscriptions door-to-door.

The policemen explained that David and two friends had been seen in Saskatoon the previous January in the same area where a 20-year-old nurse's aide named Gail Miller was raped and murdered. At approximately 8.30 on the morning of January 31, 1969, a schoolboy had found her face-down in a snowbank near her boarding house. Her white uniform was torn and stained with blood from dozens of stab wounds.

Because of a series of rapes and assaults shortly before this murder, there had been a great deal of fear in the city, I would learn later. But since I hadn't followed the news, I was blissfully unaware of this when the police arrived.

It seemed ridiculous that the police suspected David might be the killer. I knew my son was no angel. He'd been in a number of scrapes, but nothing involving violence. That simply wasn't David. He was a free spirit, a tall, shaggy-haired hippie, experimenting, like many others in the 1960s, with soft drugs and free love.

We had frequent arguments about his drug use and choice of friends. But when he got his sales job in 1968, he was a success, and I felt he was on his way to making something of himself.

A couple of days after the police visit, David phoned to say that he'd heard the police were looking for him. He told me he had visited Saskatoon in January and that he was going to turn himself in to clear the matter up. I agreed that was a good idea.

David went to the police the following day. He didn't see how anyone could seriously think he was a killer, and he voluntarily gave blood, saliva, semen and hair samples.

As David would say later: "Naïve isn't the word. I was trying my best to help the police. This had to be resolved. It was a terrible crime." Despite his hippie lifestyle, David had a typically Canadian faith in the system, and he trusted that the police would catch the real killer.

He couldn't have been more wrong.

Quirk of Fate

In May 1969, after turning himself in to the Royal Canadian Mounted Police in Prince George, David was charged with the rape and murder of Gail Miller. He was taken into custody and returned to Saskatchewan to await a preliminary hearing.

When we got the news, the whole family went into shock. Immediately, I took off to visit my son in jail, taking a copy of the Bible. I knew it would help us both now. My son was just 16 years old.

David did his best to explain to me his movements on the day Gail Miller's body was found. While waiting for his vendor's licence to come through to sell magazines in British Columbia, he had decided to take a trip. In Regina he met up with two friends, Ron Wilson and Nichol John, a pretty girl with dark, attractive eyes. They decided to drive to Saskatoon in Wilson's beat-up car and arrived there early on the morning of January 31, intent on persuading David's friend Albert Cadrain to join them.

None of them knew Saskatoon well, and they ended up asking for directions at the Trav-A-Leer Motel on the edge of town at 7am. It was –37°C, and as they approached Cadrain's neighbourhood, they stopped to help a man whose car was stuck. In the process their own car stalled. They eventually made it to Cadrain's house by 9am, only a block from where the police had found Gail Miller's body half an hour earlier. While their car was being fixed, the trio spent the rest of the day at Cadrain's house, then all four left for Edmonton.

Unknown to anyone—and by some extraordinary quirk of fate—the real killer of Gail Miller was living in the basement apartment of Cadrain's home.

No fingerprints, footprints or eyewitnesses pointed police towards him. On February 4, The Canadian Press reported: "Police are investigating the possibility that the person who slashed a 20-year-old nurse's aide to death on Friday may be the same person who attacked three women in Saskatoon last fall."

But the article didn't include a lot of information that would emerge in the years to come: the rapist attacked women who lived in his neighbourhood; he may have had a preference for women in white uniforms, like Gail Miller; and he sometimes rode the bus with his victims.

Police Grilling

My son's life changed for ever when Albert Cadrain, a boy many took advantage of, was picked up for vagrancy in Regina in February 1969. During an interrogation, police learned that Cadrain had left Saskatoon with his friends on the same day Gail Miller was murdered. Cadrain denied any involvement, but when he later learned that reward money was posted for the killer, he went back to the police. Under intense interrogation, which he later described as mental torture, he told the police he had seen blood on David's trousers the day of the murder. Before much longer, David was under investigation and brought in for an initial interview.

In May, Ron Wilson and Nichol John were picked up, too. Both told police similar stories that indicated their and David's innocence. To jar John's memory, Miller's bloodstained clothes were thrown in front of her. Still she couldn't remember anything unusual. A bloody knife was shown to her. Still no memories for the police. Horrific photos of Miller lying dead in the snow didn't help either.

Although no charges were laid, John was locked up overnight, alone, in an unfinished empty wing of the jail. Late that night the young girl snapped and began sobbing hysterically. Next morning she was taken to the murder scene and then back to the station. Something changed dramatically. John couldn't handle another night in the lockup. When she was questioned again, she began saying things the police badly wanted to hear.

> **When Nichol John was questioned again, she began saying things the police badly wanted to hear.**

As John now told the story, she had witnessed David pull a knife on Miller and kill her after he stopped her for directions. Her story didn't make sense, since Miller was found with her dress around her waist and her coat still on. There were stab cuts in the coat but none in the dress. For John's story to be true, David would have had to undress Miller, rape her, put her coat back on, then stab her.

David would also have had to rape her outdoors in –37°. There was almost no time for David to have committed such a crime, nor any motive. John's story, as well, didn't explain the other rapes in the neighbourhood, where women were attacked in the same fashion as Miller in October and November 1968. Her story, however, did satisfy the police.

The preliminary hearing in Saskatoon began in August. When a police officer noted that Miller had wounds in the left side of her throat, a light flashed in my head. In order to wound a person on the left, it would normally be done by someone holding a knife in his right hand. David was left-handed. I told this to our court-appointed lawyer, Calvin Tallis, and he was able to introduce it.

John came to the stand on September 4 as the Crown's 24th witness. Tallis told us not to worry about her lying. She was clearly a troubled young woman, and this would come out in her testimony.

John testified that David broke into a grain elevator en route to Saskatoon and returned to the car with a flashlight and a hunting knife. She also said there was a paring knife with a maroon handle in the car. Police had discovered Miller's body lying face-down over the blade of a paring knife. A month after the murder, a red handle for the knife had been found in a back yard near the lane where her body was discovered. But John no longer clung to the story she had told the police, in which she claimed to have witnessed David killing Miller.

At the hearing's close, the judge announced there was enough of a case for David to stand trial. Tallis reassured us it was no big deal. He had got a look at the Crown's case, and now that he had seen it, Tallis was certain we had nothing to fear.

Indeed, when I began to think about it logically, I calmed down. The Crown contended that David was an impulse rapist who asked a woman he had never even met for directions, didn't like her answer, so raped and stabbed her to death in bone-chilling weather. The theory seemed far-fetched at best.

Unchallenged Lies

The trial began on January 19, 1970. Looking haggard, John was a key witness for Crown prosecutor Bobs Caldwell. She told the court she had seen David holding a knife in his right hand, but she wasn't playing along as fully as Caldwell wanted. She wasn't describing a stabbing, as she had done in the police statement, and Caldwell wanted more—nothing less than a graphic description of a sex slaying.

"I don't know what happened," she replied, clearly flustered.

Caldwell asked permission to have John declared a hostile witness, which meant he could cross-examine her and test her credibility. He pulled out the police statement she had signed and began reading from it. "'Dave reached into one of his pockets and pulled out a knife . . . I can't remember which pocket . . . All I recall is him stabbing her . . .'"

Rattled, John said she couldn't remember saying those words. Caldwell pressed on, and by the time he was through, the jury had heard every word of her incriminating 11-page statement.

The damage was done. Tallis tried to get her to explain how she came to make the statement, that she had broken down under enormous police pressure. "You were anxious to get out of the place as quickly as you could?" he asked.

"Yes."

That, however, was as far as she would go. She would not say police had pressured her to lie. Her statement hung in the air unchallenged, leaving the jury with the impression that John was now lying to protect a friend.

David looked horror-stuck as he watched others turn against him. "There was a rip on the crotch of his pants and blood on his clothes," Cadrain told the court. Wilson claimed he had heard David say "I fixed her" as he was getting back into the car.

Then came a complete surprise. The Crown introduced two witnesses who hadn't testified at the preliminary hearing. George Lapchuk and Craig Melnyk told of a bizarre confession supposedly made by David during a party before he turned himself in to police in May. They said he re-enacted the murder after seeing news of it on television.

According to them, David joked that he had raped and stabbed Miller, then re-enacted the crime, repeatedly stabbing at a pillow.

Lapchuk and Melnyk said David had re-enacted the crime, stabbing a pillow. I looked at the jurors' faces. They believed it.

I looked at the jurors' faces and knew they believed it. The ironic part was that I could easily imagine how David might have jokingly re-enacted the incident, just to stop them from asking him about being questioned by the police.

The credibility of the two men should have been questioned. Nine days after testifying for the Crown, Melnyk received a relatively light sentence of six months for armed robbery. Lapchuk had a criminal record for forgery and for conspiring to use David's identification to pass cheques.

Many parts of the Crown's case went unchallenged. For one, Miller was last seen alive between 6.30 and 6.45am, and a witness had seen David at the Trav-A-Leer Motel at 7am, leaving a very short time for him to commit such a crime. What's more, a pathologist stated that Gail Miller's wounds were consistent with a right-handed killer, and David was left-handed. The court heard that the contents of Miller's purse were strewn from her body to Cadrain's house. Unfortunately, the jury would never hear that this trail also led to the killer's apartment.

After sitting in silence for more than a week, David badly wanted to testify himself. But Tallis advised against it.

"The defence calls no witnesses," he said in court, as if to say the Crown's case wasn't worthy of a response.

Mr Justice A. H. Bence did everything he could to help David. He urged the jury to consider the credibility of John and Wilson. He also noted that Lapchuk and Melnyk had testified that David had confessed to the murder, but he pointed out that even if the jury decided David had said this, they must also decide if David, who was high on drugs at the time, was telling the truth himself.

On January 31, 1970, verdict day, David half smiled at the jury as they entered the courtroom, but he clearly looked afraid. When the jury foreman said "guilty," I was flabbergasted.

David later said he hadn't actually heard the word. The verdict became clear only when he saw the horror and pain on our faces. As David was led away, he looked terribly vulnerable. He was so used to turning to us for help, and all he saw now was his father gathering me in his arms as I sobbed uncontrollably.

No Songbirds

The sentence was life imprisonment. In the days that followed, I watched my family falling apart. Our son Chris, a quiet and studious 15-year-old, came home with signs of having been in fights. Susan, 14, suddenly found herself without friends. Even little Maureen, 10, was brought home by a teacher after other children had surrounded her and taunted, "Your brother is a killer!"

In the eyes of many in Langenburg, the name Milgaard now meant "murderer." It would have been so easy for me at that point to just give up, but I turned to the Bible for strength and found it in the story of Joseph. He was also thrown in prison for something he didn't do, and he came out of it a great leader.

Prisoner—David Milgaard's life was now regimented, his freedom taken away—and all for a crime he hadn't committed.

It became evident by May 1970 that we would have to move away. In Winnipeg, Lorne found a job running a quarry. I began working three jobs at once, waitressing, handling a hospital switchboard and selling jewellery at fashion parties.

I spent every extra waking moment trying to get David out of prison: tailing his friends, looking for eyewitnesses who would vouch for his alibi, reading law books and writing to my Member of Parliament asking for support. The first setback came on January 31, 1971, when David's appeal was rejected by Saskatchewan's highest court.

David was distraught. His life was now regimented, his freedom gone—and all for a crime he hadn't committed. A caseworker noted: "Very difficult to believe that this boy could be guilty of this offence. Insists on his innocence . . . Defenceless, immature young man, incapable of facing a life sentence at this time. Deeply depressed, very emotional . . . may well become a case for the psychiatrist."

By summer David felt he had taken all he could handle. On August 17, staff discovered him lying face-down on his bunk, with several self-inflicted slashes to both forearms. He tried to kill himself again that fall by swallowing wires. He recovered from surgery enough to hear, on November 15, that he had not obtained leave to appeal from the Supreme Court of Canada.

Even worse trouble began in March 1972, when David was transferred to the notorious Dorchester Penitentiary in New Brunswick. For comfort, I sometimes read the 23rd Psalm:"I shall walk through the valley of the shadow of death."

David was in the shadow of death in that prison.

Soon after his transfer, we got a letter from a doctor saying David had been gang-raped. From then on, every time I saw David with bruises, my imagination ran wild. David would never tell me the details. Once, when he sustained a shoulder injury, he simply said, "I fell down."

In 1973 he and two other prisoners escaped from Dorchester. They didn't get far. Tracking dogs found them as they fled through a wood. David froze in terror as the dogs growled and snapped at him. He told us later the guards just stood there and let the dogs chew at them.

Three years later David was back in western Canada, at Stony Mountain, a harsh, bleak place built in 1874 on a hill outside Winnipeg. It was wonderful that we could see him often, and he was able to continue his college studies. His parole officer told us how pleased they were with his progress.

But there was a big stumbling block. David could not be considered rehabilitated and ready for parole until he showed remorse. But how could he show remorse for something he didn't do? No matter how much he hated prison, David steadfastly refused to admit he was guilty. He bluntly told me he would never bargain with his innocence. And so, year after year his parole applications were rejected.

No matter how much he hated prison, David steadfastly refused to admit he was guilty. He would never bargain with his innocence.

In the first decade that David spent behind bars, I had come a long way. I took courses in economics and property management. I also borrowed money to invest—and by 1980 I owned eight rental houses and had assets of $250,000. I was improving myself, making myself stronger to continue the fight to free my son.

Ironically, as far as David was concerned, I seemed to have reached a dead end. It made no difference whom I called or wrote to or went to see, there was nothing anyone could do. Most were polite, but their attitude was "Sure, lady, you believe him, but you're his mother."

Meanwhile, David lived vicariously through us. He would ask us to describe everyday experiences in great detail so he could picture them and feel them. He focused particularly on Maureen, who turned 15 in 1976—nearly the age David was when he was locked up. Everything she experienced from that point on was of interest to her brother. What was a first kiss like? A pizza? If Maureen went to the beach, David needed to know details about the sky, the people, the smells, the sounds. Everything. In David's prison world, there were no bright colours, no breezes, no sunsets, no songbirds.

Yet from his jail cell, David was teaching us something. We learned to look more deeply at things, at a beautiful sky, at butterflies, the feel of sand and grass and dew beneath our feet. We learned to appreciate life, which meant appreciating God.

Stolen Freedom

On August 22, 1980, David was out on a pass to attend a barbecue party for his brother Chris's 27th birthday. In the excitement of the event, David managed to steal away with help from his sister Maureen. Soon his picture was being published in newspapers as a dangerous murderer on the loose.

It wasn't long before my brother called me from Toronto and said, "The package that you sent has arrived." Of course, I hadn't sent him a package. His code was easy to follow. "Oh, that's great. I'll get in touch with you," I replied.

I called back from a phone booth and talked with David. He had hitchhiked to Toronto. There, he changed his name to Ward McAdam, got a job in telemarketing and was soon making $200 a week selling encyclopedias.

I flew to Toronto under my maiden name, Baxter. I knew that I should be turning David in. But I couldn't bring myself to do it.

We must have looked quite a pair: me in my red wig and David with his badly bleached hair sprinkled with orange patches. But there was a vibrancy about him that I hadn't seen for years. Euphoric, we both thought that if he could stay out for a while, David would show prison authorities that he could survive as a productive and peaceful person.

THE FIGHT TO FREE MY SON

We took long walks and attended church. We found a furnished apartment for David, and I bought him a bed comforter and some clothes—all the mothering things we had both missed so much. It was with a heavy heart that I finally headed home.

David's stolen freedom lasted 77 days. On November 8, acting on a tip, the police caught up with him in the city's Parkdale district. Spotting two big men who looked like police, David broke into a run. They yelled for him to stop, and he did, raising his hands. There was a shotgun blast, and David collapsed, bleeding from pellets lodged in his spine. Police said they thought David was armed when they shot him.

I flew back to Toronto. David looked so frail, so helpless, handcuffed to his bed in St Joseph's Hospital. I rubbed his feet and told him I loved him. He later explained that he'd had to escape. "I was dying a little bit, something inside, every day."

I blamed myself for David's injuries. Had I turned him in, I kept thinking, he wouldn't have been shot.

I prayed to God for a sense of direction and I got it: we would offer a reward and find the real killer.

White-Knight Lawyer

That episode was a turning point for me. I stopped placing hope in appeals or parole or politicians or any part of the justice system that had so far failed us.

Back in Winnipeg, I called a family meeting. "No one else is going to follow up on David's case," I told my children. "We'll have to do it ourselves. Are you with me?"

"Yes!" they chorused.

The die was cast. We would pour every spare penny we had into proving David's innocence. And if that meant finding the real killer ourselves, so be it.

"No one else is going to follow up on David's case," I told my children. "We'll have to do it ourselves. Are you with me?"

In December 1980 we papered Saskatoon with posters offering a $10,000 reward to anyone with information that would exonerate David. Next, I bought transcripts of David's trial and appeals, and we all pored over them, looking for cracks in the Crown's case.

We also decided to re-enact the crime to see if the Crown's version of the timing of events was plausible. I drove the car, pretending I was David, and Kathy, my son Chris's wife, played the role of Miller, walking from her boarding house to the bus-stop. Chris filmed the event. By the time I did my U-turn to circle back for Kathy, she was already at the bus-stop, rather than in the alley where the attack on Miller had supposedly taken place. We tried this several times, always with the same result. The Crown's theory simply didn't hold up.

In the meantime, we were kept busy following up leads. We wanted to talk with any Crown witnesses we could find. We managed to track down Cadrain, John and Wilson but couldn't get them to talk. I became weary of false leads and worried that our reward money was running out.

Six long years later, my son was still behind bars, with no prospect of release. It was then that a journalist friend suggested I call Hersh Wolch, a former Crown attorney who was now a respected criminal lawyer. I took the transcripts to Wolch's Winnipeg office and gave him my last $2,000 as a retainer.

"Am I banging my head against a wall," I asked, "or is there something I could really do to help my son?"

Wolch asked David Asper, a recent law-school graduate with an air of boyish vitality, to assist him on the file. The young lawyer read the transcripts and was hooked. "Did you do it?" he asked David straight away when they first met at prison.

"No."

He then hit my son with all the tough questions he could think of. David's answers convinced him that a gross injustice had been committed.

Asper revitalized our struggle. I began to see him as my knight in shining armour. He spent countless hours reviewing the transcripts and became expert on the minutest details of the case.

In January 1987 Asper rented a video camera and headed off to Saskatoon to test the Crown's version of the crime for himself. He, too, concluded that Nichol John couldn't have seen what she told police. The timing was impossible. The Crown's position meant that on one of the coldest days of the year, Gail Miller had chosen to take a meandering route to the bus-stop.

Next, Asper visited the Saskatoon courthouse and discovered that 16 years after the trial, the exhibits were still warehoused: semen samples, Miller's bloodstained clothes and undergarments, as well as graphic photos of her dead body. In ordinary cases, exhibits are destroyed after all appeals have been completed, but these had just been sitting there in a shopping cart. Asper put the court staff on notice to preserve the exhibits.

We badly wanted to gather new evidence, and an odd stroke of luck led us to Deborah Hall, a 34-year-old barber whose clients included a friend of my daughter Susan. As a teenager, Hall had attended the party at which David had supposedly bragged about raping and stabbing Miller.

When Asper and I met with her in November 1986, Hall was incredulous that police and a jury actually believed Melnyk and Lapchuk's account of David's "confession." "I don't remember any conversation like that," she said. "It would have freaked me right out."

The party had been held in a tiny motel room, Hall said, so a dramatic incident like a murder-rape confession would have been hard to miss. She recalled seeing a news report about Miller's murder on television and hearing David tell his friends that he had been questioned about it. At one point, Melnyk said to David, "You did it, didn't you?"

"Oh yeah, right," David replied, fluffing up a pillow.

That was it for the alleged confession, Hall said. There had been no crazed re-enactment of the killing, just a childish, sarcastic comment.

A statement Hall had previously made to the Saskatoon police, which contradicted Melnyk and Lapchuk's tale, was never passed on to the defence, leaving us vulnerable to the last-minute, damning testimony.

The next few years took a toll on everyone. There were times when I just wanted to pack it in. But the lengthy struggle was especially hard on David.

Once when I went to see him in Stony Mountain, prison officials said he didn't want to see me. David had suffered 45 days in solitary confinement. He was sent there for insubordination, then kept in as his behaviour got worse not better. When the assistant warden wouldn't allow me to see my son, I told him I would sit on the front steps and call the press and make things unpleasant. He relented, and I was allowed into the segregation area.

David's cell in solitary was small and stark, with no windows, no mattress, nor furniture of any kind, just a toilet without a seat. What sticks in my mind was that the lights remained on day and night.

> **David's cell in solitary was small and stark, with no windows. The person I saw wasn't the David I knew.**

The person I saw wasn't the David I knew. His hair was ratty and dishevelled, and he was shuffling like an old man. His eyes were wild, and he looked so dirty.

"Is it you, Mom?" he asked. "No, it can't be. It must be a vision."

I told him it really was me, and sobbed. I told him, "God loves you and I love you, and we're going to get you out of here."

Stunning Evidence

In the summer of 1986, David Asper and Hersh Wolch drafted an application to the justice minister for David to be released on a special power of mercy under Section 690 of the Criminal Code. For the first time in 17 years, I felt that our struggle was nearing an end. I decided to take a trip abroad.

The trip, however, didn't last beyond England, my first stop. Asper called me to say that our Section 690 application was going nowhere. Could I crank up the "Free David Milgaard" machine?

Back in Canada, as we searched for ways to bolster our Section 690 application, David called to say he had heard about a new process called genetic fingerprinting, which might help our case. "We'll look into it," I said.

Phone calls yielded the name of Dr Rex Ferris of Vancouver, who was researching the new DNA technology for its potential in homicide cases. I phoned Ferris and asked how much he would charge for testing samples in David's case.

"Don't you worry about that," he said. "I'll try to do it for you."

Soon, though, Ferris called to say that Gail Miller's clothing and other exhibits from the trial were too old for him to find anything. "But," he added, "you've got more than enough evidence here to prove that your son is innocent."

"I do?" I asked, stunned. "Will you put that in writing?"

"Of course I will."

Ferris's conclusions went further than we had hoped. The samples of blood and semen he had analyzed virtually eliminated David as a suspect. "Gail Miller may have been alive for 15 minutes after she was stabbed, slowly bleeding to death while lying in the snow," Ferris wrote in his report. "The rape was probably prolonged and wasn't likely to have taken place within the tight, 15-minute time frame suggested by the Crown."

Miller's clothing suggested that she might have been raped elsewhere and her body subsequently dumped in the alley where it was found, Ferris stated. No knife cuts were located in the dress. The black coat that Miller was wearing was found to contain cuts in the back that were approximately the same width as the knife found at the scene. It appeared that part of Miller's dress and her coat had been removed, then the coat put back on after the sexual assault but before the fatal wounds were inflicted.

Since David was on foot when the Crown said he murdered Miller, it was next to impossible for him to have done the killing in the residential neighbourhood without being seen. David had neither the means nor the time to murder Miller in the manner the Crown had suggested, Ferris concluded.

The doctor also had problems with what had been accepted in court as semen samples. They were discovered four days after the killing, when the crime scene had been badly trampled. Even so, a study of one of the samples excluded David as a suspect because of his blood type.

Ferris wrote, "On the basis of the evidence I have examined, I have no reasonable doubt that serological evidence presented at the trial failed to link David Milgaard with the offence, and that, in fact, it could be reasonably considered to exclude him from being the perpetrator of the murder."

A Wife Speaks Out

As the 1990s began, news reports referred to David as one of Canada's longest-serving prisoners. He was now semifamous in Manitoba. Cars were running around with "Free David Milgaard" bumper stickers. But we were finding the media and public easier to convince than the federal Justice Department, and our frustration built as efforts to free David seemed to be getting nowhere.

Then on February 26, 1990, someone phoned Hersh Wolch to say he knew who had killed Gail Miller. "Check out a guy named Larry Fisher," the caller suggested. "He's serving time for a bunch of rapes." The man, who identified himself as Sidney Wilson, a pseudonym, also said that he believed Fisher's wife, Linda, had already gone to the police to denounce him as the murderer.

Larry Fisher. I remembered that name, I told Wolch. We went through all the police reports and found the police had conducted an interview with him at a bus-stop near his home soon after the murder. The report showed he lived below Albert Cadrain in a basement apartment.

A family's love—everyone in the family did everything they could to refute the prosecution's case against David.

Following up on the tip, I set out in March for the hamlet of Cando, Saskatchewan, in search of Linda Fisher. I was accompanied by Paul Henderson, a private detective with Centurion Ministries, an organization that attempts to liberate people who have been wrongly convicted and imprisoned.

The plan was to show up at Linda's door unannounced, lest she bolt, as so many potential witnesses had done before.

Surprisingly, Linda looked happy to see us. She wondered why I was coming to see her now and not a decade earlier, after she had first gone to the police.

"I've heard about you only recently," I replied. "From Sidney Wilson." That drew a blank stare from Linda. She knew no one by that name.

Linda told us that Fisher stayed out the night of the Miller murder and didn't get back in time to get ready for work that morning, which was out of character. She was furious, suspecting that he was running around with other women.

As they were shouting at each other, news of the murder came on the radio, and Linda erupted, saying: "My paring knife is missing. You're probably the one who was out stabbing that girl."

Linda didn't mean it—she just wanted to upset him—but his reaction was chilling. "He looked at me like a guilty person who'd just been caught," Linda recalled. "The colour drained from his face, and he looked shocked and scared."

We drove with Linda to see her uncle, Clifford Pambrun, who worked with Fisher at the time of the murder. Pambrun said Fisher had access to cars, even though he didn't own one. That would tie in with Dr Ferris's theory that the killer may have raped and murdered Miller somewhere else, then dumped the body in the alley.

"You didn't hesitate to lend him your car?" Henderson asked Pambrun.

"No," he replied.

"It was like brainwashing"

In May 1990, we approached Dr Peter Markesteyn, chief medical examiner for the Manitoba Department of Justice. If the federal Justice Department wasn't going to respond to the Ferris report, we would give them another forensic expert.

I was ecstatic when Markesteyn's report arrived on June 4. In part, it read: "I agree with Dr Ferris that the serological evidence presented at the trial failed to link David Milgaard with the semen retrieved from vagina, snowbank and crotch of pants. In my opinion, the serological evidence was on very shaky scientific grounds to a degree that it might well be erroneous."

We sent the new report to Ottawa. As soon as it reached the department, one of its investigators finally booked an interview with Dr Ferris—two years after we had sent in his report.

On the same day we got Markesteyn's report, David Asper phoned me.

He had just received a call from Paul Henderson in British Columbia, where the private detective had finally tracked down Ron Wilson.

"Wilson's caved in," Asper reported. "He recants everything."

Henderson had got a written statement from Wilson. It said: "My testimony was coerced by the police. I was 17. I was frightened. I felt the police were trying to pin it on me."

Wilson now admitted he had never even seen David with a knife in Saskatoon. "It was like brainwashing. I started to implicate David Milgaard to tell police what they wanted to hear."

Wilson now admitted he had never even seen David with a knife in Saskatoon. "I implicated David Milgaard to tell police what they wanted."

By now we were totally disgusted with the Saskatoon police. In addition to coercing witnesses, they appeared to have deliberately kept relevant information from us. In June 1990, a CBC-TV news report revealed that back in October 1970, Larry Fisher had confessed to sexually assaulting two different women in Gail Miller's neighbourhood around the time of her murder. What's more, Fisher had used a paring knife to commit those rapes, as Miller's attacker had done.

Fisher had made these confessions after he had been caught literally with his pants down, trying to flee an attack on a woman in Fort Garry, a suburb of Winnipeg. The confessions were dynamite, the type of information that might have set David free—except that no one, including our lawyer and Fisher's victims, was told about it at the time. If David's case had been reopened then with this fresh evidence, precious little would have been lost of his life. It would have been embarrassing for the Crown and the police, but not much more.

For reasons never clear to me, Fisher's case was handled quietly in Regina rather than Saskatoon, where Fisher and his victims lived. I later learned that Crown attorney Serge Kujawa was handling David's leave to appeal to the Supreme Court of Canada and Larry Fisher's guilty plea in Saskatchewan's Court of Queen's Bench at roughly the same time in 1971. How could he have been blind to the similarities between Gail Miller's murder and Fisher's rapes?

Subsequently, in the spring of 1971—shortly before all of David's legal appeals had been exhausted—Fisher was sentenced to 13 years in prison after pleading guilty to two knife-point rapes in Fort Garry. He was paroled in 1980, and within two months he raped a 56-year-old neighbour in North Battleford, Saskatchewan, then slashed her throat.

He was soon locked up again.

Impartial Justice?

We forwarded the statements from Linda Fisher and her uncle Clifford Pambrun to Justice Minister Kim Campbell as additions to our Section 690 application for mercy. Now we had more than a powerful forensic case; we had also produced a potential suspect who had lived just a block from the murder scene and whose modus operandi fitted the attack on Gail Miller.

By autumn 1990, however, no date for a decision had been set. The delay mystified us. Our doubts about the seriousness of the Justice Department investigation grew when we heard that Eugene Williams, counsel for the federal Department of Justice, subjected Linda Fisher and Deborah Hall to tough interviews. Hall said she left her interview with Williams in tears.

I was particularly enraged when I heard a rumour that Williams was assisted in his investigation by Bobs Caldwell, the prosecutor who had gone on record as saying that David, whom he'd never spoken to, made his "blood run cold." Justice Minister Campbell infuriated all of Canada when I attempted to approach her publicly. The media caught her rebuff for the six o'clock news: "Madam, if you wish to have your son's case dealt with fairly, please do not approach me." I believe this incident became a rallying cry for the whole country.

Bad news came on February 27, 1991, when Asper phoned to say that the decision of the Justice Department was negative. I felt absolute disbelief. It wasn't justice. It was politics.

In her decision, Justice Minister Kim Campbell wrote:

> "The information provided by Deborah Hall does not detract from the evidence led at trial, and Mr Wilson's present recollection of the events in question is palpably unreliable.
>
> "The suggestion that the forensic evidence exculpates David Milgaard overstates the value of that evidence, which [at the trial] established neither guilt nor innocence. Further, there is no reliable basis to believe that Larry Fisher was connected with Gail Miller's death. The submissions concerning the location of the offence and Mr Milgaard's opportunity to commit the offence were fully canvassed by trial counsel and by the judge who properly charged them on that point.
>
> "There is no new evidence that constitutes a reasonable basis for believing that a miscarriage of justice likely occurred. Accordingly, I am not prepared to refer this case back to the courts."

Had they even studied the case? I wondered. How could they dismiss the forensic evidence when Caldwell had insisted that it didn't exclude David—an assertion that was clearly false, yet was the last thing the jury heard before they convicted my son?

After his Section 690 application was denied, I was so angry and full of disbelief. I felt like a failure. I opened my hymnal at random. "Press on, dear traveller, press thou on." Tearfully, I saw that this was the message I needed. I knew God would give me the strength I needed to go on.

> David sank deeper into depression. He wanted nothing to do with the case. When I went to visit, we left it alone.

But David sank deeper into depression. He wanted nothing to do with the case. When I went to visit, we played backgammon and talked about family matters, and left the case alone. What's more, staff and inmates at Stony Mountain now resented his media profile and were tough on him. As usual, David wouldn't tell me the details, but his missing front teeth said it all.

Candlelight Vigil

We had to figure out a new strategy. The key to David's freedom, we felt, lay in Larry Fisher's crimes. We decided to follow them up.

On April 24, 1991, Paul Henderson and I set out to interview Fisher's eight known rape victims, using court records and a tracing agency. The similarities between Fisher's attacks and Miller's murder soon emerged, and they were eerie. All of Fisher's known attacks involved a knife; he mostly targeted women getting on or off a bus; a couple of his victims were in health-related professions and wore medical uniforms, just like his mother, a hospital cleaner with whom, Linda Fisher had told us, he had had a complex relationship.

That August we launched our second bid for a ministerial review. This time, our cause got an invaluable boost from Miller's family. After watching a tape of the interviews we had put together, they issued a statement saying they joined our call for a fresh look at the case.

"Mom, you've got to talk to the Prime Minister," David pleaded during a visit. It was heartbreaking that he thought his mother could simply approach the most powerful politician in the country and appeal for justice.

On September 6, 1991, we decided to stage a candlelight vigil at Stony Mountain. But when we heard that Prime Minister Brian Mulroney was going to be in Winnipeg the next day, we moved the vigil to outside the hotel where he was going to speak. We lit 22 candles, one for each year that David had lost behind bars.

I approached one of the Prime Minister's staff to say I wasn't going to do anything to embarrass Mulroney. The man floored me when he replied, "He's planning on speaking with you." I quickly informed CBC reporter Alan Habbick, who was standing by.

Mulroney stepped out of his car, went halfway up the carpet leading into the hotel, then turned and strode towards me. He took my hand and addressed me by name, looking me squarely in the eye.

"Thank you," I said, my voice trembling. "I've been trying to see you to ask you . . . David's mental situation is not good right now, and anything you can do to get him transferred would be so helpful. And of course, the other question is, is there anything you could do for a speedy review? Because now the Saskatoon police have apparently admitted they haven't given full information to the Justice Department, that really the minister was working with just half of the things she should have had."

Key support—Canadian Prime Minister Brian Mulroney offered his help when it really mattered.

"That was the most recent information?" Mulroney asked.

"Yes, yesterday."

"I'm sure Ms Campbell will get back to the attorney general. And I've taken note of your other request and we'll do what we can."

Mulroney could have walked away any time during our conversation, but he didn't. Towards the end he remarked, "You're very courageous."

A month later David was transferred to Rockwood Institution, a minimum-security prison adjoining Stony Mountain. Shortly after, I received a hand-delivered letter from the Prime Minister, saying in part, "I am confident that the minister of justice will discharge her duties impartially, objectively and promptly."

Finally, on November 29, 1991, Kim Campbell made headlines when she referred David's conviction to the Supreme Court for review. This was only the third time in recent history that the government had referred a murder case to the top court under the power of mercy.

Mind of a Rapist

It was an imposing sight when five of the Supreme Court judges in their long robes walked into the courtroom. For years we could get no one to listen to our story, and now we had the most powerful judges in Canada

Finally, good news—Joyce and David, with sisters Susan (left) and Maureen, announce that the Supreme Court will hear the case.

to hear us. David had not testified at his trial, and now, 22 years later, on January 21, 1992, he was the first witness called before the Supreme Court hearing.

I felt immense pride as I thought of how he had refused to take the easy road and give a false confession, even though it would have bought him freedom. My son's voice was firm and strong as he said, "I did not kill Gail Miller."

Ron Wilson was on the witness stand shortly afterwards. He didn't expect an easy ride, and he didn't get one. Chief Justice Antonio Lamer was visibly frustrated, noting that Wilson had now given at least four versions of what happened the morning of the murder. What was the truth?

There was a sense of sadness about Nichol John when she took the stand. Seeing her was a reminder of how much of our lives this case had consumed. She was a mixed-up kid then, but now she looked weary and middle-aged, and continually referred to her nightmares about the case.

I was taken aback when Larry Fisher stepped up. I didn't expect him to look as nice as he did. He was well dressed and looked distinguished, his hair carefully styled.

Hersh Wolch had talked to a psychiatrist about how to handle Fisher and was told to encourage him to explain things. "You've got to get him to help you."

It worked. Wolch's tone was measured and unthreatening as he drew Fisher to explain his technique as a rapist. The judges had made it clear he was simply a witness, not someone on trial, and Fisher was so polite it was eerie as he explained what went on in the mind of a serial rapist.

Fisher described the precise pattern of his attacks—a pattern which was wholly consistent with the fatal attack on Gail Miller. These attacks weren't about sex; they were about power and control. You could almost feel pride in Fisher's voice as he described how he hurt women.

"Now, in your pattern," Wolch said at one point, "when you take her down the lane, in order to establish control, what you do is, you order them to undress. Isn't that your general pattern?"

"Yes, sir."

"You want the clothes off. And the reason you want the clothes off is because that shows you're in control."

"Yes, sir."

"Because when you do it, you don't take your clothes off, do you? When you rape?"

"No, sir."

A mother's moment—David and Joyce celebrate after the film *Hard Time* had been given six awards at the 1999 Geminis.

One of Fisher's rape victims, from North Battleford, sat in the courtroom as he testified. She was in her sixties now, and the slash mark across her neck was still visible. She sat quietly as Fisher spoke of how he was abused and ignored when he was young.

"As a child, you were controlled," Wolch said to him. "You didn't speak out. Now you were in control."

"Yes, sir."

"And when a lady walked by the alley, you'd grab her, with a knife, and drag her in," Wolch continued. "That was the real thrill, the power."

"I was looking for that power," Fisher replied.

"It was the power," Wolch said. "The sex came later."

"That's right," Fisher replied. "To fulfill it all."

In the courtroom, the atmosphere was electric, almost as if we were holding our breath.

When his testimony was completed, Fisher glared directly into my face as he walked out. His eyes were cold, like pebbles. I stared right back at him, but I was shaking inside.

The hearing was held over a period of four months and heard more than two dozen witnesses. On April 16, 1992, the Supreme Court ruled that David should have a new trial, and ordered him released. At 15 minutes past noon, my son was finally a free man.

As he walked down the narrow prison corridors and out into fresh air and freedom, Maureen said it was like a butterfly leaving a cocoon.

In the parking lot, Wolch and Asper handed David a special birth certificate bearing his new "birth date": April 16, 1992. In my son's pocket was some $240 from wages he had earned doing jobs in prison. With that, he was to start a new life.

Serving time—Canadian actor Ian Tracey, who won a Gemini Award for best actor in his portrayal of David Milgaard, is seen in a still from the film.

Clean Slate

A lot of people thought the story was now over, but we couldn't let it die. The problem was the Province of Saskatchewan. It refused to prosecute again, would not register an acquittal and refused to award compensation or hold an inquiry.

"This is a very cold trail, and it just doesn't seem productive to inquire into it further," said the Saskatchewan Justice Minister, Bob Mitchell.

Mitchell was content to leave a cloud over David's head. My son was free, but in the eyes of the law he had not been cleared of the horrible crime. In 1992 I moved to Kanata, outside Ottawa, to be close to politicians, to continue the push to totally clear David's name.

In the spring of 1997, we were granted another run at DNA testing. By now the science had advanced considerably. The testing was to be conducted in England by Dr Edward Blake, using a new method of analysis. Both the Justice Department and our side would monitor the testing.

On July 18, the results came in. The tests exonerated David and overwhelmingly suggested that Larry Fisher was the real killer.

Soon after the results were made public, Saskatchewan Justice Minister John Nilson issued a statement offering our family "the most heartfelt apology." He went on to say he was considering the questions of compensation and a public inquiry. It was music to my ears.

Three days later, at a press conference in Saskatoon, former Crown attorneys Serge Kujawa and Bobs Caldwell flanked their lawyer, Si Halyk, who spoke on their behalf:

Freedom to speak—flanked by his mother, Joyce, and DNA expert Dr Edward Blake, David Milgaard talks to reporters.

"They both extend their sincerest apologies to David Milgaard, his family and all others directly affected for the failings of the system that resulted in his wrongful conviction," Halyk said. "They fully understand that there is nothing they can say today that will ease this horrible injustice and pain that has been inflicted on Milgaard and his family."

The Saskatoon police, however, issued no such apology. Making them look even worse, Blake said that police could have tried, back in 1969, to match David's blood to the type of semen left on Miller's clothing. Then they could have discounted David as a suspect and zeroed in on the real killer, instead of waiting 28 years. The problem, Blake said, involved incompetent investigators, not poor technology.

The wonderful week after the DNA testing cleared David ended in storybook fashion with Maureen's wedding. Sometime during the celebration, David slipped away into the woods for some quiet time. He had been doing a lot of that lately. He loved to sleep alone under the stars and feel the wind against his skin.

From the sound of his voice, you would have thought he had seen the face of God. "Mom," he exclaimed, "I've just been outside, and I've seen a sunset." When I asked what he meant, he said: "You don't understand. I could see the whole sky, every bit of it. Not just a little bit through the bars. It was wonderful."

I started to cry, thinking, *How many times have I not looked at the sky?*

In May 1999 David Milgaard was awarded $10 million in compensation. In November, Larry Fisher was convicted of the murder of Gail Miller and sentenced to life imprisonment. An appeal against the conviction began in April 2003.

The government of Saskatchewan is still committed to holding a public inquiry into the investigation of the death of Gail Miller and the subsequent conviction of David Milgaard.

GUNMAN IN
THE HOUSE

Suzanne Chazin

"I'm going to kill you!" the gunman screamed, squeezing off two rounds that whizzed past Paul's arm. It was 11.30am on a sunny weekday morning, and a young father was in his house in Salem, looking after his two young sons. His wife was at work. How could he protect the boys from the desperate intruder?

P aul Hardy sank onto the living-room sofa and called to his twin four-year-old sons Kyle and Kevin, sprawled before him watching cartoons. "Fifteen minutes, boys. Then it's time to get ready for nursery." It was 11.30am on Wednesday, February 11, 1998, and sunlight streamed through the windows of their house in Salem, Massachusetts. Paul was looking after the boys while his wife Gail was at work. As he gazed at the television, he heard a distant staccato popping. He hoped the workmen down the street would quieten down later so he could sleep. A prison officer for the past five years, he'd just worked two shifts—last night and this morning.

It was hard being behind razor-wire fences, outnumbered by inmates who sometimes pummelled him as he broke up fights. Prohibited from carrying weapons, the former high-school wrestler had learned to get by on the strength of his five-foot-eight, 14-stone frame—and on his wits.

After work at the local County Correctional Facility, Paul often relaxed by having a beer with his fellow officers.

"You should be here with us," Gail would argue when he arrived home late. To Paul, family and job were separate but nearly equal parts of his life.

The boys were just about ready when Paul was startled by another, noisier pop. Two loud bangs reverberated from across the hall as bullets shattered the sliding-glass kitchen door.

Suddenly a man in a black ski mask stormed into the living room, waving a semiautomatic handgun.

"Get down!" the intruder screamed. "On the floor!"

Is this some former inmate? Paul wondered as sirens wailed and tyres screeched at the foot of his drive. The police had the house totally surrounded. The intruder, Paul realized, could only surrender—or shoot his way out.

"It's OK," Paul whispered to the frightened boys.

He wanted his children out of the line of fire, so he asked the gunman if he could put them in a corner.

"Yeah, that's OK," the intruder said, peeling off his ski mask and revealing a young, clean-shaven face.

"You boys take a little nap," Paul told his sons. "Daddy's got to talk to this man, OK?"

Kyle regarded his father warily. "It's all right, Kyle," Paul assured him. Kevin had always been sunny and outgoing. Kyle was more sensitive—and more intuitive.

When the boys finally fell asleep, the gunman ordered Paul to sit at his feet while he counted wads of notes that had been stuffed into two pillowcases. The total came to $9,000.

This man must have robbed something big, Paul realized, and is looking at a long prison sentence. If he and the kids were to survive, he'd need to forge a connection.

"I'm Paul," he said. "Those are my sons Kevin and Kyle."

The gunman just grunted. Paul noticed, however, that the man made eye contact with him and cast a quick glance at the boys. The names had registered in his mind.

"Look at all this I'll never be able to spend," he said. "I'm having a really bad day."

Paul channelled his outrage into humour. "Yeah," he said. "My day isn't much better."

The intruder picked up a cordless phone by the sofa and punched some buttons. "Mum, Dad, I'm sorry about the way things turned out. I really screwed up. I love you both. I'll see you on the other side."

The other side? If the gunman was making a final farewell, what chance of escape did Paul and the twins have?

The scene outside was just as tense. Police officers now knew that 40 miles away, at 10.20am, a gunman had robbed a bank of $9,000. Police had pursued the suspect's vehicle at speeds of up to 117mph, but he had broken through two roadblocks and fired on their cars. The chase ended when the suspect's tyre burst and he escaped on foot, shooting two more rounds at police before breaking into the Hardy house.

The suspect escaped on foot, shooting two rounds at police before breaking into the Hardy house.

Parked round the corner, police chief Robert St Pierre was getting the grim update: two children and a father in law enforcement who might have guns in the house. They were sitting on dynamite. What's more, both the gunman and the hostage were roughly the same height and build, and both were wearing light-coloured sweatshirts. If police stormed the house, could they be certain who was the gunman and who was the hostage?

"Will the suspect talk?" the chief asked police captain Paul Tucker.

"He says he'll only talk to the FBI."

"Get the FBI in Boston to send us a negotiator immediately," St Pierre ordered. "And ask the state police for negotiators along with their SWAT unit." Then he dialled the house.

"An FBI negotiator's on the way," St Pierre said. "Will the local chief of police do until they get here?"

"I want the FBI or people are going to get hurt!" The voice was young—and agitated. St Pierre looked at his watch. It was noon. Allowing for the traffic, it could take 40 minutes for the FBI to get a negotiator on the scene. By then the family could be dead.

Tense situation—when police chief Robert St Pierre arrived on the scene, he realized that he faced a gunman and a cruel dilemma.

Inside, the gunman watched a news report with live coverage of Hardy's house from a helicopter. The broadcast revealed what Paul wisely hadn't—that he was a prison officer.

"You're a prison officer?" the gunman demanded angrily. Paul choked out a yes.

The gunman paced the floor and fumed.

"Of all the houses to break into." A thought struck him. "Where's your gun?" he demanded.

"I don't keep one in the house because of the kids," Paul said.

"You're lying," screamed the intruder, his fingers dancing round the trigger of the gun.

Paul knew the rules of hostage negotiation: never lie if you can help it. Once trust is broken, you are dead.

"I'm telling the truth," he said, staring unblinkingly into the gunman's eyes.

The man's bushy eyebrows knitted together as he debated Paul's answer. Time seemed to stop. Then the man nodded slightly and relaxed his grip on the gun.

Paul exhaled.

Still furious, the intruder phoned St Pierre. "I told you to pull back," he shouted.

"I did," the chief insisted. He'd inspected the perimeter himself. From the gunman's vantage point, there wasn't a cop in sight.

"Then who's that officer with a shotgun behind the wall? I'm serious—I'll shoot these people." He hung up.

St Pierre was dumbfounded—until he heard the sound of helicopter blades whirring overhead. "Get those guys out of here now," he told Tucker. "They're going to get people killed."

Tucker radioed back. "Chief, the FBI negotiator is on the way."

Voice of reason—FBI special agent Liane McCarthy was called in to negotiate with the gunman.

Special agent Liane McCarthy, 38, had helped gain the release of kidnap victims across the globe during her six years as an FBI crisis negotiator.

Arriving on the scene, McCarthy checked her watch. It was 12.45pm. Paul and his boys had been trapped inside with the gunman for nearly an hour.

The first 45 minutes of any hostage situation are critical, because that's when suspects and victims are most likely to panic. McCarthy felt that maybe she had a chance to talk this gunman into giving himself up.

First, she requested that outgoing calls from the residence be stopped so that no one—parents or girlfriends—could interfere with the psychological bond she needed to form with the gunman. Then she got on the telephone.

"My name is Liane. I'm with the FBI. What's your name?"

"You know my name," the gunman said.

"If I knew your name, why wouldn't I just tell you?" she reasoned in a reassuring voice. The suspect was taken aback.

"It's Chad. Chad Austin."

Within minutes police data banks were spewing out a history of the gunman. Austin, 24, from Concord, New Hampshire, had been released from a state jail four months earlier after serving nearly three years on a violent assault charge for smashing a man's head with a club. Before that he had been convicted of two less serious assaults.

"I'm not going back to prison," Austin vowed.

His history and comments gave weight to what police already feared—that it wouldn't take much to force him into a shoot-out. McCarthy had to get the children out of the house—and soon.

She urged Austin to let the boys go to their mother, who was now on the scene. "Do you have children?" Austin asked her.

"No."

"I don't either," he said. He seemed curious about the woman on the other end of the line. He asked McCarthy how old she was and if she was married. She answered truthfully and noticed his tone softening.

At 3pm, after a lengthy conversation with McCarthy, Austin turned to Paul. "Would you be more comfortable if the kids were out of the house?"

Teary-eyed with relief, Paul woke the children. "Daddy's got to talk to this man a little while longer," he told them, "but Mummy wants to see you outside." Kevin rubbed his eyes. Kyle gave his father another questioning glance. "I'll be out soon—I promise," Paul said as he marched them to the front door.

Time to go—news cameras caught Paul Hardy coaxing his two young sons away from the house to safety.

But the twins froze. "Come with us, Daddy," Kyle pleaded.

Desperate, Paul tried again. "Hey, boys. How about going out to play on your cars?"

The children brightened at the suggestion, so Paul walked them down the steps to the garage to get the miniature all-terrain vehicles. While Austin watched, Paul lifted the door. Out on the driveway was the family dog.

"Go and play with Reggie, boys. Go ahead now," Paul said. "Mum's waiting for you."

The boys walked slowly out onto the drive. Two police officers wearing riot gear moved towards them. Kevin allowed one to carry him off. But Kyle ran back to his father.

"Daddy, Daddy," he cried. "Don't leave me!"

Paul crouched down and hugged his son. "Kyle, please—just follow Kevin." Then he pushed Kyle out onto the drive and closed the garage door. Upstairs he tried to get control of himself again.

The clock in the living room read 4pm. A cold winter chill now seeped into the house through the shattered kitchen door. Paul's neck and back ached with tension. He waited for Austin to begin the process of giving himself up. But for the next 25 minutes, the gunman stayed on the line with McCarthy while switching television channels.

Paul watched Austin through clenched teeth. In his mind he replayed the countless prison conversations he'd overheard from men who bragged about their crimes with callous indifference to the people they'd hurt, the lives they'd ruined. *Not this house*, Hardy vowed. *Not this family.*

When Paul's dog entered the house and walked across the broken kitchen glass, Austin jumped at the sound, letting his gun go slack. Paul saw his opportunity: he lunged for Austin's weapon, then head-butted him.

"I'm going to kill you!" Austin screamed, squeezing off two rounds that ripped through the couch and whizzed past Paul's arm. Paul saw the magazine, which carried extra ammunition, fall out of the gun. He knew that rounds already in the weapon couldn't be fired in most new guns unless the magazine was in position. Paul gambled—and wrestled the gun away from Austin, then pinned him to the floor, pounding his fists into him repeatedly.

Just then law-enforcement officers stormed the house. A flash of light and a shock wave from a stun grenade tore through the living room. Paul struggled to the front window, opened it and collapsed on the grass below. Inside, Austin resisted arrest and was shot in the thigh before being brought under control.

Home together—Paul and Gail Hardy with daughter Kristi-Lee and twins Kyle and Kevin. Family ties are even closer than they were before.

Chad Austin was convicted in Massachusetts of three counts of kidnapping and armed home invasion, five counts of simple assault, one count of unlawful possession of a firearm and two counts of assault with a dangerous weapon. He faces up to 40 years in prison. Federal prosecutors are ready to move forward with the New Hampshire bank robbery charges as well.

The twins only vaguely recall that February day, but Paul and Gail will never forget it. Now working as a drill instructor in the corrections-department training academy, Paul comes straight home after work.

"I never realized how much family meant before this happened," says Paul. "I thought that they were part of my life. Now I know they are my life."

Chad Austin requested a new trial, and a hearing to discuss that request was due to take place in 2003.

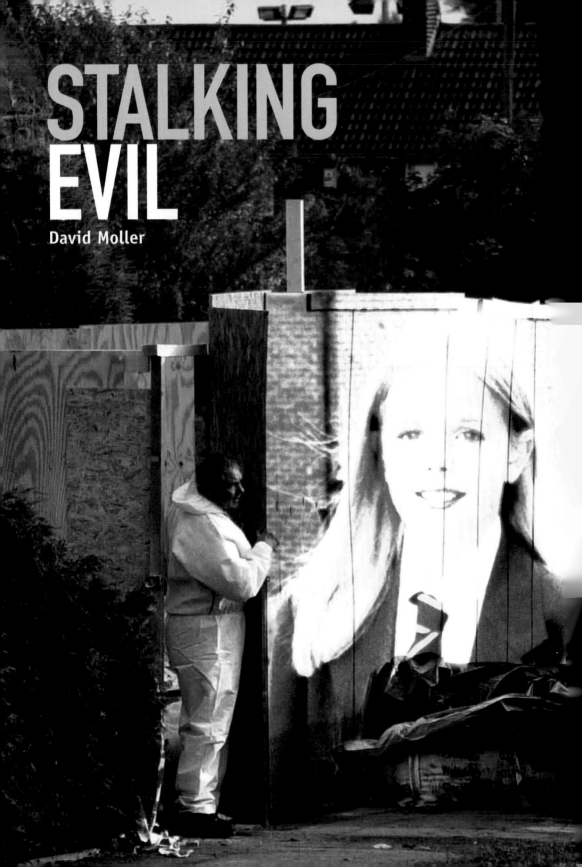

STALKING EVIL

David Moller

"I'm sorry, she's not home yet, love," Leanne's mother, Sharon Hawkhead told her daughter's best friend, Sarah Whitehouse. It was a late November afternoon in Leeds, and the two girls had been shopping. Within hours the police were out hunting for the fair-haired 16-year-old.

t was typical of Leanne Tiernan that she would spend all she had on her on a friend. Shopping in Leeds with her best friend Sarah Whitehouse, the slight, fair-haired 16-year-old insisted on buying her some jewellery as an early Christmas present.

That morning, November 26, 2000, Leanne had gone to church with her grandmother and helped out at its Sunday school. The afternoon had turned drizzly, but as the girls got off the bus in Bramley, west Leeds, they were joking about their boyfriends at home watching football.

It was 4.50pm and already dark as they parted. Leanne still had a 20-minute walk, but she'd take the short cut down Houghley Gill—a narrow strip of wooded parkland.

"Ring me later about tonight," she called.

Sarah left it nearly half an hour before phoning. "I'm sorry, she's not home yet, love," Leanne's mother Sharon Hawkhead told her.

Now Sharon felt a twinge of anxiety. She knew that Leanne was always punctual. She called her mobile phone. It rang 20 times before switching off. She tried again. This time it rang just four times—then cut off.

Briskly, Sharon called to her elder daughter, 19-year-old Michelle, and with a few friends searched the route Leanne would have taken.

Nothing.

An hour later, Sharon Hawkhead alerted the police. "Please, you've got to help me find my daughter."

WEST YORKSHIRE
POLICE

Mother and daughter—a police poster showing the sweet-natured, bubbly Leanne looms large behind her devastated mother.

Chris Gregg frowned as he scanned the map on the incident room wall inside Leeds's Weetwood police station. In his early forties, lean, with dark hair, the detective superintendent was a veteran of some 50 murder cases and several abductions. *The vast majority of missing teenagers return home within 24 hours,* he thought grimly.

Leanne had been gone two days.

On Houghley Gill, officers had found no signs of a struggle. But they still had a vast area to cover. "There are 42 water drainage shafts in the Gill," Gregg told his team. "We're going to search every one.

"Another priority is to get everything we can on Leanne's background. Could she have gone off with someone we don't yet know about?"

Gregg's detectives interviewed Leanne's divorced parents, Sharon and Michael, and her boyfriend, and took 189 statements from family and friends. All described a sweet-natured, bubbly girl, without secrets.

Drawn and hollow-eyed, Sharon recalled how, when they had kissed for the last time, Leanne had laughingly left lipstick on her cheek. "I miss the noise— her CD blasting out, her singing round the house. I just want that child to walk through the door."

At 16, Leanne was just a couple of years younger than Gregg's own son. With compassion in his brown eyes, Gregg promised: "We're going to do everything possible, Sharon, to find Leanne."

By mid-December, police had searched 800 houses, trawled the Leeds–Liverpool Canal and interviewed anyone remotely capable of abduction or sexual violence. Forensic scientists, led by 36-year-old Peter Grant at the nearby Wetherby labs, had produced a DNA profile of Leanne from saliva on her toothbrush. A set of her fingerprints had been taken from books at her home.

Gregg now had more than 200 officers working for him in what was becoming one of the biggest missing person searches in British history. He'd wasted no time in putting the inquiry onto the police computer system to correlate the mass of information: premises searched, suspects, calls from the public. As a young detective back in the pre-computerized 1970s, Gregg had worked on four of the 13 murders committed by the Yorkshire Ripper, Peter Sutcliffe. That investigation had been swamped with information, dragging on for five years. He'd learned a lot about running a big case.

> **Gregg now had more than 200 officers working for him in what was becoming one of the biggest missing person searches in British history.**

222

Relentless—Detective Superintendent Chris Gregg was now pursuing a brutal killer.

Despite working some 18 hours a day, Gregg made time to call Leanne's parents. The case rarely left his mind. *How could a young girl vanish without anyone seeing anything?*

They had one significant lead—a report of a middle-aged man seen walking a dog in Houghley Gill at the time Leanne disappeared. But despite making 1,400 house-to-house enquiries, detectives got no further clues on the sighting.

It was 1.30pm on August 21, 2001, when Gregg took a call on his mobile from Detective Inspector David Knopwood. "Boss, it's a young girl." The packaged remains of a body had been found in a grave in Lindley Woods, near Otley— 16 miles from where Leanne had last been seen.

At Harrogate District Hospital, kitted out in protective green gown and rubber boots, Gregg joined pathologist Dr Kenneth Shorrock, who was examining the body. The victim's identity had been established by her fingerprints. It was Leanne.

The teenager had been wrapped in a duvet cover and ten green bin bags— each one bound with twine. As her body was carefully lifted from the last bag, forensic scientist Samantha Warnakulasuriya suddenly called out, "Stop! I can see fibres." From the back of the victim's sweater, she extracted a half-tuft of burgundy-red carpet.

Death, so far as the pathologist could tell given the body's decomposition, was from strangulation. A double-knotted scarf and 15-inch plastic cable tie had been tied round Leanne's neck; her wrists bound behind her back with three more ties. The young girl's head was covered by a black plastic bag strapped tight with a leather dog collar.

In his investigations, Gregg tried to remain detached and clinical. But as he gazed on the teenager's pale figure on the stainless steel mortuary table, he recalled the exhaustion in Sharon Hawkhead's eyes and was filled with cold anger. *I will find whoever did this.*

It was late when Gregg arrived at Sharon's home to speak to both parents. Family liaison officers had broken the terrible news, but there were many difficult questions; some would never be answered. "Given the condition of her body, it's not possible to say whether Leanne had been sexually assaulted," Gregg said gently. Neither would anyone know how long she had suffered. Sharon and Michael lapsed often into numbed silence, and Gregg stayed with them until long past midnight.

Looking for clues—Leeds detectives searched 800 houses and made 1,400 house-to-house calls.

There was one detail Gregg daren't risk passing on: the discovery of the red carpet fibre. Straight away he'd set investigators to check the homes of Leanne's family to make sure it hadn't been picked up innocently. "It's a standard nylon carpet," Peter Grant told him. "But with something to compare it with—in the home of a suspect—it could be crucial."

Grant's team examined the materials covering Leanne for any trace of fingerprints or DNA—from blood, semen, saliva, hairs—which could then be checked with the 1.7 million profiles on the National DNA Database, or with a screening of local men. It was hopeless.

"Any DNA traces have been contaminated by the decomposition of the body," Grant told Gregg.

Dog hairs found on Leanne's sweater were taken to the world's leading experts in animal DNA: the department of veterinary pathology at Texas A&M University in the US. Tests revealed the hairs had come from a black and tan dog. But little more.

Could the killer be someone we've already interviewed? Gregg sent his detectives back to the homes of potential suspects to see if any had a red carpet that matched the fibres on Leanne's sweater. None did. And while

Gregg was convinced that there had to be a clue on the body that would lead them to the killer.

microscopic magnification of the plastic cable ties revealed the name of one manufacturer that sold almost exclusively to the Post Office, a trawl through the 5,000 people delivering around Leeds revealed no one with any clear link to the crime. For several weeks the investigation seemed to be going nowhere. Yet Gregg refused to slacken his schedule, convinced that there had to be a clue on the body that would lead them to the killer.

He assigned detectives Hayley Pedley and David Wilson to check out the tan dog collar from round Leanne's neck. Made by the Nottingham firm of Armitage, it had sold in its millions round the world. However, a change in the stitching meant that this particular collar must have been made after September 1999. But because most had been sold for cash by Leeds's four main pet shops, there were no records of who had bought it. Gregg wouldn't let the matter rest.

Photofit likeness—the police issued this E-Fit picture of a man they wanted to interview.

"There could be some corner shop that sells dog collars along with the cigarettes, the sweets and the boot polish. We'll try every wholesaler in the country." Armed with a list of 200 companies, in two days the detectives had checked 111. Then Wilson rang Pets Pyjamas in Liverpool.

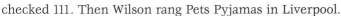

A mail order firm, it had supplied Armitage collars to three customers in West Yorkshire. In March 2000, six had been bought by a J. Taylor, of 17 Cockshott Drive, Armley, Leeds. Wilson gripped the phone more tightly. Cockshott Drive was less than a mile from where Leanne was last seen.

Detectives quickly consulted computer records for any other mention of a Taylor among the 4,000 names—informants, suspects, people still to be interviewed. A lead flashed up on the screen.

In one appeal, police had asked for information on anyone from Leeds who might also have had some connection with Lindley Woods. A woman had rung in to say a man she'd gone out with from west Leeds used to go poaching in Lindley Woods. Gregg knew that by itself the information was tenuous. But the man's name was John Taylor.

Pedley and Wilson drove to the Bradford depot where Taylor was a delivery driver. A broad-shouldered, genial 45-year-old, he was known locally as the "pet man" because he bred dogs and sold pet food.

With no criminal record, he had no objection to his home being searched: he knew other houses were being looked at. The divorced father of two offered to stay with a son who lived nearby. "No problem."

That evening, a team of boiler-suited forensic scientists entered Taylor's house. Samantha Warnakulasuriya's footsteps echoed as she walked through the hall. Bare floorboards. Except for the stairs, all the carpets had been lifted. Outside, in the garden, fragments of burnt carpet were discovered. Had evidence been destroyed?

Then, on a floor tack in a bedroom upstairs, they found a wisp of red carpet fibre. The lab confirmed it was a perfect match with the fibre on Leanne's sweater.

Searchers also found remains of an old cable tie that had supported a plant on a fence outside. It too was identical to one of the ties on Leanne's body. The twine used to secure the bin bags encasing her was shown to

"The pet man"—what lay behind the inoffensive appearance of John Taylor?

match rabbit netting found in Taylor's home. And in a grim discovery, a dog was found buried—its head cruelly bashed in.

It was a black and tan terrier.

At the end of 10 days Gregg ordered the property to be screened off with wooden boarding. He knew that would cause a stir in the press. *Mr Taylor will be wondering what exactly we have found there.*

Brought in for questioning at Killingbeck police station on October 16, 2001, Taylor was a different man—quiet and cautious. Monitoring the interview on a closed-circuit television camera from an adjoining room, Gregg noted Taylor's stocky, paunchy build. It would have been easy for him to subdue the slight teenager.

Now that Gregg had forensic evidence, Taylor would have to come up with an explanation of how Leanne came to be in his home.

He now admitted abducting Leanne. Grabbing her as she walked past him. Blindfolding her with his scarf and, with his raincoat over her head, walking her the half-mile to his home. In a bedroom, as he had taken her jacket off to bind her hands, she had kicked out. "You can't blame the poor lass."

But John Taylor swore that he was not directly responsible for Leanne's death. There had been a struggle, he said. As they'd fallen off the bed she'd hit her head on the floor. "She must have died of head injuries . . . There was a lot of bleeding."

Why, then, had the post-mortem shown no signs of head injury?

As Gregg's detectives dug deeper, they began to construct a profile of Taylor very different from the cheery "pet man". Those who had been poaching with him described how he enjoyed clubbing pheasants to death. One recalled Taylor holding a fox by its rear legs as he stabbed it repeatedly with a knife.

Women he had met through contact magazines spoke of the pleasure Taylor had taken in tying them up during their encounters. Chillingly, several months after Leanne's disappearance, he told one woman of his intense desire to tie up her 15-year-old daughter.

But Taylor was still insisting that Leanne's death was an accident, that she'd bled to death—until painstaking forensic examination of his bedroom floorboards produced clear evidence to the contrary.

The poacher was finally snared.

In Leeds Crown Court in July, 2001, John Taylor pleaded guilty to kidnap and murder and was sentenced to two life sentences.

Chris Gregg had kept his promise to Leanne's parents; but his job was not done. In October 2002, detectives began questioning Taylor about four other unsolved murders. Their enquiries are ongoing. In February 2003, at Leeds Crown Court, Taylor received two further life sentences after pleading guilty to two serious sex assaults committed in the Bramley area of Leeds in the 1980s.

TO CATCH A KILLER

Police triumvirate Chris Pryor, Bob Poole and Jo Gough stand by the grave of Jean Bellis (opposite, left to right). It was a mixture of old-fashioned police work and modern science that enabled the team to crack the perplexing case of the 38-year-old mother-of-two who was brutally murdered in the kitchen of her council house on a Birmingham estate.

No one knows for sure how long it took Jean Bellis to bleed to death. No one could have heard her cries for help as she lay on the kitchen floor of her council house on the Kingstanding estate in Birmingham. Even if someone had come through the gate onto her back garden, crossed the lawn and peered through the window, they would not have seen her: Jean's killer calculated for this and dragged her out of sight.

It wasn't until a week later that a concerned neighbour discovered her body. The police pathologist believed it was one of the five deep stab wounds, probably inflicted with a pair of scissors, that killed the 38-year-old mother-of-two—the 21 superficial wounds, including signs of strangulation, may have been an attempt to torture her into revealing the location of cash and valuables. But she was probably still conscious as the killer searched her home, as he dragged her from the living room into the stone-floored kitchen and as he fled.

All this happened two years ago and they never caught the killer, thought Detective Chief Inspector Bob Poole as he flicked through the dusty case file, his normally neat and tidy office swamped by the paper and photographs that tumbled out. There were 180 documents. It would take months to sift through it all.

Like everyone else at Erdington police station, 48-year-old Poole had been shocked by the brutality of the murder when it happened in April 1993. Forty officers were assigned to the investigation, led by DCI Geoff Mander, who had an excellent clear-up rate. Yet in July 1995 Mander retired knowing Jean's murderer still walked free.

Now the case had been passed on to Poole. He sighed as he paged through the yellowing notes. No one really expected him to solve it, but as he read on he found himself drawn into the puzzle.

The Usual Suspects
No fewer than six people had been arrested but one by one they had all come up with watertight alibis. Much evidence had pointed to 25-year-old Peter Hastings: he had known the victim and at the time of the murder he had

bragged to some schoolchildren that he had "stabbed up" Jean Bellis, before trying to sell them some of her rings. He had also been seen throwing a belt over a fence, a belt on which was found a hair that looked suspiciously like one of Jean's.

Yet Hastings was also a known fantasist, fond of surrounding himself with impressionable youngsters to whom he spun stories of being related to notorious murderers such as Peter Sutcliffe and Michael Sams. He was in reality a petty crook from Druids Heath in Birmingham, with 19 convictions for theft, burglary and car crime.

The biggest stumbling block was that on April 9 and 10, which pathologists pinpointed as the most likely dates for Jean Bellis's murder, Hastings was in Torquay, with dozens of witnesses. He had travelled down with friends on Friday, April 9, in a green Sunbeam that was in such a bad state that local police stopped them. He didn't return to Birmingham until April 12. He claimed Jean had given him the rings to sell at the beginning of March.

Poole looked up at the walls of his office, decorated with mementoes of his career and plaques from places around the world where he had lectured. It was midnight already. He had built a reputation on cracking unsolved cases, but he could tell this would be one of his toughest yet.

By now it was considered so dead in the water that Poole, at six foot two, a red-faced bear of a man, was allowed only two other officers to help him. He chose DC Chris Pryor, the exhibits officer in the original investigation, and WDC Jo Gough, who had been the family liaison officer.

They got to work straight away—which for much of the time meant sitting together in Poole's office poring over the vast case file and bouncing ideas around. All three detectives had to squeeze in work on the case around their other duties, but Poole was convinced the answer lay among the stack of papers.

"A murder inquiry is like a jigsaw. If you miss one piece in the puzzle it can change the whole picture."

"A murder inquiry fits together like a jigsaw," he insisted. "If you miss one piece in the puzzle it can change the whole picture. Sometimes you have to try rearranging the pieces in a way that doesn't obviously make sense. But then murders rarely do."

Jean Bellis was a popular woman but, despite the fact that she was looking for love, her relationships had a bad history. She already had two children by the time she married at the age of 34. However, the relationship with Stephen Bellis foundered after only 15 months.

Attractive prey—Jean Bellis was described as "a soft touch": the sort of woman who was attracted to the wrong sort of men.

Petite with long auburn hair, Jean was described in the statement of a policeman who knew her as "the sort of woman men are attracted to, but who is herself attracted to the wrong sort of men. She was a soft touch and a lot of them ended up using her."

One such man was Peter Hastings. He had befriended Jean's daughter Rhonda when the two were at school together, though Rhonda always thought it strange the way he surrounded himself with younger children. She also laughed at his obsession with polishing his black brogues. Hastings took great care over his appearance, always in his trademark drainpipe jeans and white socks— earning himself the nickname Pee Wee, after the film character Pee Wee Herman—and the shoes were his pride and joy.

At about the time Jean's marriage broke up, Rhonda, then 17, and her sister Vanessa, two years older, left home, leaving Jean lonely. When a letter arrived marked "HM Prison" Jean was interested to hear from one of Rhonda's friends—Peter Hastings—trying to get in touch with Rhonda but also asking after Jean. She wrote back and the pair struck up a relationship that endured after he left prison. Hastings became a regular visitor to the house.

The Search for Evidence

After examining the files compiled by Geoff Mander on each of the six suspects' backgrounds and alibis, Poole's team agreed that there was one who stood out—Peter Hastings.

"There's something that doesn't smell right about him," said Poole. "But he was definitely in Torquay at a disco on April 9 and at that party on April 10. That's a cast-iron alibi."

Not only that, but Hastings had been arrested and released already. From his 28 years of policing, Poole knew that the Crown Prosecution Service would demand a lot of new evidence to go to trial.

Poole began to look at exactly why Hastings had been released. It was a hair trapped in the belt, plus some spots of blood on his shoes, that had made police suspicious, but they had to prove these came from Jean. To make matters worse, Hastings had applied several layers of polish to the shoes, covering the blood. Police turned to the relatively new science of DNA analysis, but all tests had proved inconclusive, and that, along with his alibi, meant they'd had to let Hastings go.

It was then that DCI Poole saw his chance: it was now 1996 and three years was a long time in forensic science. The procedure used in 1993 on the hair and blood samples, as well as Hastings's clothes and some cigarette butts found at the crime scene, was a fairly unsophisticated one called DQ Alpha testing, which required larger samples than the ones available. But Poole had been a regular visitor to the police training centre at Bramshill, Hampshire, and had seen the technology race ahead. Could more modern DNA techniques succeed?

> **DCI Poole saw his chance: it was now 1996 and three years was a long time in forensic science.**

Poole rang the crime lab where the suspect's clothes had been sent for testing—but the staff were unhelpful. "It's no good," he said to his colleagues as he hung up. "Hastings's lawyer demanded the clothes back in 1994."

"But not the shoes," interjected Pryor. "I remember I refused to let them go. We knew those spots of blood had to be important."

Sure enough, the shoes were still at the lab. Poole rang the team at Bramshill, who put him in touch with a scientist called Dave Loxley at Birmingham's Forensic Science Service.

"Come and have a look at this!" said Loxley, as Poole arrived. There was a childlike glee in his voice as Loxley showed the detective his latest toy, a powerful new microscope. They tried it out on Hastings's shoes—and there were the blood spots. "They're like giant boulders!" gasped Poole, squinting through the lens.

> **... there were the blood spots. "They're like giant boulders!" gasped DCI Poole, squinting through the lens.**

"There's definitely a chance we can lift a sample," said Loxley. "But don't forget the spots have been polished over several times."

The shoes were sent to a specialist lab in Wetherby, near Leeds, for a state-of-the-art DNA test that looks at "short tandem repeats" (STRs) and works well on "live" matter such as blood. STRs are the basis of distinctions between individuals' genetic material and consist of brief sequences of DNA repeated end to end. Different people have different numbers of repeats.

All Poole could do was wait for the results. But would it be enough? He went to search the station's overflowing property store. Even though

Hastings's lawyer had indeed retrieved most of the suspect's clothes, it turned out that the belt was still there and the hair on it had been preserved.

Poole eagerly took the belt to Loxley—who pointed out that STR analysis wouldn't work on "dead" matter like hair. But there was another chance. The Forensic Science Service was pioneering a complex process called mitochondrial DNA (mtDNA) testing: mtDNA is passed unchanged from mother to child, with no contribution from the father, and all siblings share it. Importantly, though, mtDNA can be recovered from dead matter.

In Camera

The hair was dispatched to the lab, leaving Poole to concentrate on three further items that the property store had yielded: the original cigarette butt samples from Jean's flat, a family video and photographs from a film which was found unfinished in Jean's camera at the time of her death. The dog-ends Poole sent off for retesting.

During the original investigation, the film had been processed but largely ignored. Now Bob Poole leafed through the prints with renewed interest. They showed Jean Bellis in life, celebrating a family birthday with her daughters and grandchildren. He looked closely at one of the shots in which Jean was holding a drink—she seemed to be wearing rings but it was hard to make them out. *I wonder when these pictures were taken?* he thought.

The next day he rang Rhonda and Vanessa. They confirmed that the photographs had been taken on March 15. Then he contacted Ashley Windsor, an image-analysis expert from Mask Technology in Newbury, Berkshire, and sent him the birthday snaps, along with the original post-mortem photographs of Jean's body and the family video. Could he extract any details from them that were not visible to the naked eye?

Could image-analysis extract details from the birthday snaps that were not visible to the naked eye?

Using image-enhancement technology, Windsor assembled all the shots of Jean's hands and established a consistent colour and contrast pattern that showed, sure enough, that the five rings she was wearing in the birthday pictures and video were the same five Hastings claimed she had given him—a week and a half before the photo was taken. Hastings's story was a lie.

Windsor then turned his attention to the post-mortem photographs. He had been developing a way of analysing skin colour by removing certain tones and exaggerating others to highlight telltale marks and blemishes. His conclusions were extraordinary.

"You can see a pair of parallel lines round her neck," he told Poole. "It looks like a belt has been wrapped round her neck, with a widening of the marks at the throat where the buckle would be."

The policeman was astonished: no one had told Windsor about the belt. But the scientist had something more.

"Within the buckle area is a scratch mark that goes off at an angle," he added. "It looks as though the buckle pin was bent."

Poole fetched the belt. The buckle pin was bent.

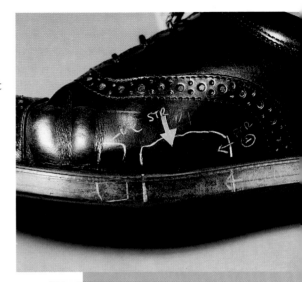

Undercover—the polish on Hastings's shoes had preserved the blood found on them, and DNA tests revealed a hidden horror story.

The Hard Facts

Eventually all the DNA test results came in. The Wetherby lab had managed to shave away leather from inside the shoe and access the blood spot from behind. Amazingly, the layers of polish that Hastings had so lovingly applied had actually preserved the blood perfectly. The STR test showed that the chances of the blood coming from anyone other than Jean Bellis were 58.9 million to one.

The mtDNA test on the hair matched too; even the saliva samples on the cigarette butts were found to be a rare strain called A-secretor—the same as Hastings's.

The evidence linking "Pee Wee" to the murder was now very strong. So how come so many people saw him in Torquay on April 9 and 10?

To bolster their case the team began rounding up witnesses to whom Hastings had tried to sell Jean's rings during the week of the murder. One testimony came in that made Poole's heart beat faster: a youth claimed Hastings had offered him the rings on the Tuesday. That was April 7, two days before the estimated date of the murder. Perhaps the time of death was incorrect and Hastings's alibi was simply for the wrong day.

Poole put his theory to pathologists who re-examined the evidence—and the final piece of the jigsaw fell into place. It turned out that a combination of cold weather in April 1993 and Jean's stone floor could have preserved the body longer than normal. More horrific, brain decomposition factors suggested Jean had somehow clung to life for 48 hours, pushing the time of the attack back. A far more likely date would have been April 6—three days before Hastings went to Torquay.

At Hastings's trial in February 1999, it emerged that he had regularly been asking Jean for money. Police even believed Hastings's letters from prison were the start of a deliberate ploy to get cash. In the end he sold her rings for a mere £9.

It took the jury just three hours to find him guilty. He collapsed in the dock and wailed as he was taken to the cells to start a life sentence.

"It sounds like something from the *X-Files*," says Rhonda. "I don't know anything about DNA or image-enhancement, but I always knew it was Hastings who killed my mum. Now, thanks to science, she can rest in peace."

HE
KILLED
MY BABY

Harry Jaffe

Missy Anastasi endured agony worse than grief after the sudden death of her thriving and happy little five-month-old baby boy, Garrett Michael. Her husband, Garrett Eldred Wilson, had often played the role of good father, but Missy was convinced that he had killed their son. Everyone else told her it was sudden infant death syndrome . . .

Missy Anastasi met Garrett Wilson at a fitness center in Rockville, Maryland. A trainer there, Garrett, 28, was in great physical shape. He was also a natural charmer. He was divorced, he told Missy. Tragically, the only child of that marriage died of sudden infant death syndrome (SIDS). Missy immediately felt compassion for Garrett. An interpreter for the deaf, Missy, 31, worked in the Montgomery County schools. But her career was not her main priority: "I wanted to get married and have a family."

Soon her dream would come true. She and Garrett were married on March 1, 1986—13 months after they first met. In July, Missy confirmed she was

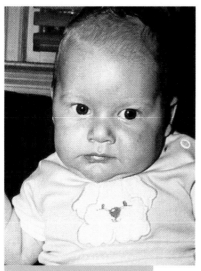

A life cut short—Garrett Michael was only five months old when he died.

pregnant. There had been only one dark note in their relationship. Shortly before the wedding, Garrett mentioned that he'd once been jailed for "misusing" money at the bank where he worked. He blamed his first wife, saying she'd gone "crazy" after their baby died and spent them into debt.

Actually, Garrett had been convicted of embezzling funds from the bank. Although he didn't serve time for that charge, he was sent to federal prison on a bank-robbery conviction. Missy wouldn't learn this until much later.

Garrett Michael Wilson was born on March 12, 1987. By five months of age, the thriving boy could walk in a walker, recognize his grandparents and kiss his delighted mother. Garrett often played the role of good father, but Missy noticed that he rarely held or cuddled his son. When he did, he turned the boy's face away.

"You seem withdrawn from the baby lately," Missy said one day.

"I don't want to get too close to him," Garrett said, "until I'm sure he's around for a while."

Chills ran up Missy's neck. She also thought it strange when Garrett told her he'd bought life insurance on the infant.

Early on Saturday, August 22, 1987, Missy awoke to the sound of crying through the baby monitor. "I'll feed him," her husband volunteered. "You have to go back to work on Monday. I'd better get used to it."

Over the monitor, Missy could hear Garrett get the bottle and sit in the rocking chair. Minutes later, she heard patting on the sheet and assumed he was burping the baby. As her two cats jumped onto her bed, Missy heard a long exhale.

She went downstairs to feed the cats, as usual. Then she checked on Garrett Michael. He was limp. She picked him up and rushed into the master bedroom. Garrett emerged from the bathroom, his face ashen.

"What did you do to him?" she shouted.

Garrett said nothing.

Missy called 911. She tried breathing life back into her baby. Garrett stood by, not saying a word.

Moments later the emergency medical team arrived and rushed the baby to Shady Grove Adventist Hospital.

Missy and Garrett ran out to their car. Instead of getting behind the wheel, Garrett unstrapped his son's car seat and put it in their other car.

"What are you doing?" Missy yelled. "Let's go!" During the 15-minute ride, Garrett was silent, but Missy's thoughts raced. Why did Garrett choose to feed the baby this one time? Why did he have insurance on an infant? Why did he take out the car seat? Because, she thought, he knew Garrett Michael would not be coming home.

> **During the 15-minute ride to hospital, Garrett was silent, but Missy's thoughts raced. Why did he have insurance on an infant?**

At the hospital, Missy tried to offer clues that her husband might have smothered their baby. But Garrett was standing there, and no one picked up on her hints. Then a doctor appeared and said that nothing else could be done—their child was dead.

The deputy medical examiner determined that Garrett Michael's demise was an "attended death." Because he'd died in the care of doctors, there'd be no police investigation.

Missy was taken to her parents' house, where she collapsed. "Garrett killed the baby for insurance money," she cried. Her family tried to comfort her. Garrett went to another part of the house.

Cold father—'I don't want to get too close to him," Wilson said of his infant son.

The autopsy determined that Garrett Michael Wilson had died of SIDS. Wanting to understand what had killed her baby, Missy read and corresponded with SIDS researchers; she attended seminars and support groups. She learned that spouses tend to blame each other and wanted to believe that her husband was not—could not be—at fault.

But the doubts always lingered. They were reinforced later that fall when Garrett dropped $10,000 in cash on their bed—part of an insurance payoff. He had yet to shed a tear.

The marriage began to unravel. Garrett lost his job, and the couple filed for bankruptcy. There were signs that he was seeing other women. The couple separated, and Missy moved in with her mother. She discovered later that Garrett, who was living in Arlington, Texas, had filed for divorce. She never saw the papers. Garrett had remarried, but what stunned her most was that he had a new child.

Blind love and foolish hope turned to rage and resolve. She feared he would try another insurance scam, that he might kill again.

There are some who would say that Missy was a woman scorned, bent on revenge. In actuality, she was a tormented mother determined to find the truth. Only now her suspicions were seven years old.

In May 1994 Missy hired Larry Robinson, a former police detective who specialized in insurance-fraud cases. "We have to track down Wilson's first wife," he said, "to see if this was a pattern."

Missy knew only her first name: Debbie. Plugging "Debbie" and "Garrett Eldred Wilson" into public-records databases, Robinson found their marriage license, Social Security numbers and divorce decree.

Robinson called Debbie Oliver Wilson.

"I'm a private investigator looking for information about Garrett Wilson," he said. "I'm working for his second wife, Missy Anastasi."

"He killed that woman's baby too," Oliver said. "Didn't he?"

Debbie Oliver was just 12 years old when she met Garrett Wilson in church. Garrett, 19, was the youth-choir director. By age 15, Debbie had had four abortions at Garrett's urging. When she became pregnant again, a doctor refused to perform an abortion—Debbie was too far along. The couple married in October 1980. Brandi Jean was born shortly afterwards.

One night when the infant was two months old, Debbie went to bed ill. Garrett gave Debbie some "vitamins," and she slept solidly until the next morning. By then, police had sealed off Brandi Jean's room. The baby's death was ruled sudden infant death syndrome.

Oliver wept as Robinson told her of Missy Anastasi's suspicions. But she made it clear that she wanted no part of the man and no part in the case.

Law and order—Detective Meredith Dominick (left) and attorney David Boynton finally believed Missy Anastasi was not merely bent on revenge.

Early on, Robinson had asked Missy, "Do you have any receipts or documents from that time?" Missy recalled that Garrett had kept two footlockers in a storage unit.

Wilson was a hoarder. He kept insurance-policy receipts, copies of letters attempting to collect on them and canceled checks for new cars bought with the cash.

Robinson learned that Garrett had taken out $40,000 in life-insurance policies on Brandi Jean. After her death he cashed them in and bought a Pontiac Trans Am.

Late in the fall of 1994, Montgomery County detective Meredith Dominick and her partner, Detective Pete Picariello, pored over the Wilson documents. Next they interviewed Debbie Oliver.

As Oliver told them her story, two things struck Dominick: the deaths of the infants seemed remarkably similar; and Garrett had asked Debbie if she would "be OK" if anything "happened" to the baby.

"What kind of man asks that?" Dominick asked Picariello.

Looking at the case through a lawyer's eyes, Assistant State's Attorney David Boynton knew he needed more evidence.

In May 1995 Dominick and Picariello knocked on the door of Garrett Wilson's house in Arlington, Texas, where he lived with his new wife, Victoria, and their 10-month-old daughter, Marysa. Garrett was shocked but polite. Calling Missy's charges "ludicrous," he said, "She could never handle the divorce. It's all about revenge."

"Why take out life insurance on an infant?" Dominick asked.

His father had taken out insurance on him from birth, he said. That's why he took out the $100,000 policy on Garrett Michael.

Dominick's stomach lurched. Finally there was a major break in the case.

Dominick's stomach lurched. She had known only of a $50,000 policy on the boy. Wilson's policies on both infants now added up to $190,000—$40,000 for Brandi Jean and $150,000 for Garrett Michael. Finally, there was a major break in the case.

By 1996 Missy Anastasi was extremely frustrated. Police and prosecutors were telling her little about the investigation. Dominick was now handling the case alone, and she was busy following up on other cases that had gone to trial. She knew that Missy was discouraged. "Missy," she told her one day, "we're still working on this case. We've gained valuable information. I believe Garrett Wilson is responsible for the deaths of both babies. But I'm not sure this case will ever go to trial."

Missy listened and said, "I'm never going to give up." Around that time, Dominick put pictures of Brandi Jean and Garrett Michael in her office. She wasn't going to give up either.

On July 15, 1997, Missy Anastasi walked into Boynton's office. Again she told her story. He was impressed by her recall of dates and details but was puzzled by one thing: "Why did you feed the cats first? Why didn't you go directly to the baby's room?"

Because, Missy explained, she had no reason to mistrust the father of her child. And then she began to cry. "Why do I still have to persuade people?" she wondered aloud.

Boynton came away from the meeting focused on two crucial goals: he had to get the cause of death changed from SIDS to homicide, and he had to persuade Debbie Oliver to cooperate in order to prove a pattern.

Boynton had already begun to seek a re-evaluation of Garrett Michael's official cause of death. Chief Medical Examiner John Smialek had sat on a 1989 National Institutes of Health panel that determined SIDS could be listed as cause of death *only after a thorough death-scene investigation.* Based on new information provided by Boynton, Smialek agreed to reopen the case.

Reviewing the autopsy, he noted that, while Garrett Michael was a healthy baby, at the time of death he had cerebral edema—swelling of the brain. Such swelling is not a feature of SIDS deaths.

Garret Michael had swelling of the brain. Such swelling is not a feature of SIDS.

On November 13, David Boynton received Smialek's new ruling: "Garrett Michael Wilson died of asphyxia due to airway obstruction, probably smothering. It is my opinion that the manner of death for Garrett Michael Wilson is homicide." Convinced that the state now had a viable case, acting State's Attorney Bob Dean gave Boynton the green light to prepare the case for prosecution.

To strengthen his case, Boynton needed an official statement from Debbie Oliver. After initially refusing, she relented and agreed to meet with him and Dominick on February 25, 1998. They told Oliver that Wilson had taken out life insurance on their baby girl. She cried. Reluctantly she began to divulge details of their relationship.

With the cause of death now a homicide and Debbie Oliver's signed statement in hand, Boynton aimed for an indictment and a warrant for Garrett Wilson's arrest.

Meredith Dominick phoned a detective in Arlington, Texas, who had been keeping tabs on Wilson. She asked him to drive by Wilson's house. He called back: it was empty, with a "For Rent" sign in front.

Dominick spent the next three days on the phone. Wilson's mail was being forwarded to bogus addresses in Texas, Oklahoma and Maryland. Then, using information from a credit report, Dominick learned that Wilson had just traded in his Ford pickup at a dealership in Texas. He told the salesman he needed four-wheel drive because he was moving to the mountains of western Maryland. The salesman also mentioned that Wilson had used his father-in-law as a credit reference: Ervin Wampler of Frostburg, Maryland.

Dawn crept cool and clear over the gently rolling farmland around Frostburg the day authorities came for Garrett Eldred Wilson. It was May 13, 1998.

A caravan of Maryland lawmen drove up the long gravel road to the Wampler house. When Garrett stepped onto the porch, the officers approached. "Are you Garrett Eldred Wilson?" a deputy sheriff asked.

Wilson nodded.

"You're under arrest," the deputy said.

"Why?"

"Homicide of your child."

Four hours later, Missy Anastasi arrived at the prosecutor's office in Rockville, Maryland. She braced herself for more empty promises.

Then acting State's Attorney Bob Dean said, "Garrett Wilson was arrested this morning."

Crying in relief, Missy said, "We finally did it."

For 11 years she had struggled with the conflict between the need to believe in her husband and the need to know what had happened to her child. The answers were not so much part of a police investigation as an investigation of the human heart. In her soul, Missy Anastasi felt she had confronted pure evil in Garrett Wilson.

On July 29, 1999, the jury took just two hours to find Garrett Eldred Wilson guilty of the first-degree murder of his son, Garrett Michael. His sentence: life in prison without parole. Wilson appealed his conviction, which was overturned in August 2002. He is now in the Maryland prison system, awaiting a new trial, when prosecutors plan to try him for the murder of his daughter, Brandi Jean.

WHO'S PRINTING ALL THIS MONEY?

Tim Bouquet

So much counterfeit currency was sluicing into Britain's economy in the summer of 1998 that police and intelligence services couldn't keep tabs on it all. They had a hunch that most of it was coming from just one ring, potentially the biggest in British history. They even had a fair idea who was behind it. But what they really needed to know was: who was printing the stuff?

t was a hot afternoon on the Isle of Wight and most of the local police officers were mingling with the thousands of tourists who had flocked there by ferry.

Not so Detective Sergeant Clive Merrett. The 42-year-old head of the island's crime and incident management unit was hurrying towards Newport police station. Detective Sergeant Paul Wright of the City of London police wanted to see him. He was their top undercover cop, but Merrett was unfazed. The black-haired father of three teenagers was a painstaking detective who knew there was more crime on the island than ever met the eye.

That day, Friday August 14, Merrett was asked to search the home and business of Bernard Farrier, a man with no criminal record.

"What's he done?" said Merrett.

"It's not what he's done, it's who he knows."

An undercover operation by the City of London's central detective unit had revealed that the 67-year-old engineer was in regular contact with a man called Stephen Jory. An East Ender with a lived-in face, Jory had heavyweight underworld connections and had already been jailed for possessing counterfeit currency. Not only had his funny money financed major crimes such as drug-dealing and gunrunning, but pensioners struggling on £60 a week found their incomes slashed by a third every time a bent Jory twenty fetched up in their wallets.

Jory had recently been released from prison so, with the flow of counterfeits continuing, was he up to his old tricks? And who were his accomplices?

Merrett rattled the door of Island Injection Mouldings, Farrier's small factory unit at Clarence Boatyard, East Cowes. It was locked.

"Search where you want, I've got nothing to hide," said the wizened, white-haired man emerging minutes later from his car. Farrier unlocked the unit. When Merrett spied five reams of brand-new, high-quality A2 paper still in its wrappings, Farrier had a ready explanation. "It's scrap. I found it in a factory skip. Thought it would be useful for packing."

Merrett didn't believe him, and torn-up £10 notes found at Farrier's house were enough to make an arrest.

Sitting in a holding cell at Newport police station, Farrier played the helpful but bemused citizen. "You've got a job to do," he assured Merrett. "I'll help you any way I can." But Farrier was about as helpful as a flat torch battery. His house was much more forthcoming, however.

When Merrett pulled up outside, the search team was waiting for him by a wooden shed in the garden. Squirrelled away at the back amid a jumble of machinery was a green tarpaulin. Merrett hauled it aside to reveal nine packs of A2 paper in the same wrappings as at the boatyard.

"Let's get it outside and see what we've got," Merrett ordered. But as an officer was lifting a pack, it split open. Sheets of £20 notes spilled out. Merrett gazed down in amazement.

> Sheets of £20 notes spilled out. Merrett gazed down in amazement.

The nine packs totalled 11,947 A2 sheets of uncut £10, £20 and £50 notes. At a rough estimate it had a face value of £5 million. The find was so valuable Merrett had it stacked in the police station's closed-circuit cell—normally reserved for prisoners likely to harm themselves—where it could be kept under 24-hour vigil.

Merrett now knew he was involved in something much bigger than a straightforward raid.

Farrier swore blind he knew nothing about the money or Stephen Jory.

"What about the diary we found in your car? There was a half-page torn out," Merrett pressed.

"It's of no significance."

That's not what Merrett thought when the missing half-page was found hidden in the gearstick housing of Farrier's car. On it he had scribbled some numbers and the name "Buzz".

One number was for a pager. It belonged to Jory. Farrier was on the hook. Merrett let him wriggle.

"My late wife knew someone called 'Steve' who once visited the island," he blurted.

"On August 4?" Merrett had done his homework, obtaining a print-out of Jory's pager log for the previous month. Eleven days before, Farrier had sent him a message: "Buzz is by the lift". On August 4 Jory had stayed at the Clifftops Hotel, Shanklin—it had a lift used by guests to reach the beach below.

Farrier now admitted that Buzz was a code name he used when he paged Jory and the records showed Farrier paging him again on August 13: "The paperwork is ready".

Tools of the trade—the counterfeit cash discovered in Farrier's garden shed had a face value of around £5 million.

So Farrier had links with Jory and with the counterfeit money, but Merrett still didn't know who the printer was.

Stephen Jory, 49, was a tough man to track and an expert at evading surveillance. City police finally caught up with him when he drove his Jaguar into the car park of a restaurant in Enfield, north London, on August 19.

Police watched as Jory handed two holdalls to small-time crook Martin Watmough. A mile down the road they pulled over Watmough's Vauxhall Corsa. The holdalls were stuffed with crisp, fake £20 notes, ready for distribution and with a face value of £750,000. Printed on a sophisticated four-colour press, they were some of the highest quality ever seen.

In Jory's car there was a shopping list of printing materials and £15,000 in genuine cash, probably downpayment for fake. A counterfeiter selling in bulk usually got paid some 5 per cent of face value for his skills. So for every £20 note he would make a pound. Every time the note was sold on, its price would increase. City police had busted other distributors who had paid up to £6, putting them way down the supply chain from Stephen Jory.

As he entered the Newport interview room where Jory was sitting, Clive Merrett weighed up his challenge: *We might have seized Farrier, Jory and millions in cash, but Jory's kept his printer so secret that even the best informers can't shed any light on him.*

Licence to print—for every counterfeit £20 note, the printer would make a pound. Each time the note was resold, its price increased.

And Stephen Jory wasn't breaking ranks. He had boiled down his vocabulary to: "No comment!"

Leads and logic pointed to the printer being on the island. While Merrett's men investigated all the printing firms with high-quality four-colour presses, there was a cell full of cash to deal with.

It was stacked as found, in different denominations with a divider sheet between each. It was standard procedure to examine the bottom and top sheets of each run of notes, as these would have been the most handled and the most likely to hold fingerprints and forensic evidence.

As officers sifted the cash, one of the dividers fell out. It was a poster advertising Cranham Caravans in Upminster, Essex. Thankful for a new lead,

Merrett called Essex police: "Can you tell us who printed it?"

Merrett then had a call from Camphill Prison where Jory was being held on remand. By mistake, Jory's diary had been returned to him when it should have been held as evidence. Warders had caught him altering the pages.

It looked like a major blunder. But Merrett realized he could turn it to his advantage and compare the amended diary with a photocopy he had of the original. Instead of following up all the names individually, he was able to home in on seven defaced entries.

One of them caught his eye.

He called City of London's Paul Wright, who had known Jory for years. "Who's Chocolate Eclair?" Merrett asked.

"She's a statuesque, 30-year-old bottle-blonde with a PA job in the City. Her name is Claire Mainstone."

So what? Merrett asked himself. She was just one of a string of young lovers on whom Jory had lavished £100,000 in the past four years.

The search for illicit printing presses on the Isle of Wight had also led nowhere. Instead, the trail swung north-east. The caravan company in Essex revealed that its poster had been printed by Upminster-based Intech Graphics. One of its directors was a 60-year-old businessman of impeccable character with a fleet of expensive cars and a private plane.

His name was Kenneth Mainstone and he had a daughter called Claire.

"Yes!" exclaimed Merrett as he headed for Essex.

Great Sunnings was a comfortable and generously proportioned 14-bedroomed house set in two secluded acres just outside Upminster. It was seven in the morning on August 27 and just light as Clive Merrett and Paul Wright knocked on the door.

"You can't do this," snapped Mainstone, still in his dressing gown, as he was arrested for conspiring to produce counterfeit currency. "I've done nothing wrong." Merrett noted how Mainstone, balding, bespectacled, quietly spoken, was far from the cliché of the criminal mastermind.

Yet in an adjoining annexe was a large four-colour litho press costing some £20,000 and taking up the space of a domestic garage. Next to it was a computer-controlled guillotine, six feet tall and eight feet wide, for cutting large sheets of paper.

Mainstone had been trying to tidy up. The image areas had been snipped out of bundles of copper printing plates. But he hadn't got rid of the rubber blankets that cushion the rollers on the press. "Clear as day," murmured Merrett looking at one. On it was the Queen's head. But the search team had still not found any money.

During that afternoon Kenneth Mainstone was in his bedroom and while he thought no one was looking, he gingerly picked up something from the bedside table and nudged it under the bed with his foot. But Paul Wright was onto him. It was a brown envelope. He pulled out a receipt from a storage firm in Rainham, Essex. It showed that Mainstone had deposited a crate there around the time of Jory's arrest.

Police found thousands of partially printed £20 notes. The stash had a face value of £11 million.

After police seized the crate, they found 58 packs of paper inside it hiding thousands of partially printed £20 notes. The stash had a face value of £11 million. The conspiracy was growing to record-breaking proportions.

In the interview room back on the Isle of Wight, Mainstone had recovered an arrogant composure. Sharp-faced, he stared at Merrett with cold eyes from behind his wire rims. He said Jory had asked him to print the crime novel he had written. End of story. "The only person who has done anything wrong is you arresting me," he told Merrett.

It was now time to build the case that would snap the trap on Mainstone's ring. Clive Merrett was put in charge of marshalling the evidence at Hampshire police's major-incident complex near Southampton. He went to work on 30,000 pieces of paper, printing paraphernalia and the bag from Mainstone's vacuum cleaner which bulged with fragments of dollar bills and Indian rupees.

Twenty-pound notes seized from Jory back in 1994 had the same physical characteristics as the forged twenties Merrett had found at Farrier's, those in the Rainham storage unit and the finished notes handed by Jory to Watmough in the Enfield car park. Mainstone's fingerprints, unidentifiable until his arrest, were on them all, side by side with Jory's.

Clive Merrett looked for more ammunition to sink the conspiracy. A list of meaningless letters and numbers found stuck to Mainstone's press turned out to be the first two letters, first two digits and last two digits of the serial numbers on the notes in all three batches discovered by police. And the handwriting on the list was not only the same as that in Mainstone's pilot's log, it was also a match for the shopping list found in Stephen Jory's car.

The log also showed that Kenneth Mainstone had flown to the Isle of Wight on August 13, 1998, the very same day that Bernard Farrier had paged Jory to tell him: "The paperwork is ready".

Clive Merrett went to Winchester Crown Court with a spring in his step. He told the court that between October 1994 and August 1998, Kenneth

Mainstone had put £50 million into Britain's black economy, two-thirds of all fake notes in circulation. Britain's biggest counterfeiting scam had thrived on Jory's criminal connections and Mainstone's squeaky-clean anonymity.

In January 2000 Kenneth Mainstone—Britain's most successful master counterfeiter—was sentenced to 12 years. Stephen Jory is serving eight years. Martin Watmough served a three-year sentence and was then released from prison. Unfit to stand trial, Bernard Farrier died in 1999.

Paul Wright and Clive Merrett were both commended by the judge. Merrett was promoted to detective inspector.

DAILY NEWS
NATIONAL EDITION
LATE RACING

WIFE MISSING; 100G REWARD

Real estate
tycoon's
son asks
for search

WHY NOT?

6

Fugitive Durst's wacky disguise drew attention

Durst's strange last days

COLONIAL REG.
POLICE - PA
I.R. NO 01- 7537
DATE 30Nov 01
NAME DURST, Robert

On Friday, he was arrested at the Wegman's supermarket in Bath, Pa., about seven miles from Bethlehem.

An employee of the Red Roof Inn on Route 22 and Airport Road South between Bethlehem and Allentown recalled seeing Durst in town.

He is being held at the Northampton County Prison in Easton, Pa.

Wednesday and Thursday, Durst went to the Golden View Diner on Route 512 on the outskirts of Bethlehem, Pa., near the Lehigh Valley Industrial Park.

By MARK STAMEY
in Bethlehem, Pa.,
FARRAH WEINSTEIN

FOUL HEIR

He was born with a silver spoon in his mouth and began living fast and hard. He stood to inherit a real-estate fortune in New York. Now police are investigating Robert Durst in connection with three grisly murders.

O nce, Bobby Durst was on top of the world. At 35, he was the first-in-line heir to one of the great real-estate fortunes in New York. With holdings of around $2 billion, the Dursts stood alongside the Trumps and Helmsleys as the city's premier owners of apartment and office buildings. It seemed only a matter of time until Bobby would take over the business, and by the late 1970s he was already acting like a mogul. He and his wife, Kathie, nearly 10 years his junior, were hot on the Manhattan social scene, frequenting cool spots like Elaine's and Studio 54, and, friends say, fueling their nights with liberal helpings of drugs. He was living fast and hard, but Bobby Durst looked like a winner.

And so if by some quirk of the universe a little voice had whispered in Bobby's ear, predicting that by the new millennium he would find himself in a Pennsylvania police station trying to explain why he'd shoplifted a chicken-salad sandwich, he would have laughed like crazy. And if the voice then told Durst he would find himself charged with one murder and investigated in connection with two others, he might have wondered what he had taken to induce such a weird nightmare.

But the voice would have been dead right.

By November 30, 2001, Durst was no longer a strutting jet-setter. He had turned into a mumbling, beady-eyed little man of 58 with a shaved head and eyebrows. Sitting in a police station in Bath, Pennsylvania, he kept telling officer Dean Benner, "I can't believe how stupid I am."

Durst had $500 in his pockets when Benner arrested him at a Wegmans supermarket, which meant he was no ordinary hard-luck case. But Durst's explanation—that he had a lifelong shoplifting addiction—didn't ring true. Benner ran a computer check on Durst's Social Security number. What popped up on the screen made him glad his prisoner was securely manacled.

"When was the last time you were in Texas?" Benner asked, wheeling to face Durst.

Bobby Durst's eyes widened. His dazed expression was replaced by a hardened stare. "I want a lawyer."

Several lawyers would have been more like it. Officer Benner discovered that Durst had been the subject of a nationwide manhunt for over a month. Police in Galveston, Texas, had charged Durst with the gruesome murder of his 71-year-old neighbor, Morris Black, and Durst had skipped out on a

$300,000 bond. Black had been dismembered, his headless torso found in Galveston Bay, his limbs in garbage bags floating nearby.

Benner phoned the Texas police. He expected his counterparts would be glad to hear from him, but never imagined his call to Galveston would also trigger urgent inquiries from California and New York.

The New York State Police were looking into the disappearance of Durst's wife, Kathie, then 29, who vanished in 1982. And the Los Angeles police wanted to chat with Durst about the 2000 gangland-style murder of his close friend, author Susan Berman, 55. Berman had been killed just as New York authorities were preparing to question her in the Kathie Durst case.

Durst was arraigned—no bail this time—and locked away in the Northampton County Correctional Facility in Easton, Pennsylvania. The charges against him were formidable. Less obvious were the circumstances that had led Durst to such a pass.

As a younger, handsomer man, Durst had hobnobbed with the likes of Jackie Onassis and Mia Farrow. He reportedly had an affair with Prudence Farrow, Mia's sister, the woman whose fragile beauty inspired the Beatles song "Dear Prudence." Durst's high living was financed by the hard work and smart investments of his family, starting with his grandfather Joseph. A Jewish immigrant from Poland, Joseph, after 13 years of working in the garment district, had saved the money to buy a midtown Manhattan office building. That purchase became the cornerstone of the family's real-estate empire.

Joseph's eldest son, Seymour, eventually took over the reins of the Durst Organization. Seymour and his wife, Bernice, had four children, but it was the eldest, then seven-year-old Bobby, who witnessed his mother's tragic end. One autumn day in 1950, Bernice climbed onto the roof of their suburban Westchester home. While her husband and son looked on, and as a fireman struggled to reach her, Bernice fell. Her death was ruled an accident.

Bobby was a quiet kid, and an undistinguished student. He earned a business-administration degree from Lehigh University, then headed to grad school at UCLA. There, in the heyday of the sixties, he was introduced to marijuana, for which he developed a lifelong passion. He also met Susan Berman. The daughter of Las Vegas hotelier Dave Berman, who counted mob figures Bugsy Siegel and Meyer Lansky as associates, Susan suspected her own mother had died as a result of a gangland hit. Susan was a fast-talking woman with a big personality. Durst was taken with her immediately, and their platonic friendship endured for decades.

After returning to New York, Durst went to work in the family business. Kathie McCormack, a 19-year-old dental hygienist from a working-class Long Island family, was a tenant in one of the Durst's Manhattan apartment buildings. Dropping off her rent check one day, she met the man who would change her life. Durst was smitten with her fresh-faced innocence; she fell for his wealth and worldly-wise demeanor.

In 1973 they married, and the early years of their relationship were a blur of exotic travel and club-hopping. The couple had two apartments in Manhattan and a rustic cottage 40 miles north of the city in the hamlet of South Salem, New York. "She was enthralled with the Dursts and the power," says Eleanor Schwank, who was one of Kathie's closest friends. "For Kathie, it was like being a kid in a candy store."

Things weren't exactly perfect, though. Unlike his bubbly wife, Durst was by nature more reserved, and drugs added to his gloom. He began to withdraw from the club scene, preferring to spend his free time with Igor, his Norwegian elkhound, and zone-out on marijuana. Kathie began pursuing her own interests. She finished nursing school and was eventually accepted into New York's Albert Einstein medical college.

Jet-set existence—Bobby Durst married Kathie McCormack on April 12, 1973, and they enjoyed a lively social life in Manhattan.

By 1981 the marriage was in trouble. Both Durst and Kathie had begun extramarital affairs, and Durst became increasingly sullen. Bobby's history was at least part of the problem. Kathie told friends that while Bernice Durst's death had been ruled an accident, Bobby had told her that in fact his mother committed suicide, something that troubled him terribly.

Kathie also discovered that following his mother's death, Bobby had been sent for psychiatric counseling after displaying extreme bouts of anger, particularly toward his father, whom she blamed for Bernice's unhappiness. In a 1953 report, written when Bobby was 10, a doctor delivered the gloomy assessment that his anger was of such intensity that it could result in personality decomposition and, possibly, schizophrenia. Bobby eventually evened out—but his fury began spewing again in the dog days of his marriage.

During a 1980 Christmas gathering with Kathie's family on Long Island, Durst pulled his wife out of a chair when she ignored his demands to return to Manhattan. "He just grabbed her by her hair and said 'We're leaving,'" says Jim McCormack, Kathie's older brother. "I wanted to punch his lights out, but Kathie said she was OK."

The following year, Durst was arrested for assaulting photographer Peter Schwartz, a friend of Kathie's who'd accompanied her home after a night of club-hopping. Schwartz was lying on the floor, innocently talking with Kathie, when Durst burst in, accusing Schwartz of trying to seduce his wife. He kicked the astonished Schwartz in the face, breaking his jaw. Criminal charges were later dropped, and a civil suit was settled out of court.

Before the year was out, Kathie was making plans to file for divorce and told Durst she wanted a lump-sum settlement of several hundred thousand dollars. Instead, Durst cut her off financially, taking away her credit cards and forcing her to borrow money from friends, who advised Kathie to just leave. "We said 'Kathie, you're going to be a doctor. You don't need his money,'" says Eleanor Schwank.

Insistent that she deserved a modest settlement, Kathie began playing a more dangerous game, threatening to publicize what she told friends were Durst's fraudulent income-tax statements. The plan backfired. On January 6, 1982, Kathie was admitted to a Bronx hospital with bruises on her face and head. She stated that her husband had flown into a rage and beaten her.

Three weeks later, Kathie showed up at a Connecticut party hosted by her friend Gilberte Najamy. Durst, furious she'd been out so long, phoned from South Salem and demanded she come home. Leaving the party about 7.15 that cold, snowy night, Kathie gave Najamy a warning. "She said, 'Gilberte, if anything ever happens to me, it was Bobby.'"

Five days later, Durst walked into Manhattan's 20th Precinct and reported Kathie missing. Kathie's family and friends immediately pointed the finger at Durst, who posted a $100,000 reward for his wife's return.

Slow to talk—Durst, pictured four months after his wife's disappearance, waited five days to tell police she was missing.

He hired a well-connected criminal attorney, Nicholas Scoppetta, now New York City's fire commissioner. Then he clammed up. Susan Berman became his spokesperson, handling queries from the rabid New York press.

With no cooperation from Durst, no solid evidence of foul play, and no probable cause to search the South Salem house, the investigation went cold. "We could never get it beyond a missing-persons case," says Michael Struk, the now-retired NYPD detective who led the inquiry.

For 10 years Durst maintained a low profile. But rumors about his role in Kathie's disappearance never went away. When Seymour Durst moved aside in 1993, he tapped Bobby's younger brother, Douglas, to take control of the business. Bobby would be the No. 2 man in the organization. Incensed, Durst walked out of the company's offices without so much as a farewell. Most of the people who worked with him never heard from him again. When Seymour died in 1995, Bobby skipped the funeral. He dropped out of sight, dabbling in real-estate deals, splitting time among homes in Northern California, Connecticut and New York. He might have remained that way, a high-living drifter, if it hadn't been for a small stroke of bad luck.

In 1999, veteran New York State Police detective Joe Becerra reopened the Kathie Durst investigation after getting a tip from a petty criminal. The information proved false, but Becerra was intrigued and did something no investigator had before. He got permission from the new owners to search what had been the Durst house in South Salem.

The search uncovered old blood mixed with mud. Investigators, convinced they were onto something, then examined telephone records obtained earlier. They indicated that Durst was in Ship Bottom, New Jersey, on February 2, 1982, less than 48 hours after he'd claimed Kathie had gone missing. Durst had told police that he'd spent that week in South Salem, waiting for his wife's return. The rough, rural southern Jersey area called the Pine Barrens is near Ship Bottom. And the Pine Barrens is a known Mafia graveyard.

Tipped off about the reopened investigation, Durst headed to Galveston. In November 2000, wearing a wig and masquerading as a deaf-mute woman named Dorothy Ciner, a

Durst headed to Galveston and rented a $300-a-month apartment—wearing a wig and masquerading as a woman.

name he pulled out of his Scarsdale High School yearbook, he rented a $300-a-month, two-room apartment in a nondescript neighborhood. The following month, in a private New York ceremony, Durst wed Debrah Lee Charatan, a commercial real-estate agent he'd seen off and on for a dozen years.

Less than two weeks after the wedding, as New York police were preparing to interview Susan Berman, her Los Angeles neighbors spotted her dog wandering the neighborhood. They called the police, who found Berman's door unlocked. Her body was inside, face-down in a pool of blood. There was no sign of forced entry or struggle, suggesting she knew the person who shot her. Police are currently investigating Durst.

Various reports indicate that Durst mailed two checks for $25,000 each to Berman in the months before her death. Although she showed early promise as a writer—in 1981 she published *Easy Street*, a memoir detailing her life as a "Mafia princess"—Berman had fallen on hard times. More than once she asked Durst for financial help. Some of Berman's friends theorize the checks were hush money to keep Berman from saying anything incriminating to New York investigators. Others scoff at the notion that Durst would have harmed her. They suggest she was killed by mob figures concerned about the new book Berman planned to write.

Close confidante—gangster's daughter Susan Berman (right) and Durst had an enduring friendship going back to their college days.

Back in Galveston, Durst had inevitably crossed paths with his neighbor, Morris Black. Originally from Massachusetts, Black was down on his luck. He had been arrested in 1997, after threatening to bomb the local phone company during a billing dispute. Before he was killed, Black clearly made someone mad. Says Galveston police sergeant Cody Cazalas, "I'm a hunter and could tell whoever did this was either a hunter or had done this before." Black's arms were neatly sliced below the shoulder. The legs were pared around the upper thighs, the large femur bones cut straight through. Even the head, yet to be found, was expertly removed from the body.

Down on his luck— Morris Black, Durst's neighbor in Galveston.

Police were led to Black's apartment after discovering a newspaper address label inside one of the garbage bags floating in the bay. The place had been cleaned, but forensic experts discovered a blood trail leading across the hall to Durst's apartment. Inside, they found bloodstains in the bathroom, on the walls, on the kitchen floor and on a paring knife. They

Blood trail—police followed a trail of clues which led to Durst's extradition and arrest.

later discovered that for some reason Durst had paid Black's $300 October rent, and that Black, who'd held only a series of menial jobs his entire life, had $137,000 in a bank account.

Durst was charged with murdering Black on October 9, 2001, but was immediately freed on bail when his wife, Charatan, wired the money. Then he became a fugitive until his shoplifting arrest weeks later. In his car, Pennsylvania police found two .38-caliber handguns, $38,000 in cash, a rental receipt in the name of Morris Black, and a stash of marijuana.

In February 2002, Durst was extradited to Texas. He pled not guilty to the murder. "The best we could tell they had a strained neighbor relationship—a lot of petty bickering," says Sergeant Cazalas, acknowledging that investigators have yet to uncover a clear motive in the Black killing. Durst himself suggested one on March 27 when his attorney suddenly indicated he would enter a revised plea—not guilty by reason of self-defense and accident.

After she learned of Durst's arrest in Texas, Westchester County district attorney Jeanine Pirro, who is overseeing the investigation into Kathie Durst's disappearance, offered a cryptic comparison. "I see even at this point some striking similarities with what allegedly happened in Texas and what happened in Westchester County."

Kathie's Durst's survivors say all these events have given them new hope. "Our family always felt this guy was prone to violence, and we believe the last two years of increased pressure tilted his psyche and brought on more irrational behavior," says Jim McCormack. "We're anxious to see a painful ordeal coming to a resolution." Sadly, many others have now joined the McCormacks in their wish.

Bobby Durst remains in jail in Galveston without bond. A trial date was set for August 2003.

SHATTERED PEACE

Candice DeLong and
Elisa Petrini

Like Hannibal Lecter's Clarice Starling, real-life FBI special agent Candice DeLong must track down dangerous and elusive predators, whose crimes sometimes strike close—too close—to home.

W hen I bought my first house in La Grange, Illinois, I felt that it would be a wonderful place for my eight-year-old son, Seth, to grow up.

A small suburb west of Chicago, La Grange was famous for Victorian homes and graceful American elms arching in 50-foot canopies over the streets. It was close enough to Chicago to let us enjoy the city's cultural offerings, yet it was still the quintessential Midwestern small town. Norman Rockwell could have painted it.

Much as I loved the town's charm, I hardly felt like a Norman Rockwell mother. For one thing, I was divorced, still something of a stigma in the early 1980s. For another, unlike most of the other women with school-age children, I had a full-time job, and an unusual one at that. I was a special agent for the FBI.

I worried that Seth would feel deprived and conspicuously different in a neighborhood where most fathers lived at home and most mothers waited to greet children after school. So I made it a frequent ritual to hurry out on my lunch hour to treat him at our favorite restaurant. I also tried to participate in as many of his school activities as I could.

"Seth's mommy has a gun!"

When we moved to La Grange, Seth was just starting third grade. Not long into the first term, his homeroom teacher, Mrs Kinnear, called to see if I would be a "hot dog mother."

Apparently on the first Tuesday of every month, the class had a special lunch, with mothers doing the serving.

"Sure," I said. "Sign me up."

On my first visit I arrived dressed for work in my suit and Seth beamed. As I reached across the table to pass out hot dogs, I wasn't paying much attention to the children's whispers. Then one little boy piped up, loudly, "Seth's mommy has a gun!"

Mrs Kinnear rushed over in alarm. "It's OK," I told her, holding out my empty hands. "I'm an FBI agent."

While on duty, I was required to carry my weapon at all times. In those days I wore it in a shoulder holster, hidden under my suit jacket. I hadn't realized how visible it was from below when I stretched out my arm.

The teacher must have suddenly recalled Seth's school records because she said, "Oh, right. That's so interesting! Why don't you tell the class all about your work?"

"She catches bad guys," my son announced proudly, and a crowd of eight-year-olds began bombarding me with questions. That much attention proved too much for Seth, who buried his face in his arms on the desk, but I could tell that he was pleased.

As the weeks went by, I was delighted at how quickly we were settling into La Grange. But a shocking string of crimes was throwing our community into turmoil, and I would need to draw on all of my FBI training to help track down a predator in my own neighborhood.

Rough Stuff

Growing up in the black-and-white TV era, I had longed to be a crime-fighter like Eliot Ness on *The Untouchables*, my family's favorite show. Ness was a mythic figure in our house, for during the Great Depression, my then-teenage father had actually worked for him as an informant. When the feds raided the speakeasy where my dad was busing tables, the great man himself had shoved a gun in my dad's face, just for show, before moving on to arrest the real criminals. Ness was our hero.

Dream come true—crime-fighter Eliot Ness, pictured here in 1936, became a formative influence on Candice DeLong when she determined to follow his example.

My father had gently tried to quash my childhood dreams by telling me that Ness had to do a lot of "rough stuff" with "tough customers" no woman could handle.

Indeed, J. Edgar Hoover, the all-powerful director of the FBI, had decreed: "Because of the nature of the duties our special agents are called upon to perform, we do not employ women in this position."

That edict remained in effect until 1972, when Hoover died, and a few

On the ropes—Candice (above) was a young mother with a four-year-old son, Seth (left), when she fulfilled the harsh demands of the FBI training.

*Name changed to protect privacy

brave souls were finally able to scale the walls of the impenetrable male preserve. These women were an intrepid group, and a chance meeting with one of them led me to make the most important decision of my life.

At the time, I was pushing 30 and having a crisis of faith. My nine-year marriage had dissolved, and my four-year-old son was showing signs of craving independence. I had worked as a psychiatric nurse for almost 10 years and was disillusioned by the knowledge that most of the time I could only comfort patients, I couldn't help them get well.

I was ripe for change when I met Clay Carlson*, an FBI special agent who became a good friend. He introduced me to a Bureau colleague, a petite woman who could barely have weighed 100 pounds. I was amazed, but Clay assured me that though diminutive, she was well trained and plenty capable of dealing with any "tough customers" who came her way.

Though I was only five foot five inches and weighed 110 pounds, I knew that if this woman could join the FBI, then I could too. I took the Bureau exam in January 1980, and four months later was summoned for my "face test"—an interview by a panel of agents. To my surprise, I passed muster and was sent to the FBI Academy, which was in Quantico, Virginia.

My subsequent 16 weeks of training were grueling. On my second day at the Academy I watched while a female agent took her final, pregraduation physical-training test. A colleague cheered her on as she struggled with her push-up quota, while a gym instructor kept count.

The trainee had to do 35 perfect push-ups to earn the minimum cumulative score to pass, and she was tiring as she reached 30, 31 and then 32. She barely squeaked out 33, her arms trembling with fatigue, but managed to summon the strength to crank out No. 34.

Someone mentioned that the woman had taken a master's degree in computer science and was also a certified public accountant, two impressive accomplishments. The Bureau would benefit tremendously by having an agent with her credentials on the white-collar-crime task force—that is, if she could do just one more push-up! I couldn't take my eyes off her as she lowered her chest almost to the floor that last time, the sweat dripping off her. I heard her groan in frustration as she fought to push herself up—and made it!

But then I heard the instructor say, "No go." Her form on the final push-up wasn't flawless, so with a smirk on his face, he flunked her—not just on the test but, because it was her second try, out of the Academy. She had no recourse. Later, a few of us heard the instructor boasting that he had "washed out one more female."

I resolved right then and there that no self-important jackass of an instructor was going to wash me out. Having grown up roughhousing with three brothers, I was never one to back off from a fight, and my experience as a psych nurse had left me pretty hard to intimidate.

I stuck it out and made it to graduation day. As I celebrated with my family, my father gave me an unexpected present.

He had watched bemused as I was admitted to Quantico, endured the rigorous training and graduated with an assignment to the FBI's Chicago squad.

The gift of a gun—when Candice DeLong graduated with an assignment to the FBI's Chicago squad, her father's present of a gun felt like "the keys to the world."

When I opened his gift, I found a blue steel, snub-nosed Smith & Wesson .38. I felt as if he had given me the keys to the world and, by extension, to my entire generation of women.

Probing a Twisted Psyche

In my first three years with the Bureau, I was used to wearing my gun on duty. And since some of my early assignments involved tracking down suspected terrorists and fugitive felons, I was glad for the protection it gave me. Still, I hadn't expected to need it in the quiet community my son and I had settled in.

But then came a frightening attack that put the entire town of La Grange on edge. A woman was sexually assaulted as she got off the Burlington Northern commuter train from Chicago, becoming the sixth victim in the vicinity of the rail line that year.

Because rape is so often a crime of opportunity, pleasant suburban neighborhoods like ours, which have plenty of green, open spaces, can unfortunately be an ideal setting for an assault.

It was now all too apparent that a serial rapist was on the loose—right in my own back yard.

The recent attacks had occurred at train stops in different jurisdictions, so it had taken authorities a while to compare notes and determine that these were probably not isolated incidents. In fact, it was now all too apparent that a serial rapist was on the loose—right in my own back yard.

As soon as I heard about the case, I called Gene Stapleton, the FBI's profile coordinator for Chicago.

At the time, profiling was a little-known tool that provided law enforcement with the likely characteristics and traits of an unidentified offender. Pioneered by psychiatrist James Brussel in the 1950s, it was introduced to the Bureau in the early 1970s.

By the time I attended the FBI Academy in 1980, it was just starting to be codified as a formal discipline by Roy Hazelwood and others in the Bureau's Behavioral Science Unit.

Profiling is part science, part art. The science part employs statistics compiled from thousands of violent crimes, as well as interviews with offenders themselves.

Profilers analyze the "what, when, where and how" of an attack, scrutinizing even the most minute details to see if they suggest a pattern or offer a useful clue to the offender's personality.

By comparing the attack to similar crimes committed in the same way, and determining the most common characteristics among known offenders, profilers can create a personality and lifestyle sketch of the UNSUB, or "unknown subject," being sought by investigators.

The approach works best for offenders who act out of psychopathological compulsion, rather than, say, the kid who holds up a liquor store, and then panics and shoots the clerk.

In the past, many cops investigating sex crimes were too embarrassed or uncomfortable asking victims for the details. You'd see police reports that were very specific as to the location, the circumstances, and so on—up to the point of the attack, which would be summarized in a single line: "And then he raped her." Buried within that line was precisely the information most critical to investigators: it could reveal the verbal, physical and sexual behavior of the assailant.

A comprehensive profile should anticipate the perpetrator's behavior: what type of victim he may target, where he is liable to surface (at a victim's funeral, for example) or whether the level of violence in his attacks will escalate. It can also suggest the kind of public appeals that may flush a suspect out (by encouraging him to communicate with the police or the press, for example), or the lines of questioning that may elicit a confession.

An Unexpected Factor

Many law-enforcement professionals, even within the Bureau, considered profiling little better than hocus-pocus. But Gene Stapleton took a chance and called Roy Lane, Sr, the La Grange chief of police, to offer the Bureau's assistance in developing a profile.

Fortunately, Roy Lane was more sophisticated than the average suburban police chief. He had taken advanced course work at Quantico and was the father of Roy Lane, Jr, the agent who had coordinated the FBI's investigation of the 1982 Tylenol murder case. Lane accepted Stapleton's offer.

At the time, I was on the foreign counterintelligence squad, so the La Grange case wouldn't ordinarily have been assigned to me. My boss was understanding, though, and agreed to let me join the investigation. So I went with Gene to a meeting of the police task force representing most of the municipalities hit by the rapist.

The victims ranged in age from a young girl to a woman in her forties—evidently, our suspect was not targeting any special type of woman—and their descriptions of the attacker varied just as widely. They placed his age at anywhere from 20 to 35, and estimates of his height ran the gamut from five foot seven to six foot four.

These widely varying details raised the question: was more than one rapist at work?

Not necessarily. Conflicting descriptions are common in assaults. Under such high stress few victims—or even witnesses—can zero in on the assailant's looks. Fortunately, the different artists' sketches bore enough similarities to suggest a single perpetrator.

We also had an unexpected factor working in our favor. Around this time the Chicago Bears were enjoying some success after a series of losing football seasons. As a result, the distinctive, chiseled features of the Bears' coach were showing up daily under front-page headlines and on the nightly TV news. So even women who weren't sports fans were describing the assailant in terms every cop could visualize: "He looks like a young Mike Ditka."

But the assailant's appearance only took us so far. We still had to figure out where to look for him. "Let me go back and re-interview all the victims," I volunteered. "Maybe with a single questioner juggling all the stories, we can plug some holes."

To my surprise, the detectives agreed to this—possibly because I was the only woman present. People tend to assume that a woman will more effectively question female sexual-assault victims than will a man. But actually this is not true. Anyone can be a good interviewer: it's a matter of personality and training more than gender. But regardless of their reasons, I eagerly grasped at any opportunity that would help us stop the rapist before he attacked again.

Victims' Voices

If I found myself with a little downtime from the investigation, I worked on fixing up our new house, and getting to know our neighbors.

Some of the other mothers watched Seth for me after school, and in exchange, I'd take six or seven youngsters out to the movies on Friday nights. Afterward we would all go out for dessert, and I enjoyed listening to the kids discuss the film.

But what brought me even greater pleasure was my nightly run. I would go for a jog after dinner and Seth would ride alongside me on his bike to keep me company.

One night a couple of neighborhood children started following us. I waved to acknowledge them and then just kept going. A few miles from home, I glanced back and was surprised to find them still on our tail. They didn't peel off until we turned back onto our own front sidewalk.

A few nights later when I came out in my sweatsuit, they were waiting, riding in little circles on the driveway. "How come you go running, Mrs DeLong?" one boy asked.

"Well, I do it to stay strong and so I don't get fat," I said.

I did a few stretches and set off, with Seth beside me. The boys trailed in our wake like a couple of seagulls after a yacht. Soon we were joined by a third child and a fourth.

On nights when I stayed home because I was just too tired or the weather looked threatening, one of the kids would ring the bell. "Aren't you coming out, Mrs DeLong? You're gonna get fat . . ." My little squad of personal trainers didn't brook many excuses.

Eventually we formed a regular band that would assemble most nights. As I ran, I was lulled by a new kind of music—the meditative thrumming of bicycle wheels and the rustling of leaves in the trees high above us—and it filled me with peace.

My growing familiarity with our neighbors proved unexpectedly helpful as I moved ahead with the investigation of the man we now identified as the "Burlington rapist."

Though Chief Roy Lane remained committed to developing a profile, some detectives were skeptical. I was paired with one of the scoffers, Gary Konzak, who dismissed it as "crystal ball stuff."

Luckily, we discovered the bonds of living a few blocks apart and having children at the same school. And even luckier, my re-interviewing scheme soon paid off with a solid hit that resolved the height discrepancies.

One of the victims was very tall. "Agent DeLong," she told me, "I am six-one. When he grabbed me, I could feel his chin jamming into the top of my head. He had to be taller than me."

A sensation that vivid was very likely a reliable memory, and it established that our man was perhaps six foot four or six foot five—significantly taller, at any rate, than average. Gary Konzak now had to agree that we were on the right track.

Most of the victims portrayed the rapist as regretful. Having committed the rape, he would berate himself for the abuse.

I also noted that most of the victims portrayed the rapist as seeming regretful. Having committed the rape, he would apologize, berate himself for the abuse, and sometimes begin to cry.

One of the most telling descriptions came from the second woman assailed, whom the rapist pinned in her car. He kept asking, "You like my kissing you, don't you? Do you like the way I'm touching you?"

Calmly and gently, she replied that she didn't like it, but only because she didn't know him. That seemed to confuse him, she reported. After 15 minutes of groping, he kissed her goodbye and let her go, saying that he was sparing her as a "Valentine's Day present."

Conventional wisdom suggests that fighting back is the best way to foil a rape. Unfortunately, this is often not the case.

In a recent Department of Justice poll of rape and sexual-assault victims, 81 per cent reported that they had taken some form of "self-protective" action. This was defined as anything from appeasing to attacking an assailant.

More than half of the victims believed their efforts had helped the situation, while 10 per cent claimed that they had made matters worse. (Of course, we can never poll those who did not survive an assault.)

Clearly, there is no one "best" way.

The FBI's pioneering profiler, Roy Hazelwood, classified rapists in six categories, depending on whether they were driven by the need for power, the need to act out their anger at women, or by other factors. Few attacks arise out of actual sexual desire.

The Burlington rapist's "pseudo-unselfish" acts—cushioning one victim with his raincoat, expressing the hope that another enjoyed his caresses and giving her a "Valentine's Day present"—placed him in the "power–reassurance" category. According to Hazelwood, this kind of rapist tries to reassure himself of his own masculinity by asserting his power over a woman. Yet he still wants to feel that he is an adequate, sexually desirable man.

Unfortunately, as their experience and confidence grow, these predators may become increasingly hell-bent on completing the act, no matter how their victims respond.

Because of her calm self-possession, Woman No. 2 managed to escape with just back-seat pawing. The other victims weren't so lucky, but at least they weren't otherwise injured if they didn't resist (after their initial efforts to escape).

Screaming and fighting may scare off a nervous assailant in a setting where he risks discovery, but it may also provoke him into unintended violence. One victim of the Burlington rapist fought back hard, even trying to bite her attacker. She was beaten and nearly strangled to death.

Another seriously injured victim was so angry that she could hardly talk to me. After choking out that she was never going to testify, she just clammed up, burning with fury.

Of course I could sympathize with her pain and sense of violation, but finally I had to say, "Look, talk to me or not, we're going to catch this guy, but being mad does nothing to help us get him off the streets."

When the task force next reconvened, I was able to offer the detectives a great deal of new information. To my relief, they welcomed it—it had been nerve-racking to stick my neck out in a roomful of older men.

We were now ready to present my findings, along with the detectives' original battery of reports, to the Bureau's Behavioral Science Unit. Finally, the profilers could go to work.

Compelling Portrait

Assisted by Gene Stapleton from our Chicago office, I developed a portrait of our suspect with Roy Hazelwood, the master profiler. After reviewing all the evidence, we estimated the rapist to be in his mid- to late twenties. He would be a loner with few friends who had never experienced a normal, consenting, intimate relationship with a woman.

Probably a high-school graduate at best, he would have served in the military. He would currently hold an unskilled or semiskilled job, with little public contact, if he worked at all.

He would have a police record of some kind and probably indulge in peeping-Tom activities.

Most likely, our assailant lived within the vicinity of the La Grange train station, where some of the attacks had occurred, either in a rented apartment or with his mother in her home, given his low income. Our analysis even suggested the kind of car he would drive, an old "beater," and the clothes he would wear, a dingy T-shirt and worn jeans.

Some detectives were gung ho about the profile, but others shrugged it off, disdainful of the "fortunetellers" at the FBI. Only time would tell us who was right.

Our quarry, meanwhile, was picking up steam, attacking two more women in quick succession.

The first victim was relatively fortunate. A petite young woman, about five feet tall, she weighed no more than 100 pounds and must have looked like an easy mark. But the rapist had misjudged her. She luckily had some martial-arts training. As he grabbed her from behind in a bear hug, she ducked out of his grasp, whirled around, and kicked him hard in the solar plexus. She then fled, leaving him gasping for breath.

A short time later in La Grange, a middle-aged shop employee was closing up for the night when she heard a noise at the back door. When she went to investigate, a man startled her and forced her into a storeroom.

Screaming, she turned to run, but he grabbed her, clubbing her to the ground with a telephone. "I'm going to kill you!" he snarled.

Screaming, she turned to run, but he grabbed her, clubbing her to the ground with a telephone. "I'm going to kill you!" he snarled.

Then, tearing at her clothing, he raped her. She lay still, too frightened for her life to try to fight back. Finally he pulled himself off her and beat a retreat, leaving her dazed with terror and, later, too flooded with shame even to tell her family about the assault.

Fortunately, the shop worker, like the other victims, found the strength and courage to come forward. We met, at her insistence, at a place where no one knew her, a local restaurant called Marc's Big Boy. We chose a table up front, a few feet from the door, and I sat facing the kitchen, giving her the window view.

How easily the case might have been solved had our positions been reversed that day!

As she told me her story, I could see that she was painfully unnerved by the rape—tense and edgy, drinking cup after cup of coffee, peering warily at every male who walked by. There was a visible bump on her head.

"He hit you," I said. I had read the initial police report, but I wanted to encourage her to talk.

"Yes," she replied. "I was terrified. He was so angry, and I thought he was going to kill me."

It was the first time that the UNSUB had battered a victim who hadn't resisted—probably a reaction to the little kickboxer who got away, I thought. At about six foot four inches, he must have been shocked and humiliated that such a tiny woman could thwart him, and he wasn't about to take no for an answer again.

It is a very different kind of rapist who derives pleasure from inflicting pain.

"Why did he pick me?" the shop worker kept agonizing. "What did I do to provoke him?"

"Why did he pick me?" the shop worker kept agonizing. "What did I do to provoke him?"

"Nothing," I assured her. "You did nothing wrong. You were just the unlucky woman he happened to come across. This wasn't your fault, so you can't blame yourself."

But she would, I knew, even then. Between my careers as a nurse and an agent, I have seen hundreds of rape victims, and for virtually every one, among their harshest psychic burdens was that tormenting self-recrimination.

Despite her emotional upheaval, which was entirely understandable, I found the victim to be an exceptionally reliable witness. Unlike some of the others, she was certain of her attacker's height, confirming that he was very tall. And because he had confronted her in a lighted room rather than seizing her from behind in the dark, she had been able to see his face.

Moreover, the woman seemed levelheaded and steady—considerations no cop or agent can ever overlook. If we managed to prosecute her attacker, her gray hair and maturity would make her eminently believable on the witness stand.

So Gary Konzak and I were elated when the shop worker called a short time later to report that she had spotted her assailant around town.

She had even noted his license-plate number. Gary quickly tracked the man down, convinced that this was the break we were hoping for, and—sure enough—he matched the artists' sketches of the Burlington rapist.

A few days later, the detective called me, defeat in his voice. The police had verified that the man had been out of town the night of the attack.

This setback was bigger than a simple misidentification, for by a good defense attorney's lights, our star witness had just "cried wolf"—thereby impugning her credibility, perhaps irrevocably. When we caught the guy, it would be that much harder to prove our case.

Eyes of Evil

Looking for a new strategy, we re-examined what we knew about our suspect. It was improbable that the rapist had sprung out of nowhere. And in a year-long rampage, it seemed likely he had claimed more victims than we were currently aware of.

Many people in law enforcement believe that serial rapists tend to operate on a 28-day rhythm comparable to a woman's menstrual cycle. During certain predictable periods, they can be astonishingly active. In the research conducted by Roy Hazelwood, 41 offenders were studied because each had raped at least 10 times. Cumulatively they were responsible for 837 rapes and 400 attempted rapes.

With this in mind, some of us believed that our perpetrator had at least approached—whether successfully or not—two or three times the number of women who had called the police.

Some of these potential victims may have gotten a glimpse of his car or picked up other critical information. Strange as it may seem, power-reassurance rapists quite often tell victims their first name.

We had tried an intense publicity blitz about the rapist, but this had failed to flush out the victims too skittish to come forward. Now I suggested we set up a hot line manned by counselors from a mental-health center.

We held a press conference, well covered by the TV, radio stations and newspapers, to announce that we weren't looking for more victims to testify—all we wanted was information on the attacker. Callers could remain anonymous.

The first two days alone 100 people contacted us, most of whom we easily dismissed as the usual cranky neighbors, vengeful ex-wives, and other grudge-holders. We got a few good leads but none were solid enough to pan out.

Two weeks passed, and then our middle-aged shop worker came forward again to report another sighting of her attacker. This time she was positive, she told Gary Konzak.

"I saw him. I looked straight at him. I know it's him. I will never forget that face."

Gary gently tried to put her off, explaining that if we kept bringing in men for questioning on her say-so, it would damage her reliability—and possibly her case—beyond repair.

"I understand," she insisted, "but you have to believe me. There is no doubt at all in my mind that he's the one. And I even know where he works."

She was so convincing that Gary had to ask, "Where?"

"At Marc's Big Boy on La Grange Road. He's the cook."

I could tell that Gary still had his doubts, but I said, "Hey, what's the harm in looking? Besides, I love their omelets. Let's go there for breakfast together and check it out."

We went to the restaurant the next morning, and again I took a seat facing the kitchen. By then I had been staring at the artists' sketches for months, so the UNSUB's sharp-featured face, with his close-cropped hair and mustache, were acid-etched on my mind.

Gary and I chattered like a normal couple, but over my open menu, I kept my eyes fixed on the kitchen, which was some 15 feet away. When a tall man bobbed up in the doorway for an instant, I had to steady myself so I didn't jerk with surprise.

He looked like a young Mike Ditka.

The server arrived to take our order, and when she moved out of earshot, I told Gary, "The victim is right. It's got to be him."

> **When a tall man bobbed up in the doorway for an instant, I had to steady myself. "The victim is right. It's got to be him."**

He laughed. "Come on, DeLong," he said. "I'd like to believe it too, but nothing is that easy in police work. She was wrong before."

"Not this time," I told him.

"You liked her, so now you want her to be right. Don't lose your objectivity. That last guy also looked like Mike Ditka, don't forget."

I felt like he was patronizing me, so I smiled and stood up. "OK, I'll go take a better look."

"Candice—" he warned, but before he could stop me, I was gone.

He was probably worried that I'd gape at the cook and tip him off that he was under suspicion. Or maybe he was afraid I would confront him when we didn't have the evidence to pick him up. But he couldn't intervene without creating a scene.

I poked my head in the kitchen. "Excuse me," I said to the man. "Are you the cook?"

He didn't answer.

Moving fully into the kitchen so I could study him, I pressed on. "My husband and I just ordered Denver omelets, but I'd like to change mine to cheese. I couldn't catch the waitress, so I thought I'd better tell you myself."

Everything about the cook—his height, his angular face, the way he looked me over with his piercing blue eyes, his surliness, his sarcastic reply—"Sure, lady"—matched the descriptions I'd collected from the victims. I felt a chill, and was glad to leave the kitchen for the safety of our table.

Once I was seated again, Gary's panicky look relaxed into relief at my returning without incident. "You know—" he began, but I cut him off, declaring: "Bingo. He's our guy."

Takedown

Once the police started digging, it turned out that the cook fitted the profile on a number of key counts. He was a single white male, 21 years old, who had finished high school and enlisted in the military.

As a short-order cook at Marc's Big Boy, he was working at a semiskilled job requiring little public contact. Before being hired he had been living with his mother. Only recently had he moved into his own rented apartment, two miles from the train station. We even discovered he had recently sold a car, which was an 11-year-old Datsun—an old "beater." Roy Hazelwood helped turn some skeptics into converts with that profile.

The evidence tying our suspect to the rapes now started falling into place. A discreet check of the restaurant's records showed that the cook was off duty at the time the recent assaults took place.

Finally, the police felt confident that they had enough "probable cause" for an arrest warrant.

"Do you want to come along on the bust?" Gary asked. Did I ever.

"You bet," I said.

I had been living and breathing the Burlington rapist case for months.

The police arrested the cook at his home. As they led him out in handcuffs, I stood watching and noticed with satisfaction that he was dressed exactly as we had predicted, in a T-shirt and old jeans. I hoped he was feeling at least some of the terror I had heard in his victims' voices. Before ducking the cook's head into the patrol car, Gary gestured in my direction.

"See that woman?" he said to the prisoner. "She helped capture you."

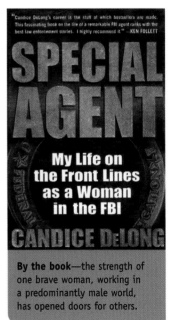

"Candice DeLong's career is the stuff of which bestsellers are made. This fascinating book on the life of a remarkable FBI agent ranks with the best law enforcement stories. I highly recommend it." —KEN FOLLETT

SPECIAL AGENT

My Life on the Front Lines as a Woman in the FBI

CANDICE DeLONG

By the book—the strength of one brave woman, working in a predominantly male world, has opened doors for others.

The cook fixed me with a glare so chilling that I froze. But I held his gaze until they hustled him away.

He was indeed "our guy." Later he would be convicted and sentenced to multiple terms in prison. He would have to serve a minimum of 18 years before becoming eligible for parole.

With the Burlington rapist safely locked up, I found a renewed pleasure in my evening runs. Once again all was right in our little world. Seth and the neighborhood kids joined me each night as I ran through the streets. The familiar sounds of spinning wheels and rustling leaves filled my ears, and I reveled in the peace.

ACE
AND THE
DOG MAN

Margo Pfeiff

Together they form a potent crime-fighting team. Chasing down car thieves, drug dealers and murderers has forged a bond between Canadian Glen MacKenzie and his police service dog Ace. "They're so close, I swear they could finish each other's sentences," says Inspector Mike Chadwick, head of Saanich Uniform Division.

"K-9," radios Constable Glen MacKenzie of the Saanich Police Canine Section, "I'm en route to that red Mustang." A stolen car racing down the Malahat Highway on Vancouver Island has evaded police in a high-speed chase. By the time police locate the car in a Victoria suburb, the driver has vanished.

Police service dog Ace is immediately on the case—37 kilograms of muscular black and tan German shepherd straining eagerly on his lead as he picks up the thief's scent. MacKenzie, his handler, jogs behind at the end of a 10-metre leash.

At a picnic area filled with people, Ace heads straight for the shore of Langford Lake and wades into the water. "Where you going, buddy?" a puzzled MacKenzie asks his partner as he follows, thigh deep. Some metres out, Ace suddenly turns left and swims parallel to the shoreline.

Downshore, standing on a small dock, another officer waves his arms. "He didn't come this way!" he shouts. But Ace continues to swim towards him. Reaching the dock, he dives underneath and seconds later resurfaces—dragging the suspect with him.

MacKenzie and Ace are a potent crime-fighting team. During seven years working with MacKenzie, the dog has been directly responsible for more than 300 arrests—everyone from shoplifters to drug dealers to murderers. But most remarkable of all is the close relationship between MacKenzie and his canine sidekick.

"In 24 years of police work, I've never seen anything like it," says Inspector Mike Chadwick, head of the Saanich Uniform Division. "They're so close, I swear they could finish each other's sentences."

At 7pm on a rainy, windy February night, I arrive at Saanich police headquarters just as MacKenzie and Ace are readying for a night shift. Ace rolls on the floor, paws in the air, shamelessly soliciting belly rubs. "Some tough police dog you are," 38-year-old MacKenzie scoffs.

Ace jumps into a large cage in the back of MacKenzie's Ford Explorer and we set off to cruise the municipality, a bedroom community for the city of Victoria. Three police radios mounted on the dashboard crackle with calls.

One announces the licence-plate number of a stolen red Nissan, and MacKenzie adds it to his "hot sheet" list above the driver's door.

Just after 11pm MacKenzie picks up the radio and mutters a few words. Ace leaps to his feet and yips excitedly. "That dog can read my mind," MacKenzie chuckles as he plants his foot on the accelerator. "They've spotted that Nissan."

First on the scene, we find the car abandoned on a front lawn, doors wide open. "Two 'runners,'" MacKenzie notes. Ace is frantic with anticipation as MacKenzie slips on the dog's vestlike tracking harness and clips on the lead.

Without a word from MacKenzie, Ace heads to the driver's side of the car, turns a circle and dashes off into the rainy night, head and tail down, ears forward. Ace is tracking a "scent cone," a cocktail of smells from the suspect's body, clothing, and even the grass he's trampled.

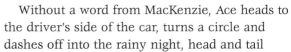

Partners—Constable Glen MacKenzie with his trusty police service dog, Ace.

I struggle to keep up as the pair weave through a maze of back yards. Ace tracks up a driveway, raises his head and tail for an instant and looks to the right. "That's the direction the second suspect took," MacKenzie pants. "We'll get back to him in a minute."

Ace is already inside the garage, barking at a parked car. Using the abrupt German commands many handlers prefer, MacKenzie shouts: "*Platz!*" ("Get down!") and the dog crouches on the spot. "Come out or I'll send in the dog!" he yells. A teenage male crawls out from beneath the car. It has been only two minutes since we spotted the stolen Nissan.

As back-up officers handcuff the suspect, MacKenzie takes Ace back to the spot where the two suspects separated. "Heavy rain washes scent away quickly," MacKenzie says. Nevertheless, Ace picks up the track and we're off again.

Soon there is tension on the leash, which tells MacKenzie the scent is getting stronger. Suddenly the dog stops and barks. MacKenzie searches with his flashlight. Five metres up a tree perches another young man. "Call off your dog," he shouts, fear in his voice.

Other incidents have not ended so peacefully. Once, MacKenzie was awakened at 3am by dispatch: an officer had pulled over an impaired driver, who then knocked her to the ground before fleeing.

At the scene, Ace tracked the suspect into a thick clump of evergreens. Following behind, MacKenzie heard a sickening thud. He rushed into the grove just as the suspect kicked the dog. Ace lunged, sank his teeth deep into the man's thigh and hauled him down screaming. Although Ace had been smashed across the shoulder with a large rock, he didn't flinch when MacKenzie carefully examined him that night. Two weeks and eight arrests later, it was discovered the dog had a broken rib.

"Ace lives for me," says MacKenzie, "and he would die for me."

Raised in Kamloops, British Columbia, MacKenzie joined the Royal Canadian Mounted Police in 1982 at age 20. After four years with the RCMP in Alberta, the sandy-haired, blue-eyed officer moved with his young wife, Shannon, to Saanich, where he joined the municipal police force.

Proud possessions—MacKenzie joined the municipal police force in Saanich at the age of 24.

MacKenzie often volunteered to be the "bad guy" during police dog training and became fascinated by the intelligence of K-9s. "I want to be a dog man," he told his superior one day in 1990. MacKenzie's request was granted, and he was given German shepherds with good bloodlines to "test drive" for persistence, courage and intelligence. But six months and 16 dogs later, MacKenzie was becoming discouraged. Finally he contacted Sergeant Doug Deacon, an instructor with the New Westminster Police Service. In February 1992, Deacon found 14-month-old Ace.

At a dog trial, MacKenzie set his stopwatch and sent Ace into a field of tall grass after a ball. If a dog searches for seven or eight minutes before giving up, it has potential. Ace searched for 40 minutes. MacKenzie knew he'd found his dog.

In a test for courage, a "bad guy" runs from the dog, then turns and threatens him. Ninety-nine per cent of dogs flee in fear, but Ace stood his ground. Under gunfire he didn't flinch. As for tracking skills, Ace had only to be given a scent once and he remembered. After three months' training, he sailed through certification, and on June 22, 1992, MacKenzie hit the streets with his new partner.

A very real test of the dog's courage occurred in 1994. A man had fired three shots at Saanich police as they arrived at a farmhouse to answer a domestic-dispute call. An emergency-response team, along with MacKenzie and Ace, were called in. Close to 40 officers surrounded the site. For six hours the man refused to respond.

Finally, at dawn, police fired tear gas through the windows, and the suspect staggered out clad in a heavy winter coat, hands deep in his pockets. "Show your hands!" shouted the team leader. Ignoring him, the man continued towards the bushes where MacKenzie and other officers were thinly shielded by shrubbery.

MacKenzie commanded the dog to take the suspect: "*Haggemup!*" he shouted. Ace hit the suspect shoulder high and knocked him flat.

One of Ace's most famous tracks began late one day after a woman walked into her upstairs bedroom and found an intruder. For an exhausting 40 minutes after MacKenzie was called to the scene, he followed Ace over dozens of suburban fences. Suddenly the dog stopped, looked up and barked, his signal that "the bad guy is right here." MacKenzie could see nothing. "Where is he, buddy?" he asked. The dog jumped onto a rickety platform and then to the roof of a woodshed. MacKenzie scrambled up to find himself face to face with the burglar, lying flat on the roof.

Ace's tracking has proved reliable in court as well. When a repeat offender, a house burglar, was about to be acquitted because no witnesses could make a positive identification, MacKenzie stepped in to testify. He recalled how Ace had located the stolen goods in bushes the night of the crime, then tracked the suspect down as he attempted to stroll away.

"A dog's nose is between 3,000 and 30,000 times more sensitive than our own," he explained. "While we smell our mother's stew, a dog smells carrots, potatoes, onions and meat."

Persuaded that the dog had found the right man, the judge sentenced the thief to two years.

In June 1995, MacKenzie noticed Ace walking strangely. *Shepherds can have bad hips,* he thought, and took the dog to local vet Dave Kirby. After weeks of testing, Dr Kirby called MacKenzie into his office. "I'm afraid it's degenerative myelopathy, a disease similar to multiple sclerosis," the vet said. The paralysis would move up his spine until it paralysed his lungs. "It's unlikely

Ace could continue to work for more than a month or two. His hind legs could become paralysed within six months."

Reluctantly MacKenzie set about training another dog. Before Ace got sick, the team had been training to go to the Canadian Police Canine Association Trials in Vancouver. Kirby advised against it. "But Ace lives to track," MacKenzie told the vet. "He'll die faster if I leave him at home."

On Labour Day 1995, Ace's fierce concentration and sheer will won the competition over 35 other teams. But for MacKenzie the victory was bittersweet; he was sure his friend would soon be gone.

A month later, through persistent research, Kirby located Dr R. M. Clemmons of the University of Florida, who had been working with an experimental medication that looked as though it might slow Ace's disease. They decided to try it. Miraculously, within two months Ace's paralysis seemed to stop and he was tracking like his old self again.

Off duty on June 8, 1998, MacKenzie was training Ace in an open field outside Saanich in the sweltering heat when his pager rang out: five teenagers were robbing a home nearby. By the time he arrived, three had been arrested and two had fled. Ace took off across a field of chest-deep hay. Running flat out to keep up with the dog, MacKenzie could see the pair fleeing 500 metres ahead. MacKenzie let Ace off the leash. He leaped across a stream and pulled down one of the youths. MacKenzie had no handcuffs. "Put your hands behind your back, and don't move or the dog will get you," he warned the thief. "Stay!" he instructed Ace, then raced off towards the main road to flag down a police car.

With the first of the runners in custody, MacKenzie and Ace set off after the second. They tracked through forest and across fields for eight kilometres until they reached a golf course. Following their progress, several police cars patrolled the perimeter of the course. Suddenly Ace collapsed, panting furiously, his eyes glazed over. *Heat stroke! I've got to get him to water!* thought MacKenzie. "Police emergency!" he shouted to a golfer. "I need your cart!"

At the first water hole, he held the dog's head above water and Ace began to come around. A police officer shouted across the green, "We got him!" Ace's tracking had forced the suspect into the open.

Less than a month later, on July 1, MacKenzie opened the back door of his truck to send Ace on a drug search. The dog was so weak he could barely stand up.

This time Ace was diagnosed with autoimmune hemolytic anemia, a rare condition in which the body rejects and kills off red blood cells, which carry oxygen from the lungs.

Devastated, MacKenzie headed home. Around midnight Kirby phoned. "Can you find another dog for a blood transfusion? It's our last chance."

It was after 2am when MacKenzie arrived at the clinic with another dog. All night MacKenzie stayed at Ace's side, and by morning the dog's red-blood-cell count had risen slightly. "If he makes it through the next four days, we might get him back," said Kirby.

When the day is done— MacKenzie's son, Max, shares a police dog's love.

During the next two weeks, Ace's red-blood-cell count continued to rise, but he remained very weak. "Let's take him off the drugs and see what happens," Kirby advised. Within days, Ace began to improve.

For two months MacKenzie kept Ace off the job. Then, one evening in late August, the dog whined so piteously as his partner headed out on shift that MacKenzie relented. "Let's go tracking, " he said, slipping on the harness. Ace worked like he'd never been away. The following morning MacKenzie told Kirby he was taking Ace with him to the Nationals the following weekend.

On September 4, without a single training session, Ace tracked, searched and apprehended "criminals" with such skill that he won the Canadian Police Canine Association Trials for the third time. "He's some kind of wonder dog," Kirby confesses. "Most dogs just don't have his kind of inner strength."

Ace continued his career until his retirement in February 2001, just after Constable Glen MacKenzie left the Saanich Police Canine Section after being promoted to sergeant. He went on living with Glen and his family, spending many happy days rolling around with the kids in the yard. His medical condition finally caught up with him and he passed away in April 2003—a day Glen describes as "the worst day of my life". After his cremation, and in memory of his faithful friend, Glen scattered Ace's ashes over the training field, the place that Ace loved and where they had spent many joyous hours perfecting their skills together.

HIJACK ON
THE HIGH SEAS

Today's pirates no longer fly the skull and crossbones, but their intentions are just as deadly. Opposite, a brigand on the South China Sea shows off a watch he has pocketed for himself after a raid. In modern-day piracy everything is up for grabs and it's each man for himself.

aptain Ken Blyth watched impatiently as shore crews, now 12 hours behind schedule, finished loading his ship in Singapore. He was skipper of the *Petro Ranger*, a tanker bound for Vietnam that would be carrying a cargo of jet fuel and diesel oil worth some $2.5 million. It would be a three-day turnaround. Then he would fly home to Queensland for a celebration of his 25th wedding anniversary.

When the *Petro Ranger* finally slipped its berth at 4.30 on the afternoon of April 16, 1998, it joined the daily parade of cargo vessels that make Singapore the busiest port in the world. Just outside the harbour is the Horsburgh Lighthouse, the last outpost of domestic law in the region. From Horsburgh on, you enter international waters. Not technically possessed or patrolled by anyone, these waters are the no-man's-land of the New World economy. They also serve as an arena for the revival of an age-old crime: piracy.

> International waters, not technically possessed or patrolled by anyone, are the no-man's-land of the New World economy.

The *Petro Ranger* cruised past Horsburgh at about 9.30pm and headed north into the South China Sea. Relieved and tired, Blyth put the ship on automatic pilot, crawled into bed and fell asleep. One floor above the captain's fourth-storey quarters was the bridge, where a crew member was stationed as lookout.

Despite the sophisticated technology aboard the *Petro Ranger*, radar detection at the rear of the vessel was difficult because the ship's funnel created a blind spot. No one on board realized that hovering in the ship's wake was a small speedboat.

Just after 1am the speedboat opened its engines and pulled alongside the ship's stern. Twelve pirates were on board: seven Indonesians, three Malaysians and two Thais. They had learned the layout of the ship beforehand and knew Blyth had a crew of only 20 men.

Securing ladders to the stern, the men scrambled to the main deck. Then, using a fixed ladder outside the accommodation housing—the six-storey structure containing the men's quarters and the mess halls—they climbed to the open bridge. Their faces disguised by balaclavas, they appeared in the bridge's doorway. They overtook the lookout in a struggle loud enough to wake up the captain below.

Blyth sat up in the dark. *Had someone been drinking?* Putting on a dressing gown, he went to check.

Suddenly, there was a crashing blow at his door, and four hooded men rushed in, waving machetes. A fifth stepped forward and held a gun to Blyth's head. They bound his wrists with cord, then ordered him to help them round up the crew.

When Mohiuddin Ahmed Farooq, the chief engineer, heard Blyth just outside his quarters, he knew something was wrong. Blyth, 52, was a tall, sinewy Scot who usually radiated a hardheaded intensity. But when he called out, "Chief, Chief," his voice was quavering. Farooq quickly opened the door. Four or five knives were pointed at Blyth's neck.

One by one, every crew member was taken, tied up and dumped in the captain's day room. The pirates took Blyth to the bridge, forced him to be seated and then taped his arms and legs to a chair.

Chilling pattern—Captain Ken Blyth knew the usual fate of crews aboard captured ships.

Baffled by touch-screen computerized piloting, they ordered Blyth to show them how the controls worked. "You're going to kill me anyway," Blyth responded. "Why should I cooperate?"

When a pirate said they would kill the crew one by one until he obeyed, Blyth promised to help.

The pirates released Blyth's bonds long enough for him to divert the tanker from the main shipping lanes and into the maritime equivalent of a dark alley. They wanted to winch their speedboat onto the larger vessel's deck and have Blyth teach their pilot how to use the ship's navigation equipment.

Then they had Blyth put the ship on autopilot, following the original northward course.

Blyth was taken to his men in the officers' mess, which was filled with mattresses. Guards were stationed at the door. Lights blazed 24 hours a day, making sleep difficult.

Two days into captivity, Blyth was allowed to shower. The pirates had taped over the portholes in the mess, but he could see through his shower window that the bottom half of his ship's identifying blue funnel had been painted red. Had he been able to see the stern, he would have found that the *Petro Ranger* no longer existed. He was now aboard the *Wilby*, just another vessel bobbing along in international sea lanes.

Over the next few days, changes in the weather convinced Blyth they were nearing the China coast. Blyth theorized that the pirates intended to meet some black-market tankers to off-load the fuel cargo. They would need Blyth's crew to help make that transfer. But then what? Would he and his crew go over the side?

Piracy on the high seas resurfaced in the mid-1980s and in recent years has escalated to a true crisis. Reported acts of piracy have doubled in Asia in the past decade. Last year, 354 of the 469 attacks reported worldwide occurred in Asian waters.

The cause of piracy's revival is no different from the reason for its appearance centuries ago. Ships serving the top trading nations (America, Germany and Japan) are transiting through a global geography of poverty, envy and desperation. Often these vessels are carrying commodities like alkali, aluminium ingots and various types of fuel—all easily turned into quick money on the black market.

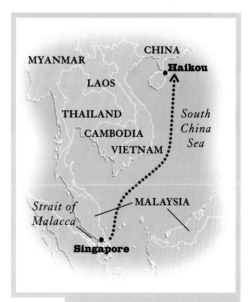

Modern piracy ranges from desperate fishermen pulling off petty larcenies to highly organized syndicates slaughtering crews to steal multimillion-dollar vessels and their cargo. According to Noel Choong, director of the Piracy Reporting Centre in Malaysia's capital, Kuala Lumpur: "Ninety-five per cent of pirates are armed and will not hesitate to use weapons to escape."

Rerouted—the *Petro Ranger* left Singapore bound for Vietnam, but pirates altered course for China.

The captured seamen may end up like the crew of the *Global Mars*, seized by pirates in February 2000. The 17 crewmen were bound,

Floating target—hundreds of attacks have been reported on both small recreational boats and large vessels like the *Petro Ranger*.

blindfolded and set adrift in lifeboats. Or they could suffer the fate of the sailors aboard the *Cheung Son*. In 1998 all 23 crewmen were systematically murdered by 13 pirates, who photographed their act. Later captured by Chinese officials, the pirates were convicted of murder and executed. Blyth was thinking about these incidents when he asked to meet with the pirate leader. The 49-year-old Indonesian, who called himself Herman, spoke several languages, including perfect English.

Blyth began negotiating right off, complaining that the cords were cutting into their wrists. Herman agreed to a less chafing form of handcuffs, using a rubber O-ring and strong tape.

Blyth was surprised that Herman wanted to linger and chat. The pirate king seemed so exhilarated at what he'd accomplished that he wanted to share it with someone.

Soon Blyth realized that, with the mildest prodding, Herman would provide details he thought were irrelevant. He told Blyth that four of the pirates, those carrying guns, were in leadership positions. Herman and a second officer were the brains of the operation; the other two, Blyth surmised, were executioners. The junior pirates were basically thugs; one had just been released from prison.

The syndicate he worked for, Herman explained, had four men in leadership positions: one each from China, Hong Kong, Indonesia and Singapore.

He claimed they had "inside access" to Petroships, the *Petro Ranger*'s parent company. They knew it would be sailing with fuel; they knew all about Blyth and most of the crew. Further, Herman had all the documents he would need: registration for the *Wilby*, papers identifying Herman as captain and bills of lading indicating the cargo was part of a legitimate charter. As Blyth was returned to his mattress, he worried. *Why would Herman tell him all this if he did not intend to kill him?*

Six days later, two tankers pulled up alongside the *Wilby* to siphon off diesel. Blyth's chief officer was forced to help off-load thousands of tonnes of fuel. A third tanker was delayed, Blyth learned, and the *Wilby* idled for several days. Then one pirate made a huge mistake: he called the missing tanker on the public VHF frequency. The Chinese heard him.

Soon afterwards, officers aboard a Chinese patrol vessel stopped and inspected what they thought was the *Wilby*. But Herman handled it smoothly. He locked Blyth and a few of his men down below in crew cabins. He presented papers indicating he was the captain and passed off both Blyth's sailors and his own henchmen as his crew. (The pirates kept Blyth's crew in check by reminding them they knew the whereabouts of their families.)

Suspecting a smuggling operation, the Chinese withdrew and waited to see what might happen. When the third tanker arrived, the Chinese sped in and escorted it and the *Wilby* to Haikou harbour on the island of Hainan in southern China.

Since the Chinese were now convinced the *Wilby* was a smuggling ship, Herman contacted his syndicate and got a lawyer to facilitate the usual round of bribes. Blyth learned this from Herman, who enjoyed boasting of his caginess.

Blyth knew that if Herman pulled this off, the *Wilby* would push out to sea and his crew would be killed. He had to get to Chinese officers, who he hoped were not corrupt.

For help, Blyth turned to two crew members: Saini Ugie, a Malaysian, and Ebenezer "Benny" Gakpey, a Ghanaian. Ugie, who spoke Mandarin, managed to ask a Chinese lieutenant to meet him at midnight on the monkey island, the colloquial name for the roof of the bridge.

The pirate guards checked on Blyth every half-hour or so. Often that meant just jiggling the handle on the door to make sure it was still locked. Knowing this, Blyth, Gakpey and Ugie concocted a plan. Ugie would watch for the pirates. When he determined the stairwell to the bridge was clear, Gakpey would knock three times on Blyth's door.

The scheme began as planned. Ugie and Blyth hurried to the bridge while Gakpey went back into the captain's cabin and locked the door. If the guards tried the handle, everything would seem to be in order.

Ugie and the captain bolted up to the monkey island, where the Chinese lieutenant was keeping watch. Blyth handed the officer papers he'd managed to hide from the pirates: his passport and documents stating he commanded the *Petro Ranger*.

Reassured that Blyth would now be protected, Ugie and Gakpey returned to their cabins. The Chinese dressed Blyth in a Chinese army uniform and asked him to sit atop the monkey island. From below, the pirates could see only the silhouette of a man in battle fatigues and army hat.

The Chinese dressed Blyth in a Chinese army uniform and asked him to sit atop the monkey island.

The next morning, Chinese soldiers came to the ship. Still perched atop the monkey island, Blyth watched as the Chinese herded Herman and the mix of pirates and legitimate crew onto their boat. Told they were going ashore to sign documents granting port clearance, they complied as 30 armed Chinese soldiers held their weapons at the ready.

The Chinese lieutenant then called out to Blyth, who stood up. We are left to imagine what Herman must have thought when he looked up to see the Chinese guard descend to the deck as Ken Blyth. The captain pointed at each man in turn, identifying him as either pirate or crew.

After the pirates were arrested, Blyth was taken ashore and interrogated by the People's Liberation Army (PLA) and the Public Security Bureau (PSB). Days of interviews gave the captain the impression his ship had become ensnared in a major power play. Blyth felt the PLA was deeply concerned with how this might look internationally. The PSB seemed more beholden to provincial powers in southern China, which are widely suspected of not only tolerating piracy but organizing it.

What finally happened still baffles those involved. C. M. Tan, executive director of Petroships of Singapore, retrieved his stolen ship, but the Chinese kept 5,100 tonnes of fuel as "evidence" before later selling it off. "What the Chinese authorities did was deplorable," Tan says.

Four months later, the Chinese authorities quietly released Herman and all his men. The Chinese have refused to offer a credible explanation for why they let the pirates go.

"One of my old crew members phoned me up in early August," Blyth says. "He told me that five of our pirates have been spotted doing piracy again. You just can't believe it, but they're back out there."

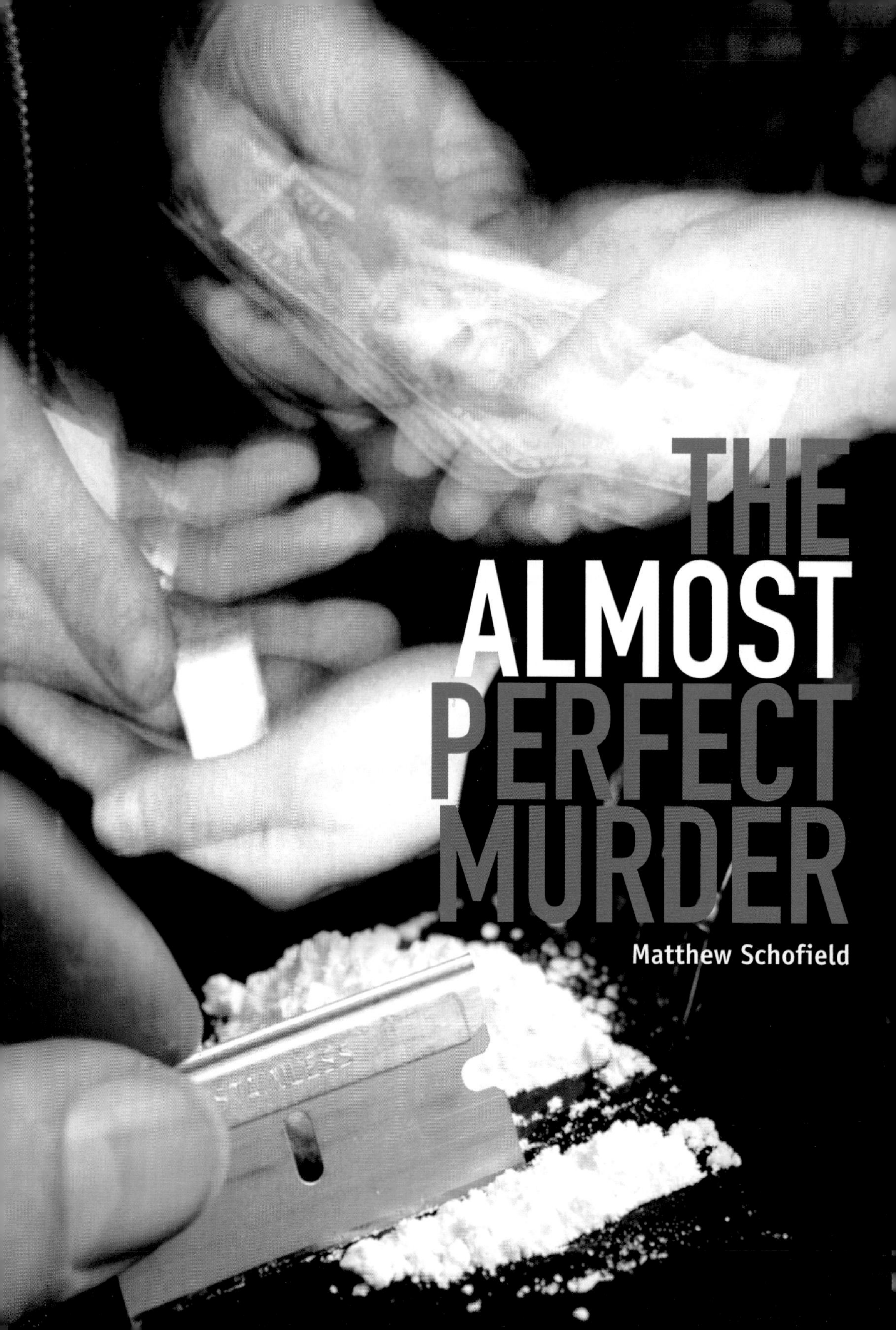

THE
ALMOST
PERFECT
MURDER

Matthew Schofield

In the small town of Maryville, Missouri, drug-dealing is rife. So when one dealer-turned-informant went missing, police feared the worst. But they had no witness, no body and no leads.

Christine Elkins hesitates in the dark doorway. Tony Emery, a muscular 34-year-old, is urging her to step inside the shadows, past the strip of dusty floor and onto the braided rug. Elkins had dealt methamphetamine for Emery in this small town of Maryville, Missouri. But now she is a federal informant—and knows this meeting could be dangerous.

Elkins plants her feet and refuses to budge. Emery's powerful arms push her and she stumbles through the doorway . . .

On Monday, August 6, 1990, Special Agent Michael Schmitz, 28, arrives early at the Kansas City offices of the Bureau of Alcohol, Tobacco and Firearms (ATF). After ten tough weeks at the Bureau's National Academy in Georgia, Schmitz is finally a federal agent. And he can't wait to get started.

While he was at the academy, he was kept abreast of the Emery case by his mentor, Special Agent Mark James, a maverick ATF agent known for cracking a high percentage of cases. Duane Nichols, 47, revered by lawmen throughout the region for his no-nonsense leadership, is their supervising agent.

According to investigators, Tony Emery controlled methamphetamine sales in the north-west corner of Missouri. People were scared of him, and for good reason. When a prosecutor started pursuing an assault case against a friend of Emery's, bullets blasted into the wall above the bed of the prosecutor's young daughter. Emery was never charged with this, though he was a suspect.

The feds had just gotten a woman inside Emery's empire: Christine Elkins, 32, a recovering meth addict and mother of two. For several months she had dealt meth for the drug dealer. But after cops busted her in December 1989, she said she'd help them get Emery.

Sure, she was afraid of Emery. But she had her kids to think about, so she agreed to do what no one else would.

On July 26, 1990, Special Agent James had met Elkins at a small airport in Maryville. He handed her a microcassette recorder, which she slipped into the waistband of her jeans.

She left the airport in her maroon Olds Cutlass. James and a trooper pulled their unmarked car into a parking lot, from which they could see Emery's house.

Fifteen minutes later Emery walked toward their car, staring straight at James. *We're burned!* James thought. *How did he know we were here?* The officers pulled out of the parking lot, realizing their surveillance was blown.

Back at the airport 45 minutes later, Elkins's Cutlass came screeching up to them.

"He saw you!" Elkins screamed.

Sobbing and shaking, she explained that Emery had taken her to a dark, deserted house. He'd run his hands up her sides, looking for a wire. Emery didn't find it, she said, but he told her he'd seen the cops. "If you assist law enforcement," he said, "I'll kill you."

After calming her down, James told Elkins to stay away from Emery. She promised she would.

On Thursday, August 2, James heard from Elkins again. "Tony wants to know if I'm ready to leave town for good," she said. "He says he's trying to get three to four thousand dollars together for me to leave on. He says he's set up a place for me to live far from here, where you'll never find me, where I won't have to testify against him."

"Stay clear of that man," James warned. "It sounds like a set-up."

"OK. I'll stay away."

But now, during Schmitz's first week on the job, James is worried. He hasn't heard from Elkins for several days. Is she still alive?

As the summer of 1990 wanes, Elkins misses work—something she isn't known to do. Also, she hasn't spoken to her mother at all, and the two are close. James's instinct is telling him that Christine Elkins is probably dead.

Adding to James's foreboding is a conversation he has had with Jerry Moser, a friend of Elkins's, which indicates that she'd met one last time with Tony Emery.

It was late on the night of August 4 when Elkins showed up at Moser's door with her younger son. "Can you watch [my son] for 10 minutes?" she'd asked. "I've got to go get some money." Then she added, "If you don't see me in 10 minutes, you'll see me in the morgue."

Sinister, but there is no evidence of a murder. No body, no blood, no witnesses. On top of that, her car—a Cutlass with Missouri plate number B6E-652—has also vanished, so she might have just taken off.

In September 1990, Colorado drug dealer James Witt is driving near Fort Collins when he hears a small airplane behind him. *I'm being tailed,* he thinks. He knows he is looking at a federal bust—maybe 10 years in prison.

He contacts the Greeley, Colorado, Police Department to make a deal, offering some attractive bait to lessen the charges against him. It seems he has something on a couple of guys in a drug operation—two men named Emery. "I might know of a murder that happened," he tells the police. *There was a girl missing in Maryville, Missouri,* he says. *Some guys killed her over something to do with drugs.*

At 5pm on December 18, 1990, Witt watches Tug Emery, Tony's cousin, pull into the parking lot of the Lucky Star restaurant north of Greeley. Witt, now a wired federal informant, motions for Tug to get in. Their conversation is to be transmitted to a nearby van.

Witt broaches the topic of murder by mentioning that he has a man he needs to "do." He adds, "But I don't know what to do with the body."

Tug's advice: "A mine shaft is what you need, but if he's driving something, you've got to get rid of it too."

But how do you get a body out of a house? Witt asks.

"Wrap him in the rug. You can't tell what's in there." Tug, not often in a position to play the wise professional, has an answer for every concern.

Without referring to Elkins by name, Witt asks, "Was there a lot of blood?"

"A little. She went."

How do you hold down the pedal to sink the car? Witt asks.

"Put a stick in there," Tug says.

From the tape, James and Schmitz deduce that Elkins has been murdered. But her name never came up—and Tug didn't really confess to a murder so much as describe a hypothetical crime. They still have no case against Tony.

Without referring to Elkins by name, Witt asks: "Was there a lot of blood?"

Eight months after Elkins disappeared, Tony Emery pleads guilty to conspiracy to possess with intent to distribute methamphetamine. He is sentenced to 110 months in Leavenworth on the drug charges, but the feds aren't stopping there.

Prosecutors ask them whether it is wise to pursue a murder charge that still has no body, no weapon, no witnesses, no blood. But supervising agent Nichols has no intention of letting a killer go free. "If we don't have a case now," he says, "we work until we build one."

Schmitz and James interview everyone believed connected to Emery's drug organization. The interviews yield little. "Look, you can send me to jail," they are told time after time, "but if Tony finds out that I talked to you, I'm dead."

"We can protect you."

"Is that what you told Christine?"

———

295

In January 1992, the Maryville Police Department promotes Randy Strong to investigator and assigns him to the Elkins case. He is awed. Here he is, a wet-behind-the-ears local cop, working on a high-profile murder case with federal agents. *What do they need with me?* he wonders.

The answer, he decides, is effort. He studies every detail of the case, looking for a crack.

After two years of research, Schmitz thinks he knows where Emery killed Elkins—in a house on the north-east corner of town. In December 1992, he arrives at the house with several officers. They hope that luminol, a chemical that turns blue when it comes into contact with even traces of human blood, will identify this place as the scene of the murder.

Schmitz knocks on the door. A woman answers. She is renting the place from Tony Emery's family. Inside, the floorboards, the drywall, the carpets are all new. Schmitz is stunned. "He remodeled the whole house," he says. Luminol would be pointless.

Time is running out on nailing Tony Emery. In December 1998, he will be eligible for parole on his drug conviction.

During the summer of 1995, Assistant US Attorney Mike Green offers immunity from prosecution to a man named Bobby Miller, a friend of Tug Emery's. Miller, it seems, was around for the planning of the murder, and he heard screams coming from the house. But he claims he panicked and bolted from the scene, never saw a body, didn't see a killing.

Miller heard screams coming from the house. He panicked and bolted from the scene.

Still, with the tape recording of Tug Emery, that was enough to make a case against Tug. If Tug is facing life without parole, he might give us Tony, Green thinks.

On November 20, 1996, Mark James carries a sheaf of papers and a photo into a Colorado federal detention-center interview room. Tug Emery, serving time for the same drug bust that imprisoned Tony, is seated at a table.

James walks to the table and lays down the papers. Emery's eyes only need a few seconds to tell him the papers are an indictment against him for the murder of Elkins.

Next to the indictment, James places a photo of Elkins. Emery looks briefly at it, then jerks his head away.

"This woman was a mother of a couple of young boys. She was a daughter," James says. "There are people who need closure, and she deserves a decent burial."

With that, James leaves.

Every phone call from Leavenworth is taped. Inmates know, however, that with hundreds of calls each day, the volume of recordings can be impossible for investigators to sort through. So sometimes crimes are discussed, even if only in code.

It is this knowledge that repeatedly brings Schmitz and Strong to the Leavenworth tapes. Finally, a week after Thanksgiving, 1996, they discover a conversation. From prison, Tony Emery calls his mother for the holiday.

Mother: "You know what's going on? Nationwide news. Tuggy."

Tony: "Oh, no."

Mother: "That's right. First-degree murder charges. Something to do with a person being missed. You know what I'm saying."

Tony: "Yeah."

As he listens to the conversation, a grin spreads across Schmitz's face. For six years Emery has been smug, confident he would get away with murder. Now, for the first time, Schmitz can hear panic setting in.

Tony: "Somebody needs to tell him to stand his ground."

Schmitz and Strong slap hands. "He's feeling the pressure," Schmitz says.

Schmitz and Strong commit to re-checking every detail of the case. In June 1997 they show up at the farmhouse of Dana Clizer, who is among the more than 200 people connected to Tony Emery who have been investigated. The brother of Tony's ex-girlfriend, he was interviewed the first time only because he bought a car from Emery.

After about half an hour of talking with Clizer on the front porch, the conversation seems to be going nowhere. Strong prepares to leave. But Clizer's next words freeze him. Clizer says he has a good story about Tony, if they want to hear it.

"Yes, we do," Schmitz says.

Clizer explains that it was back in 1990, right before the time he laid some carpet for Tony in one of his houses.

"We were getting ready to go to bed. I seen headlights—Tony pulling in my farm."

Clizer said Tony told him he had to get rid of the car. "He wanted me to show him the fastest way to where I put my boat in the river, and stay off 71 Highway as much as I could."

Schmitz and Strong spat out questions. "Did he tell you what was in the car?"

"No."

"What model of car?"

"Later model, GM car."

They know now where Elkins vanished. She must have been in the trunk.

Murky depths—the muddy riverbed of the Missouri proved to be the resting place of the murder victim and the car.

Several days later, at the Amazonia boat ramp, Schmitz stares at the muddy water of the Missouri river. The US army Corps of Engineers has warned him chances of finding the car in the murky depths are slim. *There must be a way to find that car,* Schmitz thinks. He arranges to bring in NecroSearch International, a group of scientists and lawmen who specialize in finding bodies.

On July 26 and 27, 1997, the NecroSearch team trolls more than a half-mile stretch of the river. At the end of the second day, they hand Schmitz a map. "We identified seven anomalies that could be the car," one explains. "We'd say you should start your search here." He points to a slight bend in the river, not 200 yards from the boat ramp.

The next morning, Schmitz and Strong watch as a diver jumps into the river and descends to the riverbed.

At 12.51pm the diver emerges holding a Missouri license plate above his head. It's muddy, but white numbers shine through: B6E-652. "That's the car!" someone shouts.

Nobody speaks much as a tow truck drags the car into a circle of cops who've waited seven years to see it. They note a piece of wood jammed behind the gas pedal, and in the trunk they find rolled-up carpet padding.

Soon they discover Elkins's skull, which has a soup-can-sized hole on the right side.

In July 1998, a Kansas City jury listens as Tug Emery tells how Elkins died. Tony wanted Elkins dead, he says, convinced a drug case against him would vanish if she wasn't around to testify. So Tug came from out of state to help plan the killing. His friend Miller joined him and learned of the scheme when he and Tug arrived in Maryville.

Tony lured Elkins to the house on August 4, 1990, telling her he was going to give her money to start a new life. Tug was hiding inside, waiting to hit her and wrap her up in a rug. Miller was outside, ready to haul away the body.

When Tony pushed Elkins inside, Tug slammed a blackjack down on her head. But it didn't knock her out. Elkins fought back, so he struck her again and again. But the plan wasn't working—they were now fighting. Tug took another swing, and Elkins managed to grab the blackjack. As she wrested it away, she tumbled down the basement steps.

Tony told Tug, "Get a pipe and finish her off. I've got to get rid of her car." Then Tony walked away from the house.

Tug headed from the house and asked Miller to help him. Miller refused, saying, "I'm not a killer." The two decided to leave the scene.

The next afternoon, Tug told Tony why he fled. "It was better that way," Tony said. "I took care of the dirty laundry."

Later, Tony told Tug how he'd returned to the house with a friend and struck Elkins one more time with a flashlight. Evidently, they wrapped her up in some carpet padding, carried her to the car and stuffed her in the trunk. Then they dumped the Cutlass in the river.

On July 14, 1998, the jury finds Tony Emery guilty of murder. Several months later, before sentencing, Mike Green plays a tape recording of Christine's mother, Patricia. Her words are to Emery: "The hardest thing I've ever had to do, other than to hear my daughter had been murdered, was to sit in the courtroom and listen in horror—the manner of her death."

Emery looks away from the Elkins family. But Schmitz's eyes never leave Emery's face, hoping to see some sign of remorse, pain, fear.

"She was Christine Ann. You murdered our daughter. It sickens me to realize your face was the last thing my daughter saw. We curse your soul."

For the first time, Emery looks troubled. His face reddens and he vigorously shakes his head.

The judge announces a sentence of life in prison without chance for parole and adjourns the court.

Schmitz, James and other agents gather in a conference room. They shake hands and exchange hugs. ATF supervisor Nichols steps forward. The room quiets as he starts to speak. "You have no idea how much this means to me," he says, his eyes filling with tears. "I'm announcing my retirement today. I put it off to see this case closed—to see that no matter how corrupt this world might look, in the end, justice will prevail.

"And, gentlemen, justice did prevail."

INTO THE MIND OF TERROR

Lou Michel and Dan Herbeck

Throughout his capture and conviction, Oklahoma City bomber Timothy McVeigh maintained a stony silence. What was it that drove him to commit an act of such unspeakable cruelty?

When a bomb blew up a federal building in Oklahoma City, the whole world wanted to know: who was Timothy McVeigh and why would anyone do such a thing? Veteran newsmen Lou Michel and Dan Herbeck, of the *Buffalo News*, started digging for answers—and ended up in their own back yards. Timothy McVeigh had grown up in his father's house in Pendleton, New York, about 20 minutes away from where Lou Michel lived. Capitalizing on local contacts as well as their best investigative instincts, Michel and Herbeck were able to get to McVeigh's father, and then to Timothy McVeigh himself—who, from his death-row cell, divulged what was going through his murderous mind that fateful day.

Dawn, April 19, 1995. He awoke with the sun on this Wednesday, yawning and stretching in the cab of the Ryder truck.

He'd slept like a baby in the rental, two feet in front of a 7,000-pound bomb. The padded seat in the big yellow truck had been like a fine hotel bed compared with many of the places he'd slept in recent years. Back in the army, he'd learned how to sleep without being comfortable.

He had also learned how crucial rest was when you were preparing for action, and there would be plenty of action today. Timothy McVeigh was going to teach the government a lesson. He intended to strike back for Waco, for Ruby Ridge, for high taxes, for gun laws and a host of other grievances he'd been amassing for years.

He reached below the seat and pulled out an envelope made of thick brown plastic. He peeled open the wrapping, pulled out a food packet and tore it open. This was breakfast, a spaghetti MRE, or meal-ready-to-eat. High in calories and carbohydrates, it was specially formulated for soldiers on the move. Energy food. He would need every ounce of it to steel himself for what was to come.

After finishing his meal, McVeigh got out and thoroughly examined his truck, checking the tires, making sure that the rear and side doors to the cargo box were securely locked.

All this came naturally to him. He was a detail man—meticulous and tireless. He was not, those who knew him would agree, an overtly violent or nasty person. Yet here he was, four days shy of his 27th birthday, preparing to use a truck-bomb to destroy an office building filled with people he had never met—a mission he considered an act of war.

McVeigh checked the .45-caliber Glock semiautomatic handgun that he carried close to his heart, in a leather holster across his chest. It could fire

16 bullets without reloading, and he was prepared to use it to kill anyone who interfered with his task.

He was dressed in faded black jeans and army boots, with a windbreaker over his favorite T-shirt, worn as a token of his defiance. On the front was a drawing of Abraham Lincoln. Underneath was the Latin refrain that John Wilkes Booth screamed after he assassinated Lincoln—*Sic semper tyrannis* ("Thus ever to tyrants").

On the back of the shirt was a picture of a tree dripping blood, bearing a quotation from Thomas Jefferson: "The tree of liberty must be refreshed from time to time with the blood of patriots and tyrants."

A lot of blood will be shed today, McVeigh thought. *Innocent people will suffer. But there is no other way.*

He found the truck to be in good running order. He'd checked all the fluid levels the night before, when he stopped for gas in southern Kansas, topping off the tank with $40 worth of unleaded.

Timothy J. McVeigh turned the key in the ignition, threw the Ryder truck into gear and headed for Oklahoma City.

Calculations

As he drove down the highway, McVeigh carefully obeyed the speed limit. With 7,000 pounds of explosives behind him, he could hardly afford a traffic accident. But he had another tactical reason for taking his time. He had planned the bombing for 9am. He did not want to get there too early—before the Alfred P. Murrah Federal Building in Oklahoma City filled up with people. He wanted his body count.

At least two of the agencies he most despised—the Bureau of Alcohol, Tobacco and Firearms (ATF) and the Drug Enforcement Administration—had offices in the Murrah Building, as did the Secret Service. The other agencies housed there—the Social Security Administration, and the departments of Housing and Urban Development and Agriculture—were all part of a government McVeigh regarded as evil and out of control.

To justify what he was about to do, he summoned up a favorite movie from childhood: *Star Wars*. McVeigh likened himself to Luke Skywalker, the heroic Jedi knight whose attack on the Death Star is the climax of the film. McVeigh dismissed the killing of secretaries, receptionists and other personnel with the same cold-blooded calculation. They were all part of an evil empire.

McVeigh had carefully scouted every aspect of his plan. On a previous trip to Oklahoma City, he had worked out the exact route he would take, looking for speed traps, highway construction, possible road hazards and, especially, underpasses too low for the Ryder truck.

About 8.50am McVeigh entered Oklahoma City, a proud community of 460,000 people. The weather was warm and sunny, the sky a brilliant blue. Most people were just settling in to what promised to be an ordinary workday.

McVeigh wore no expression as he sat at the wheel of the truck. He drove on, scanning his surroundings and reviewing every contingency he might face in the moments ahead.

Expecting to be either captured or killed after the bombing, he had filled a plain white envelope with articles explaining his antigovernment ideology.

No matter how things turned out, he counted on police getting hold of the documents and leaking them to the news media.

At a stoplight he took a moment to cram a pair of green foam ear-plugs into his ears. As the rental vehicle rumbled up Northwest 5th Street, nobody in downtown Oklahoma City thought anything of it. Ryder trucks drove through the city all the time. That was one reason McVeigh had picked it.

He was surprised at how little traffic there was. Keeping his eyes peeled for onlookers, McVeigh pulled to the side of the road, just long enough to take out a lighter and ignite the five-minute fuse to his bomb.

Soon the truck cab filled with the acrid smell of burning gunpowder. As McVeigh continued along Northwest 5th Street, he rolled down both windows to let out some of the smoke.

A block from the target, he stopped for a traffic light. Now he lit a second, shorter fuse—the one he had measured at approximately two minutes.

For 30 seconds, McVeigh sat watching the red light. With both fuses burning and his fingers tight on the steering wheel, he glared up at the light, willing it to change.

When it finally turned green, McVeigh made sure to ease away from the intersection. No stomping on the gas pedal. No frantic movements.

With both fuses burning and his fingers tight on the steering wheel, McVeigh glared at the light, willing it to change.

Approaching the building, he spotted the location he had chosen for the bomb—a drop-off point, several car-lengths long, cut into the sidewalk on the north side of the structure. No other vehicle was there when he arrived. McVeigh breathed a sigh of relief. If the drop-off spot had been filled, he had planned to drive onto the sidewalk and crash his truck into the building. That would not be necessary now.

As calmly as any ordinary deliveryman, McVeigh parked his vehicle. He was right below the tinted windows of the America's Kids day-care center on the second floor.

He looked over his creation one last time. The fuses were burning. The

After the bombing—planted by a young American, the blast that tore off the front of the Murrah Building shook a country's faith in itself.

vehicle was exactly where he wanted it, its back close to the building. He grabbed the envelope full of antigovernment articles, locked the truck and walked away.

McVeigh counted off the seconds to himself as he headed north into an alley. He was about 150 yards from ground zero when he broke into a jog.

That bomb should have blown by now, he thought. For an instant he wondered if something might have gone wrong. Then he heard the roar.

And felt it.

Devastating Blast

When the Murrah Building exploded, it lifted Tim McVeigh an inch off the ground. Even muffled by ear-plugs, the sound was deafening. The blast rocked hundreds of buildings in the downtown area.

Looking up, McVeigh could see the buildings near him wobbling from side to side, plate glass showering down into the street. He felt the concussion buffeting his cheeks.

A live power line snapped and whipped toward him. Some falling bricks struck him in the leg, but he was able to hop out of the way of the power line. Smoke and dust billowed high into the air. Fires erupted.

Just like at Waco, thought McVeigh.

Reap what you sow.

He reached his getaway car. The yellow Mercury was still parked in a lot several blocks from the blast site. He had placed a "Do Not Tow" sign in the windshield. It was still there. No one, it seemed, had messed with it.

But when McVeigh got behind the wheel, the car didn't start. He tried several times; the engine would not turn over.

He stomped the gas pedal to the floor. Finally the engine coughed to life. Tires squealed as he peeled out of the parking lot. *I do not want to get caught in Oklahoma City,* he thought.

The automatic transmission was slipping badly as McVeigh headed north toward Kansas. By 9.10am, eight minutes after the bombing, he was heading out of the city, driving carefully under the speed limit.

An observer watching the scene from a helicopter would have seen many Oklahomans rushing toward the crippled federal office building. They would have seen drivers abandoning cars and running to the blast scene. They would have seen the flashing emergency lights on police cars, firetrucks and ambulances, all heading toward the rising dust and smoke.

McVeigh's bomb killed 167 people, including 19 children aged five and younger; 163 of the victims had been inside the building. A 168th victim died while assisting in rescue efforts. Over half of the dead worked for the federal government. The others did not. Many of the dead would not be positively identified for several days.

In the chaos, few would have noticed an old yellow sedan heading slowly away from the blast site.

Once on the highway, McVeigh watched for helicopters and police cars. Though he wasn't exactly eager to get caught, there was a part of him that was curious to see how things would play out if he did.

He'd put his future in the hands of fate by leaving the Arizona license plate off his car. Ultimately, he figured, some officer would pull him over for the missing plate, but he hoped it would happen in another state. He was counting on the Oklahoma cops being too busy with the bombing to bother with anything else.

McVeigh rolled on through the countryside along Interstate 35. Sixty miles

Image of a nation's grief—fire-fighter Chris Fields cradles the body of one-year-old Baylee Almon, killed in the blast. She was one of 168 victims.

north of Oklahoma City, he saw a highway patrol car by the roadside. A state trooper stood outside the vehicle, looking over a minivan. *Probably a speeding arrest,* McVeigh thought, although he wondered why the troopers would bother with speeders at a time like this. About 20 minutes later McVeigh saw what looked like the same state trooper in his rearview mirror. The cop was in the passing lane, roaring up alongside McVeigh.

The car was almost past him when McVeigh noticed the front end dip slightly. The police cruiser slowed down and fell alongside McVeigh's Mercury.

The trooper at the wheel was Charles J. Hanger, a 19-year police veteran. For Hanger, the morning had already been hectic. Shortly after the bombing, he and other troopers had been directed to hurry to the command post in Oklahoma City. But the order was soon canceled. They already had enough help at the post.

Hanger was indeed the trooper McVeigh had seen by the roadside. He wasn't stopping speeders, though; he'd been helping two women get assistance for their disabled minivan. Then, as Hanger headed back north, he saw McVeigh's car without the license plate.

As he drove wheel-to-wheel with the Mercury, Hanger glanced over and nodded. McVeigh nodded back. The trooper then fell behind him and turned on his emergency flasher, directing him to pull over.

McVeigh complied, easing the right tires of his car onto the grass. It was decision time. He considered pulling out his Glock and killing the trooper. It had a Black Talon bullet, known for expanding with lethal effect on contact, ready in the chamber.

If I want him, I can take him, McVeigh thought.

Minor Misdemeanors

As Hanger stepped out of his car, McVeigh emerged from his as well. He sized up the trooper. If he drew on him, he figured the element of surprise—plus his expertise as a former army marksman—would put the officer at a severe disadvantage.

Then McVeigh thought again: *No, not a state trooper. Stand down.* If Hanger had been a federal agent, McVeigh would have probably started shooting. But he had a grudging respect for local and state cops and their right to do their jobs.

He would not draw his gun on this officer of the law.

For his part, Hanger wondered what McVeigh was up to as he watched the younger man step out. Most people just sat in their cars, nervously waiting for the trooper to approach. Hanger stood behind his open car door, watching McVeigh's hands closely as he came forward.

Cautiously, the trooper began walking toward the other man. He looked at the Mercury. "You don't have a license plate," Hanger said.

McVeigh glanced at the rear bumper of his car. "Huh. No," he said.

The trooper kept a wary eye on him. "Do you have insurance?"

"No, I just bought the car."

"You have a registration? Do you have a bill of sale?"

"Not yet, but I have a license."

McVeigh pulled out his wallet. As he took out his driver's license, Hanger noticed a bulge under McVeigh's windbreaker. "What's that?" he asked.

"I have a gun," McVeigh replied calmly.

Hanger felt for the Glock. Then he pulled out his own gun and pointed it at McVeigh. "Move your hands away, slowly," he instructed. "Get both hands up in the air."

The trooper pointed his gun at McVeigh's head and reached around to remove the Glock from its shoulder holster.

"My gun is loaded," he warned the officer.

"So is mine," Hanger said, and he directed him to put his hands on the trunk of the car and spread his legs.

McVeigh told the officer he would find a clip of ammunition and a knife attached to his belt. Hanger removed them and the Glock, and tossed them onto the shoulder. He then cuffed McVeigh's hands and asked why he was carrying a weapon.

It was his legal right to carry it, he insisted.

"You know, when you carry a gun around like that, one wrong move could get you shot," the trooper told him.

"Possible," McVeigh said.

Hanger marched his handcuffed prisoner to the police cruiser. He then asked the dispatcher to run a computer check on McVeigh. The report came back quickly: no arrest warrants, no criminal record. Timothy McVeigh had never been arrested in his life.

Hanger also gave the dispatcher the Glock's serial number to check. The gun was not stolen.

With McVeigh's permission, the trooper then searched the Mercury but noted nothing unusual except for a sealed white envelope in the front seat. Soon they were heading toward the Noble County jail in Perry, Oklahoma. At about 11am they pulled into the parking lot.

McVeigh took off his jacket, and Hanger got his first look at the odd T-shirt that his prisoner was wearing. The trooper had never seen one like this, with its picture of Lincoln on the front and illustration of a tree on the back. But he didn't really read the slogans.

Marsha Moritz, the jailer, booked McVeigh on four misdemeanor charges: transporting a loaded firearm in a motor vehicle, unlawfully carrying a weapon, failing to display a current license plate, and failing to maintain proof of insurance.

The booking process went routinely until Moritz told McVeigh that she needed to know his next of kin, in case he got sick or something happened to him in jail. After an awkward silence, he gave the name of James Nichols. McVeigh's driver's license listed the Nichols farm in Michigan as his home address.

Moritz took the prisoner's mugshot. In his thick-soled combat boots, McVeigh was well over six foot two. He seemed surprisingly loose for a man being arrested. As Moritz prepared to fingerprint him, he was asked to wipe the perspiration off his hands, as prisoners tend to sweat from nervousness.

"No problem," McVeigh said. "My hands are dry."

The two chatted briefly, McVeigh even kidding around with Moritz a little. But the light mood didn't last long.

A TV set was in the office, and the ongoing broadcast about the bombing cast a pall over everyone in the jail.

McVeigh, pretending to be paying little attention, was watching and listening to every word. His initial reaction to what his bomb had done was disappointment.

Damn, he thought. *The whole building didn't come down.*

McVeigh then heard someone in the jail office mention how horrible it was that the blast had destroyed a day-care center in the federal building, killing a group of children. This news stopped him; he had not planned for children to be among his victims. Then a more cold-blooded reaction kicked in. The deaths of innocent children would overshadow his political message. In the court of public opinion, this would be a disaster for his cause. *The media's going to latch on to that,* he thought.

Defiant stare—in this mugshot, taken at the Noble County jail in Perry, Oklahoma, McVeigh wears his *Sic semper tyrannis* T-shirt.

Everyone in the office listened closely as a TV reporter gave the first sketchy descriptions of a possible suspect: white male, somewhere between five foot nine and six foot one. A deputy looked over and eyeballed McVeigh. "Gee, you're a recent arrival," he said.

"That ain't me," said McVeigh, laughing off the suggestion.

Rescuers were still pulling bodies out of the building. Everyone—both jailers and prisoners alike—watched in stunned disbelief. *How did this happen? Who would do such a thing?* they wondered.

310

McVeigh concentrated, maintaining his poker face. More than anyone, he knew that the answers were elusive. As a psychiatrist would later suggest, the path he had traveled to this point stretched back through his unsettled life: the breakup of his parents, his Gulf War experiences, the tragedy at Waco.

An Unsatisfactory Reality

In many ways Timothy McVeigh was like millions of young, middle-class American men. He had grown up the son of a factory worker, in love with TV, movies and the outdoors. He liked football and comic books about superheroes.

McVeigh was raised in western New York. His mother, Mickey, was a travel agent who loved the excitement of visiting new places. She was boisterous, and enjoyed swapping stories and jokes with friends. In contrast, McVeigh's father, Bill, was shy and quiet, a homebody. He was a caring parent and a good provider, and put in long hours at the factory.

Small and scrawny for his age, Timothy McVeigh was 10 when, in the spring of 1978, his Little League team was having a practice. Tim took the field under the watchful eyes of his father. But the boy's size made him an easy target. Another kid walked up to him and grabbed his baseball cap. The two wound up in a tugging match, until the other boy walloped Tim.

Stunned, the youngster ran to his father's car, hid in the back seat and cried. He was scared and embarrassed: the men of the McVeigh family were not supposed to shed tears. Now here he was, bawling his eyes out.

Indeed, Timothy McVeigh felt like a failure in the eyes of his father. He lacked the aggressive jock mentality, the muscle coordination and the size to be a star athlete; he would come to be known as Noodle McVeigh.

By adolescence, size and coordination caught up with Tim. But his humiliation at the hands of the bully on the baseball field was something he remembered forever. Over time, he developed a seething hatred of bullies—of any person or institution that he perceived to be picking on the weak.

Bill McVeigh, for his part, wished that maintaining the happy family life he cherished was as simple as playing baseball. But his marriage of 13 years was unraveling.

The truth was, Mickey McVeigh was bored with Bill. Working long hours, he was hardly ever around. And at times, despite his congenial nature, he had a nasty temper. He could explode in anger about something as minor as misplacing his car keys.

The fundamental differences between him and his wife finally became too much. In December 1979 the couple separated, letting the children decide where they wanted to live.

Their two daughters, Patty and Jennifer, wanted to stay together with their mother. But Tim cast his lot with his father.

"I don't want Dad to be alone," he said.

The real problem, Tim McVeigh said later, was that he never really felt close to his parents. With both of them working full time, he never had an adult to talk with when he came home from school.

Even when Tim's mother returned to try to work out her differences with Bill, it didn't bring the boy any closer to his family. The only person he would actually and unabashedly say he loved was his paternal grandfather, Ed McVeigh.

Tim was devoted to the graying and bespectacled older man, and his feelings were met with unconditional love. Their relationship revolved around a common interest: guns. On

Different paths—Patty McVeigh would grow up to save lives as a nurse. Her brother, Tim, would choose the opposite course.

regular outings the two would walk beside the Erie Canal to a ravine where they practiced target shooting with a .22-caliber rifle. There Grandpa McVeigh would offer bits of wisdom.

"When you're carrying a gun on the road, the ammunition is always in your back pocket," Ed would say. "When you're shooting, make sure you have a backstop and consider the possibility of a bullet ricocheting."

Again and again Tim saw things in his grandpa that he wished he could see in his dad. The words *I love you* never rolled easily off shy Bill McVeigh's tongue. So long as he provided the necessities—a good home, food and a few extras—Bill felt his actions bespoke love.

Blessed with a high IQ, Tim stayed out of trouble in school. He became a devotee of action heroes and filled his bedroom with boxes of superhero comics. These fantasy adventures were a welcome distraction from the furious words he heard more and more often coming from his parents' bedroom. Some nights he lay in bed frightened; at times his parents seemed so angry he feared they might kill each other.

Looking increasingly to escape, Tim took refuge in imaginary games. One neighbor, Liz McDermott, recalled that when the youngster came over, he'd transform the house into a battleground filled with GI Joe action figures. Tim also engineered elaborate games of flashlight tag. He would draw down the shades and turn off the lights, then he'd move through the house trying to catch the others with the flashlight beam. "We'd fall on the floor and freeze for a while," his younger sister, Jennifer, recalled.

But his superhero imaginings were only temporary, and Tim would always find himself once more facing an unsatisfactory reality.

Something Missing

When the McVeighs' marriage ended for good in 1986, Tim was a senior in high school. It was during this year that he found Sarah, his first real girlfriend. A senior at nearby Sweet Home High School, she thought he was "loud and goofy" sometimes, like a lot of boys she knew, but he could also be nice and thoughtful.

By this time Tim had acquired an old Ford Thunderbird and he drove it very fast, which both scared and thrilled Sarah.

Like Tim, she had endured the divorce of her parents. She felt that his experience had left him feeling "lost," and she sensed the anger he harbored toward his mother. Often, Sarah noticed, he was the only person at his house. It was almost like Tim was raising himself.

No ties—McVeigh in 1986 with his grandfather, Ed. After Ed died, Tim no longer cared how his actions would impact on his family.

For six months they became very close, going steady, attending the senior prom together. But not long after his graduation, Tim abruptly broke off the relationship. "I'm not ready to get serious," he explained.

After high school he briefly attended a business school, aided by a small scholarship, but soon quit, opting to work instead. For self-education he read gun magazines and ordered books from back-page ads. One title that captivated him was *To Ride, Shoot Straight, and Speak the Truth* by Jeff Cooper, an expert on self-defense and firearms. A sort of training manual, the book's broader messages resonated in Tim's fertile young mind. He liked the idea of going through life in a combat mind-set, aware of his surroundings at all times.

313

The Turner Diaries was another book that hit a nerve. The 1978 novel by white supremacist William L. Pierce told the story of Earl Turner, a gun enthusiast who reacts to tighter firearms laws by making a truck-bomb and destroying FBI headquarters in Washington.

The possibility that Congress and federal agents might take guns away from law-abiding citizens seemed a very real threat to Tim. He decided to start collecting his own firearms. To finance his appetite, he became an armed security guard.

At work his friends called him "The Kid," as in "Billy the Kid." Once, as a joke, he showed up at work dressed like a gunslinger, a bandoleer filled with shotgun shells strapped across his chest. But it was more than just image that earned McVeigh his outlaw nickname. He could outshoot just about everyone; hours of practice had given him a deadeye aim.

Tim enjoyed his guns and new-found independence, but he still felt something was missing from his life. When a family friend suggested he enlist in the military, he listened carefully. By May 1988 he had made up his mind.

"When are you going?" asked Bill McVeigh, who was accustomed to his son's independent ways.

"Tomorrow," Tim replied.

Killing Zone

His first stop was Fort Benning, Georgia, where he arrived for three months of training. McVeigh threw himself into army life. He enjoyed it all—the 5am wake-ups, the crass jokes, even the uniform inspections. Mostly he loved anything to do with firearms.

William David Dilly, his room-mate for over a year, saw potential in McVeigh, who had struck him as frail and meek when he first got there. Dilly noticed the attention McVeigh paid to detail, and his desire to perform his duties better than anyone else.

McVeigh reveled in things that other recruits seemed to hate—long marches in the scorching sun, crawling on his belly under the barbed wire. What Tim really loved was pulling night guard duty, when he could be alone with nature, gazing in silence at a sky so rich and black that he could see the outlines of the Milky Way.

At Fort Benning, McVeigh also formed a powerful bond with Terry Lynn Nichols, a Michigan native who at 33 was the oldest recruit in the company. An intense, oddly compelling man, Nichols had had a number of jobs before the army, and made it clear he deeply disliked the government.

With his spectacles and slight build, he looked no more imposing than Woody Allen in an army uniform. But he had a commanding presence and carried himself with an air of maturity that made McVeigh and others look up to him.

"Two days into training, Tim and Terry were like brothers," Dilly said. "They were drawn to each other. It was almost like Tim idolized Terry."

One sweltering afternoon, the recruits were out on a long march when they stopped for a rest. McVeigh and another soldier, a powerfully built man who weighed around 250 pounds, got into a quarrel. The recruit gave McVeigh a shove and brought up his fists.

McVeigh didn't call for his drill sergeant. He called for his friend.

"Nichols came running over, got right into the middle of it and broke it up," another soldier recalled. "He was not a wimp."

After Fort Benning, McVeigh headed off to Fort Riley, Kansas, for more training with the First Infantry Division. Joining him were Nichols and another soldier, Michael J. Fortier, an Arizona native who shared many of McVeigh's political views.

At Fort Riley, McVeigh was devoted—fanatically, some would say—to becoming the best soldier on the entire base. He even went to the expense of keeping a separate uniform, specially starched and dry-cleaned, and buying an extra pair of boots and additional gear just so he could have them in immaculate condition for inspections.

His fellow soldiers noticed he kept dozens of books and magazines on firearms stacked next to his bunk. Though not particularly talkative, whenever the subject of gun rights came up, McVeigh's blue eyes would flash in anger. He would then launch into intense speeches about guns, the Declaration of Independence, and Revolutionary War patriots—men who stood for liberty and freedom from government oppression, no matter what the cost.

Determined to be the top gunner in his unit, McVeigh trained hard on Bradley fighting vehicles. Eventually, he nailed a perfect score of 1000—the best in his battalion.

His sterling record resulted in his receiving orders to try out for the army's elite Special Forces, better known as the Green Berets. But before he could report, Iraq's dictator, Saddam Hussein, invaded Kuwait, and McVeigh's company was told to prepare for combat duty in the Persian Gulf.

The young soldier did not like to see the United States meddling in the affairs of smaller nations. At the same time, Saddam appeared to be the kind of leader he hated most—a bully, brutally attacking a smaller and weaker neighbor. Someone had to stand up to him, McVeigh figured.

He arrived in Saudi Arabia in January 1991, part of a huge Allied force. On February 24 a huge explosion in the pre-dawn hours told McVeigh that he was about to get his chance to fight.

On the second day of the ground war, his crew spotted a dug-in enemy machine-gun nest more than a mile away. McVeigh's platoon leader ordered him to fire.

Pressing his forehead against the viewfinder, Sergeant McVeigh zeroed in on the target, adjusting his shot to allow for the movement of the Bradley. An Iraqi soldier popped his head up for a second. McVeigh fired, and everything above the soldier's shoulders disappeared. The same shot, a 25-mm high-explosive round, killed another Iraqi soldier standing a few feet away.

"Did you see that?" a fellow gunner exclaimed. "Great shot!"

Yet the would-be Rambo was emotionally torn about what he had done. This was the first time he had fired at a human being. In a way, it had been a great thrill, putting his skills to the test and succeeding. But later, McVeigh found this first taste of killing made him angry and uncomfortable.

The carnage he saw in the hundred-hour war left him with a feeling of sorrow. Beating the Iraqis was almost too easy. It rankled McVeigh further to be part of a United Nations force that, he feared, was eventually planning to take over the world.

Despite his misgivings, the sergeant was proud of the Allied victory, and in late March

Dead shot—Sergeant McVeigh, dispatched to the Persian Gulf in 1991, felt that beating the Iraqis was almost too easy.

1991 he got some good news. He was ordered back to the United States, to the Special Forces Selection and Assessment Course at Fort Bragg, North Carolina. At last he had his chance to become a Green Beret. His future was brimming with promise.

Rude Awakening

On the flight to North Carolina, McVeigh sat with a fellow serviceman. Civilian passengers noticed McVeigh's clothes and haircut. "Hey," one man asked, "were you over there?"

"Yes, I was," McVeigh replied, beaming. When the pilot heard a couple of Desert Storm vets were aboard the plane, he made an announcement over the PA honoring the soldiers, "who have just come back from the Gulf War."

What followed was a show of adulation the likes of which Americans usually reserve for their top athletes and movie stars. Passengers got out of their seats and stood in line in the aisle to shake hands with the two soldiers.

Then the plane touched down in Fayetteville, North Carolina, and the high times were over. There were no slaps on the back from the Green Berets. Since the day he enlisted, McVeigh had been hoping for a chance to join one of these special units. But once he reported to Fort Bragg, he quickly realized he wasn't ready.

The three months he spent in the Persian Gulf had broken him down, physically and emotionally. The commanding officers recognized this difficulty, and they called all the Gulf War veterans together, inviting them to defer their tryouts.

"No way," one of the proud Desert Storm vets yelled out. "We're ready!"

Peer pressure took hold. Asking to delay the tryout might be seen as a sign of weakness, McVeigh thought. He decided to go ahead.

It was a mistake—and a critical one. The grueling 24-day program was designed to push the soldiers much further than anything they had seen in basic training. Just two days into the assessment program, McVeigh surrendered. Though still a couple of weeks short of his 23rd birthday, he felt like a tired old man.

"I just can't hack it," McVeigh told the commanding officer. His three years in the military had been one success after another, but now his star was falling. By late 1991, tired and disillusioned, he decided to leave the army altogether.

When he returned home to Pendleton, McVeigh still had high expectations for his future. After all, he had gone off to war and come back with a chestful of medals. But it didn't work out that way. Western New York, its economy still struggling, didn't have much to offer. A disappointed McVeigh soon found himself trading in his crisp green army uniform for the dull shirt and slacks of a security guard.

He made the best of it, but the demanding schedule—80 hours some weeks—took a toll. Becoming angry and sullen, he began to request posts giving him the least possible exposure to the public.

During this time, McVeigh was back staying with his father. Even with just three people living there—Bill, Tim and Jennifer, who had rejoined her father—the little house felt crowded. Tim McVeigh was unable to get enough rest, and he grew increasingly irritable. A disheartening realization finally hit him: *I don't fit in here anymore.*

Downward Spin

Less than three months after returning from the army, McVeigh hurried out of his father's house one snowy day in a state of panic, dressed only in sweatpants. He had to get away, but where? He climbed into his car and drove over to his grandfather's home. Tears streaming down his face, McVeigh knocked on the door.

"Timmy, what are you doing?" said Ed McVeigh, ushering him inside. He saw the tears. His grandson was having a breakdown.

"Tim," Ed said, "what's wrong?"

"Grandpa . . . I can't tell you," McVeigh answered.

"Do I need to call someone?" asked Ed.

"No. Just leave me alone. I'll get through it."

Ed suggested his grandson come in and lie down for a while. As Tim lay there, he was overcome by dark thoughts. He even considered killing himself, but stopped because he knew how much it would hurt his grandfather. Finally, his anxiety subsiding, he fell into a deep sleep.

Later Tim would come to believe he had suffered from post-traumatic stress disorder brought on by the Gulf War. Whatever the cause of his depression, he began reading more antigovernment books and sharing them with his inquisitive younger sister. Some of the literature struck Jennifer as bizarre, but she looked up to her older brother and was flattered he would share his political views with her.

In the summer of 1992 McVeigh pointed to the events of Ruby Ridge, Idaho, as proof that his theories were correct. On August 21 federal agents got into a shoot-out at the cabin of Randy Weaver, a white separatist accused of selling illegal shotguns to a government informant. By the time Weaver was finally arrested, his wife and son and a US marshal had been killed.

Ruby Ridge became a rallying cry for militia and survivalist groups, and reinforced McVeigh's belief that America was becoming a police state. Yet unlike Jennifer, who hung on her brother's every word, Bill McVeigh had little interest in his son's views. The American flag proudly flying from a pole in the center of his front lawn left no question where Bill stood.

He watched in alarm as his son turned into a harsh critic of the government he had once served. Now, whenever Tim saw a newscast detailing some inept government operation, or any example of faltering leadership, he'd shout and throw things at the TV.

Bill, who rarely said an unkind word about anyone, did little to reproach his son. "Timmy is strong-willed" was all he could find to say.

Frustrated and restless, Tim McVeigh felt he had to make a change. He told his dad he was leaving New York to search for a place where he could find more personal freedom. Tim spent the next 26 months traveling to some 40 states, mostly from gun show to gun show, selling books and survival items.

During this time something happened that would galvanize him. In February 1993 federal agents raided the home and church of a religious group known as the Branch Davidians in Waco, Texas. Agents from the ATF arrived to execute a search warrant for illegal weapons. A shoot-out erupted, taking the lives of four agents and injuring more than a dozen. On the Branch Davidian side, six people died and more were wounded, including David Koresh, their strange and charismatic leader.

The ATF then retreated, and Koresh and his followers remained inside their compound.

Nobody in America followed the stand-off closer than McVeigh. Day after day he devoured every article and broadcast account he could find. Finally, he decided he had to go see for himself. He packed up his car with a supply of antigovernment materials and headed for Waco.

When he arrived, he was stopped at a checkpoint about three miles from the compound.

As McVeigh reluctantly turned his car around, he watched as the federal agents gathered in a circle. His mind swung into military mode. *I could take them all out with one hand grenade,* he thought.

McVeigh left Waco after a few days. He attended a gun show in Tulsa, and finally found his way to the farm of army buddy Terry Nichols, who lived with his mother in Decker, Michigan.

With the help of Terry and his brother James, McVeigh hoped to learn how to live self-sufficiently off the land.

On the afternoon of April 19, 1993, as McVeigh was changing the oil in his car, a voice hollered from inside the farmhouse, "Tim! Tim! Get in here! It's on fire!"

McVeigh raced inside. On the TV the Branch Davidian complex was burning. He stood, transfixed, in the parlor with the Nichols brothers, watching the flames and the armored vehicles ramming the walls.

The blaze in Waco, more than any single event, was a turning point in McVeigh's life. He felt it epitomized the arrogance of federal law-enforcement agents in dealing with the public—everything that was wrong with intrusive government.

Last, Thin Thread

A month later McVeigh traveled to Kingman, Arizona, to visit his old friend Michael Fortier. His hatred for the government had taken on a sharp new edge, and he angrily shared his views with his friend.

McVeigh continued to bounce from one gun show to the next, from one state to the next. He was still seething about Waco when news hit the gun-show circuit in September 1994 that a new assault-weapons ban was becoming law. To McVeigh, his heritage, his income and perhaps his very life were threatened. It was time to take action.

Back in Kingman, McVeigh revealed to Michael Fortier that he was going to blow up a federal building, and he extended an invitation for Fortier to join him.

"No," his friend answered. "I would never do anything like that, unless there was a tank in my front yard."

Undaunted, on October 4, 1994, McVeigh signed a rental agreement for a storage locker in Kingman. Soon afterward, McVeigh appeared at Fortier's home and told Michael he wanted to show him something. Fortier came outside and found Terry Nichols waiting for them in his pickup. They drove to the storage unit, where McVeigh pulled back a blanket covering a stack of boxes. Fortier saw that the top box contained explosives.

McVeigh pulled back a blanket covering a stack of boxes. The top box contained explosives.

McVeigh said the explosives had come from a quarry in Marion, Kansas, near where Nichols was now living. He described how, a few nights earlier, he and Nichols had robbed it.

It was drizzling when the two men arrived at the quarry. McVeigh walked around each of the lockers to make sure there weren't any burglar alarms. He drilled out the padlocks, and the door swung open. His flashlight shined on crates of Tovex, a high-explosive gel shaped like 16-inch-long sausages.

McVeigh carefully examined each 55-pound box, checking the dates. He knew the older the material, the less effective it was. He grabbed seven of the fresher boxes. *Like shopping for milk,* he thought.

Then McVeigh and Nichols drove in separate vehicles to Kingman. If Kansas authorities made a big deal of the theft, McVeigh figured, they'd be much better off stashing the explosives a few states away in Arizona.

He had already managed to assemble 4,000 pounds of ammonium nitrate, and was now eager to conduct a test of the ingredients he planned to use in his bomb's main charge.

He loaded the materials in a truck and invited Fortier to watch the detonation. Fortier refused, commenting, "It looks like a lot of trouble." So McVeigh, on his own, exploded the bomb out in the desert.

Later, alone with Fortier and his wife, Lori, McVeigh told them that he had figured out how to convert a truck into a bomb. He had also chosen a target: the Alfred P. Murrah Federal Building in Oklahoma City. The explosion would occur on the second anniversary of Waco: April 19, 1995.

"What about all the people?" Fortier asked.

"Think about the people as if they were storm troopers in *Star Wars*," McVeigh answered. "They may be individually innocent, but they are guilty because they work for the evil Empire."

Before settling on Oklahoma City, McVeigh's possible targets included federal buildings in Arkansas, Missouri, Arizona and Texas. He chose the Murrah Building for several reasons. The front of the structure was made of glass, which would shatter from the explosion. The parking lot across the street would minimize collateral damage—deaths and injuries to people in nearby nonfederal buildings. This was something, McVeigh claimed, he was genuinely concerned about.

But another colder calculation influenced his final choice—the photo opportunities. He wanted a site with open space around it, to allow for the best possible news photos and television footage. He wanted to create a stark, horrifying image that would make everyone who saw it stop and take notice.

In late October, McVeigh's plans were disrupted when he got the news that his grandfather, Ed, had died. McVeigh returned home to Pendleton to help his father.

In a sense, his grandfather's death freed him. He no longer had to worry about him ever finding out about his grandson's involvement in the bombing. McVeigh knew the crime would have emotionally destroyed Ed, but now that thin thread of restraint was gone.

The rest of the family was a different matter. As long as none of them wound up being thrown in prison, McVeigh could live with the consequences.

He did try to prepare Jennifer for his plan to go afoul of the law, promising in a letter "something big is going to happen in the month of the Bull"—which she understood to mean April.

A TWISTED MIND

Three years before the Oklahoma City bombing, on February 11, 1992, the Lockport, New York, *Union-Sun & Journal* published a letter from Timothy McVeigh. After spouting off about a variety of issues, ranging from government and its leaders to crime, taxes and racism, McVeigh concluded:

> America is in serious decline! We have no proverbial tea to dump, should we instead sink a ship full of Japanese imports? Is a Civil War Imminent? Do we have to shed blood to reform the current system? I hope it doesn't come to that. But it might.

In February 1995, while staying in Arizona, McVeigh wrote this disturbing passage in a letter to a friend:

> Hell, you only live once and I KNOW you know it's better to burn out, then …… rot away in some nursing home. My philosophy is the same — in only a short 1-2 years, my body will slowly start giving away — first maybe knee pains, or back pains. Might as well do some good while I can be 100% effective! My whole mindset has shifted from intellectual to … animal, (Rip the bastards heads off.)

In another letter to his sister he wrote: "Why am I running? I am trying to keep my path 'cool,' so in case someone is looking to 'shut up someone who knows too much' I will not be easy to find. I have also been establishing a network of friends so when I go completely underground, it will be very difficult for anyone to find me."

Later he warned her to be careful: "private investigators" might be tailing her into bars.

A Frightening Rage

On Friday, April 14, 1995, McVeigh registered at the Dreamland Motel in Junction City, Kansas, giving the Nichols farm in Michigan as his address. The next morning he finalized the rental of a 20-foot Ryder truck, using the name Robert D. Kling. On Easter Sunday, McVeigh arranged to meet Terry Nichols at a pizzeria. But Nichols failed to show.

In the last few weeks McVeigh had begun to suspect that his friend's enthusiasm for the bombing had begun to wane. As he waited impatiently, his anger grew.

Infuriated, McVeigh finally called him. When he answered, McVeigh let loose, screaming so loud that Nichols's son, Josh, could hear his voice through the phone 10 feet away. McVeigh cursed Nichols, threatening him and his family. "Get in your f—— truck," he screamed. "Now! This is for keeps!"

Finally Nichols gave in, perhaps afraid that McVeigh would make good his threats.

The men arrived in Oklahoma City in the evening. McVeigh parked his yellow Mercury, the getaway car, several blocks from the Murrah Building. He placed a note on the windshield: *Not Abandoned. Please Do Not Tow. Will Move by April 23 (Needs Battery & Cable).*

The two then drove back to Kansas in Nichols's pickup. The next day McVeigh got the Ryder truck, and the following morning he and Nichols headed for Geary Lake. Once by the lake, McVeigh later said, the two men went to work in the back of the truck. McVeigh combined nitromethane fluid with ammonium nitrate fertilizer. It was a big job. The thirteen 55-gallon drums were each large enough to hold several bags of fertilizer and about 100 pounds of liquid fuel.

At about 9am McVeigh and Nichols saw a man and boy unexpectedly launch a boat onto the lake's choppy waters and start fishing offshore.

McVeigh closed the side door and cracked open the rear roll-up door of the truck, letting in just enough light for them to continue their work. Every few minutes McVeigh peeked outside to make sure the fisherman and his young companion weren't coming over.

Luckily for them, they didn't. McVeigh later admitted he was prepared to murder the fisherman if he got too curious.

The boy was a different story. McVeigh decided he would let him live. He would tie him up and hide him, and by the time the boy was discovered, McVeigh would be far away.

As work continued, the barrels were roughly arranged to form a letter T, with the top flush against the front of the cargo-bay wall closest to the truck's cab. The 7,000 pounds needed to be equally distributed, McVeigh realized, or the truck might flip over.

He then set up the dual ignition system he had designed. There would be a two-minute fuse, as well as a second, five-minute fuse, which would serve as a back-up.

The job of mixing the bomb completed, McVeigh wiped down the inside of the truck's cab for fingerprints. Then he changed into a fresh set of clothes, put on a pair of gloves and climbed back into the cab. More than three hours had passed since he and Nichols had started building the bomb. Now they parted company; it was the last time they would see each other as free, unshackled men.

Leaving Geary Lake, McVeigh drove into Oklahoma and headed south, stopping for the night in a small gravel lot near a roadside motel.

When dawn broke on Wednesday, April 19, McVeigh arose and set his sights southward. Just hours later, he would shower hell on Oklahoma City.

"We found him!"

Waking up in his cell on the morning of April 21, two days after the bombing, McVeigh wondered why federal agents hadn't come for him yet. Hadn't they discovered that stuff in his getaway car?

He would soon find out. Hundreds of federal agents and police officers had begun chasing leads all across the United States, hoping for a break that would lead them to the Murrah Building bomber.

To many observers—from politicians to average citizens—the obvious assumption was that foreign terrorists were responsible. After all, the bombing of the World Trade Center had been masterminded by Arab extremists operating out of New Jersey.

However, at the FBI's Behavioral Science Unit in Quantico, Virginia, Special Agent Clinton R. Van Zandt was offering a different opinion. Asked to put together a psychological profile of the Oklahoma bomber, Van Zandt said immediately that the date—April 19, the anniversary of the deaths at Waco—was the key.

"You're going to have a white male, acting alone, or with one other person," Van Zandt told colleagues. "He'll be in his mid-twenties. He'll have military experience and be a fringe member of some militia group. He'll be angry at the government for what happened at Ruby Ridge and Waco."

The first break was recovering the 250-pound rear axle from the Ryder truck, which hurtled through the air for a full city block before landing on a Ford Festiva. Federal agents found a confidential vehicle identification number stamped on the axle. Later, Oklahoma County sheriff's deputies digging through the rubble found the rear bumper from the same truck, its Florida license plate intact.

A series of computer checks showed that the axle and bumper came from a truck owned by Ryder Rental Inc., of Miami. The 1993 Ford truck, with a 20-foot cargo box, had been rented two days earlier at a body shop in Junction City, Kansas. The renter was someone named Robert Kling.

Less than eight hours after the bombing, agents were on their way to Junction City to talk with the shop's owner.

The next morning, using information from workers who had seen Robert Kling, an FBI artist drew up composite sketches of both him and another man who was in the shop. The possible suspects were designated John Doe No. 1 and John Doe No. 2.

The evening after the bombing, agents hit pay dirt at the Dreamland Motel. The manager recognized John Doe No. 1.

Agents spent the day taking the sketches door-to-door through the Junction City area. On Thursday, April 20, the evening after the bombing, they hit pay dirt at the Dreamland Motel. The manager recognized John Doe No. 1 as a recent guest. But she didn't know him as Robert Kling. She knew him as Timothy McVeigh.

And yes, she recalled, she saw him in a Ryder truck, one of those big yellow rentals. And he had an old yellow Mercury too. The authorities had their suspect.

And soon they had another lead. When he registered for his motel room, McVeigh had listed his residence as the Nichols family farm in Decker, Michigan. Before long, investigators would be looking in the direction of his old army buddy, Terry Nichols.

McVeigh was now the subject of an intense manhunt. A huge task force of investigators, working out of Oklahoma City, began making phone calls to police stations throughout the state.

Maybe, the investigators thought, this guy was already sitting in a jail somewhere.

Again, a computer came through. A check with the National Crime Information Center at FBI headquarters in Washington showed that less than two hours after the bombing, an Oklahoma trooper named Hanger had run a computer check on one Timothy McVeigh.

On Friday morning, two days after the bombing, an ATF agent called the Noble County sheriff's office. Did the sheriff's department know anything about this Timothy McVeigh?

The sheriff, Jerry R. Cook, remembered the name. He checked his records, then said, "Yeah. We got him incarcerated."

"Put a hold on him!" the ATF agent told Sheriff Cook. "Don't let him go."

In the task-force office in Oklahoma City, agents shouted out, "We found him! We found him!" Within minutes several of them bolted from the room for a waiting helicopter. Meanwhile, others started typing up an arrest warrant. Later one would also be drawn up for Terry Nichols.

Co-conspirator—Terry Nichols's mild appearance masked a towering rage against the American government.

McVeigh knew nothing of this as he sat in his cell on April 21, waiting to appear on his misdemeanor charges before a county judge. Assistant district attorney Mark Gibson would prosecute the case. The appearance was expected to be brief. More than likely, the judge would release McVeigh on minimal bail. The matter was about as routine as it could get.

Gibson stood in the courtroom, waiting for the court session to begin. Sheriff Cook walked in and handed him a note.

"This guy, McVeigh, is the one the FBI has been looking for in the bombing case," the note said. "We need to keep him in custody."

Gibson looked at the sheriff. "You're yanking my chain," he said.

"No, I'm not," Cook said.

There was a prickly new vibration in the jail, and McVeigh instantly picked up on it. He could sense a change in the demeanor of the employees and the other prisoners as well. The people around him, he noticed, were giving him sideways glances.

McVeigh could sense a change in the demeanor of the employees and other prisoners. People were giving him sideways glances.

It's happening, he told himself.

McVeigh could see that word was getting around fast. One by one, the four prisoners who shared the cellblock with him were taken away for a few minutes.

They're questioning these guys, asking them if I made any admissions about the bombing, McVeigh thought.

He looked out of a window and saw a police officer on the roof of a nearby building.

A prisoner hollered to McVeigh, "Hey, dude, did you do it? Are you the bomber?"

He didn't answer.

Overwhelming sorrow—mourners at a makeshift memorial for the bombing victims, during McVeigh's 1997 trial. Their lives had been changed forever.

"McVeigh," a deputy said, "there are some government agents here. They want to talk with you." McVeigh agreed to see the agents; he wanted to find out what the government was up to.

Two FBI men from the bombing task force, Special Agents Floyd Zimms and James Norman, Jr, were waiting in a room for him. As he walked in, wearing handcuffs, McVeigh looked around. He bent down to look under a table for recording devices. Finding none, he sat down at the table. He was in combat mind-set, but working hard to control his emotions. These were federal agents: he was determined not to show signs of weakness or give them any satisfaction.

"Any idea why the FBI wants to talk to you?" Zimms asked him.

"That thing in Oklahoma City, I guess," McVeigh said.

327

"Exactly right," Zimms replied. "Our investigation has showed you may have information about the bombing. Before we ask you questions about it, I'm going to read you your rights."

McVeigh gave the agents his name, height and weight.

"Place of birth?" one agent asked.

McVeigh refused to answer. "I guess I shouldn't talk to you guys without talking to a lawyer first," he said.

"I just want to tell you what's happening right now," Zimms said. "Federal charges are being filed against you in connection with this bombing. Later today, you'll be transported back to Oklahoma City."

McVeigh's face stayed blank, expressionless.

As they prepared for the journey, McVeigh became concerned about his safety. Already an angry mob was gathering outside.

"Can I have a bulletproof vest?" McVeigh asked. No, he was told. None was available.

McVeigh still had to appear before the judge on the charges from the Hanger arrest. A guard came to take him to court and—except for the large number of deputies in the courtroom—the matter was handled routinely. During the proceeding McVeigh was asked where he lived.

"I really don't live anywhere," he said. Assistant D.A. Gibson recognized McVeigh's military bearing. He also noticed the cold, soulless look in the prisoner's eyes, which would linger in his mind.

By 5pm, 56 hours after the bombing, a team of agents from the FBI and ATF had arrived, with orders to bring McVeigh back to Oklahoma City. Another team had already secured his getaway car, which had been left by the highway, completely unattended, for more than two days.

No remorse—McVeigh (in 1997 photograph) refused to apologize for his crime. A prison inmate asked him where he had gone wrong. McVeigh replied: "I didn't."

Later the FBI would find and open the white envelope packed with the antigovernment materials McVeigh had left behind.

A convoy of vehicles pulled up outside the courthouse to await the prisoner's emergence. The world now got its first look at the bomber. McVeigh was still wearing the orange jail jumpsuit as he left the courthouse. The news photos and videos sent around the globe by satellite showed the prisoner, tall, wiry and grim, his eyes cold and narrow.

As cameras whirred, McVeigh squinted into the afternoon sun. He scanned the buildings for snipers, moving his eyes slowly from left to right and then up and down in a Z pattern he'd learned in the army.

If there's a sniper, he'll be standing back, McVeigh thought. *He won't be hanging the gun barrel out the window where everyone can see it.*

He heard the screams of the crowd as he made his way toward a van, his shackled feet unable to move quickly. "Look over here," one man shouted, cursing at him. "Baby killer! Look me in the eye!"

McVeigh did not turn his head, nor hunch his shoulders. He walked erect, still scanning the area. He and a team of federal agents got into the van and left, as millions of Americans tuned in to see him on the evening news.

Guilty As Charged

United States magistrate Judge Ronald J. Howland called the hearing to order at 8.30pm on April 21, almost 60 hours after the bombing. Prosecutors introduced the FBI arrest warrant accusing McVeigh of using an explosive device to "maliciously damage or destroy" the Murrah Building.

McVeigh sat ramrod straight, looking forward most of the time. With his court-appointed defense lawyers beside him, the accused bomber told the judge that he understood the charges.

Afterward marshals took McVeigh to a nearby federal prison, a medium-security facility in El Reno, Oklahoma.

On August 10, 1995, a federal grand jury indicted McVeigh. He was accused of using a weapon of mass destruction to "kill and injure innocent persons and to damage property of the United States."

McVeigh's new court-appointed attorney, Stephen Jones, brought in a psychiatrist to help determine whether McVeigh was competent to stand trial.

The doctor talked with the prisoner for nearly 25 hours, but found no signs of remorse as McVeigh dispassionately discussed the bombing.

"I expect to be convicted, and I expect to receive the death penalty," McVeigh told the psychiatrist.

He was right. In June of 1997 a federal-court jury in Denver found him guilty. A few days later, they sentenced him to death.

His fellow conspirator, Terry Nichols, would be sentenced to life in prison. Nichols continues to proclaim his innocence even as he faces a separate state trial for 160 counts of capital murder. Michael Fortier later received 12 years for crimes including failing to warn the government of the bombing.

In his summation during the McVeigh trial, prosecutor Larry Mackey lashed out at the defendant for the T-shirt he wore on the day of the bombing, and its slogan celebrating the spilling of patriots' and tyrants' blood. The 168 people who were killed were not tyrants, the prosecutor said. McVeigh had a right to protest the events at Ruby Ridge and Waco, he allowed, but he had no right to turn his political agenda into an assault on innocent people.

"In America," Mackey said, "everybody has a right to their beliefs, a right to think and say what they do. This is not a prosecution of Tim McVeigh for his political beliefs. This is a prosecution of Tim McVeigh because of what he did. He committed murder."

Mackey asked jurors to take one more thought with them to the deliberation room. "Who are the real patriots?" he asked. "And who is the traitor?"

When they were finished, 12 jurors, 12 of Timothy McVeigh's fellow citizens, gave him their answer.

Timothy McVeigh was executed by lethal injection at Terre Haute prison, Indiana, on June 11, 2001. On May 13, 2003, a judge ruled that Terry Nichols, already serving a life sentence in federal prison, must stand trial in a state court on 160 counts of first-degree murder. Michael Fortier's lawyers are appealing against Fortier's 12-year sentence.

THE REDEMPTION OF ENZO LO SICCO

Christopher Matthews

Innocenzo Lo Sicco had been employed in the building trade for years, and then, at the age of 40, he had achieved his dream. He had become his own boss. He knew he could be a successful developer, and he knew that, on the quiet, he'd have to pay his dues to the Mafia. This was Sicily, after all. But it wasn't so simple. For years he suffered in silence, and then misery struck deep into the heart of his family . . .

Innocenzo Lo Sicco was strolling down a narrow street in Florence when his gaze fell on the little stone plaque. It was set into a historic wall, just around the corner from the famed Uffizi Gallery, one of the world's greatest treasure houses of Renaissance art.

His curiosity aroused, the businessman from Palermo came closer to the spot where, three years before, a bomb planted by the Mafia had exploded and killed five people, one of them a baby girl.

"On 27.5.1993," the inscription on the plaque read, "a murdering bomb ended the life of a little poetess (Nadia Nencioni), and of her infant sister Caterina, of her parents Fabrizio and Angela-Maria and of Dario Capolicchio, a student. They live on in the hearts of all Florentines."

Standing there on that summer day, Enzo, as he is known to his friends, was terrified by what he knew he must do next. And yet, strangely, he also felt something he hadn't felt for years: exhilaration.

Five years before, the future had seemed so bright. Enzo was in his early forties, a lifelong construction executive who'd always dreamed of being his own boss—and his dream was coming true.

The wiry man with close-cropped black hair knew the building trade inside and out. He had a gift for resolving the endless problems that came up; he was sure he could be a successful developer. And so, cashing in his savings, Enzo set up a business in Palermo.

At a celebration dinner with his wife Rosalia and children Giuseppe, 15, and Valentina, 12, he raised his glass in a toast. "To the new business. To us."

His first project was a small apartment building close to the railway station. The land was cheap and the prospects were good. All he needed was to get permission—and make a payoff—to the Mafiosi.

This was Sicily after all; Enzo knew the score. Still, he wasn't concerned. Through an intermediary he contacted a man known to have links with the local Mafia, who officially made his living as a lawyer. The terms were easy: he had only to use certain firms as his suppliers. Work began.

Gazing over the site each morning, Enzo felt proud of his little kingdom with its churning concrete mixer, its heaps of sand and gravel, its brawny labourers pushing wheelbarrows and nailing planks. Then a man named Sebastiano Lombardo showed up.

You made a serious mistake, he said: the Gravianos should have been consulted. "Don't ever do anything like that again," Lombardo warned.

Giuseppe and Filippo Graviano were known to be gangsters—men so terrifying that people wouldn't speak their names, referring to them instead as "the lads." They controlled the Brancaccio district on the eastern side of the city of Palermo, where he, Enzo, lived; and Enzo avoided building there because of them.

Yet the message he'd just received was clear. The Gravianos didn't just own territory. They owned him.

Mafia control—the Graviano gangsters controlled the district of Palermo where Enzo lived, and wanted a stake in his business.

In mid 1992, a site came up for development on Corso dei Mille, the broad avenue on which Enzo lived. Stifling his misgivings, he contacted Lombardo. Permission to build, he was told, would cost him half his profits. "That's ridiculous!" The words were out before Enzo could stop himself. "Tell the Gravianos the answer's no."

Lombardo tapped his forehead as if Enzo was crazy. But later that week he was back, inviting him to a meeting.

Filippo "Fifo" Graviano, a slight young man in his early thirties, had the coldest eyes Enzo had ever seen. At the time he was implicated in various crimes, including the murder of Paolo Borsellino, one of Italy's most famous anti-Mafia magistrates. A car bomb had blown Borsellino to pieces.

334

Murdered magistrate—in 1992, Paolo Borsellino, one of Italy's courageous anti-Mafia magistrates, fell victim to a bomb in Palermo.

But that didn't stop Fifo doing business in a suite of banqueting rooms called, ironically, "Happy Days."

"We thought we were doing you a favour offering to go 50–50," he said. "We usually ask for 60 per cent."

Enzo swallowed nervously as Fifo went on to say that the Gravianos believed in him. They'd settle instead for 200 million lire (£73,000) in cash.

There were further conditions. Bricks, mortar, cement and steel— even nails—would have to be bought from certain Mafia-controlled firms, as would earth-moving equipment, plumbing and electrical contractors. Enzo agreed.

Enzo got down to work, but without the joy. It wasn't the price or quality of the supplies he had to buy—they were average. But the daily visits to the worksite were another matter.

Lombardo, or some other goon, would strut about as though they owned the place. If they ordered a man fired, or another hired, Enzo had to comply. What had become of his dream—to be his own boss?

There were financial problems too. The apartments were slow to sell, and by late 1992 Enzo didn't have the money he had promised the Gravianos.

He stalled and stalled, until one day Fifo delivered an ultimatum—two apartments in lieu of cash. They were worth much more than he owed, but Enzo agreed—as he would agree to give the Gravianos two more apartments on another housing project located nearby.

Self-respect, Enzo's father had said, was the most precious thing you could have—and he'd taught his son to look a man straight in the eyes. Enzo was finding it difficult even to look at his own in the bathroom mirror. "I'm sorry, Dad," he would whisper.

But he only realized how low he'd sunk when the local parish priest, Don Giuseppe Puglisi, was murdered.

From his pulpit in the little parish church of San Gaetano in Brancaccio,

Puglisi preached against the Mafia every Sunday. The Gravianos and their henchmen were thugs. At catechism, he taught children that to be a Mafioso was a sin.

One day in September, 1993, a man walked up behind the fearless priest and shot him in the back of the neck. It happened not 100 yards from one of Enzo's building sites.

A few hundred protesters gathered to wave placards and shout slogans of defiance. Enzo, watching them from behind his wire-mesh fence, felt like weeping.

He too would have liked to express his indignation at Puglisi's murder. But he dared not do so. *What have I become?* he asked himself.

When Fifo Graviano was arrested the following year, Enzo felt a rush of euphoria; his problems must be over.

He was wrong. They were about to get worse.

Another Graviano thug, Cesare Lupo, forced Enzo to sign away three more apartments. Lupo (which means wolf in Italian) came back later for yet another apartment, then demanded a personal "present" of 20 million

Priest and martyr—Don Giuseppe Puglisi preached against the Mafia every Sunday in the church of San Gaetano. He, too, was murdered.

"We've no time to waste on people who don't pull their weight. Be careful!" Lupo shouted. "We'll get rid of you!"

lire (£7,300). Enzo had to borrow the money from the bank. But when he delayed handing over the apartments, Lupo bawled him out. "We've no time to waste on people who don't pull their weight. Be careful!" he shouted. "We'll get rid of you!"

The tongue-lashing took place in full view of Enzo's son.

Enzo's financial situation was becoming disastrous. The sum of what he had given or owed to the Mafiosi was close on two billion lire (£730,000).

Strapped for cash, he'd borrowed against his unsold apartments and was in trouble with the banks. But weighing most heavily was the effect on his family life. He was often sullen and irritable and, as he struggled to keep his guilty secret, he felt himself growing apart from Rosalia and the children. At night, Enzo would close his eyes, pretending to go to sleep. He didn't want Rosalia to know that he spent much of the night tossing and turning.

Rosalia knew something was on Enzo's mind. But she knew it was no use prying. When Enzo was ready, he would tell her.

One day in 1995, Enzo opened his newspaper and spat at the picture on the page. Lupo had been arrested!

No matter. Another Graviano henchman, Vittorio Tutino, showed up and demanded an apartment himself.

When Enzo tried to stall, he was told to watch out for his son. Giuseppe, now 21, had joined the business as soon as he left school.

When Enzo arrived at work one morning not long afterwards, he was told that Giuseppe had gone for a drive with Tutino. Enzo was beside himself. What could he do? But one thing was clear. If he called the police, it could make matters worse.

An hour went by, then another. Enzo checked his watch compulsively, his gut knotted.

At last Tutino drove through the gates and Giuseppe climbed out unscathed. Enzo, shaking with relief, threw his arms around his son, who looked at him, puzzled. Giuseppe hadn't realized the danger.

"You see how simple it would have been?" Tutino told Enzo.

After years of frustration and humiliation, Enzo could not bear the sight of another Mafioso. He hated everything about them—their arrogance, their allusive way of talking, the violence lurking behind their every word.

He bought a notebook and filled its pages with the details of how the Gravianos and their henchmen had extorted a fortune from him. He hid the notebook in a safe place at home, where Rosalia would never normally look but where she would be sure to find it if anything happened.

He wasn't sure what he would do next; he needed time to think. He went to Tuscany in search of peace of mind.

Enzo was alone on that June day in 1996 when he chanced upon the stone plaque on the Via dei Georgofili in Florence. After reading the inscription, he looked down at his hands.

What he saw was blood.

For if these monsters could spread such evil with impunity, it was thanks to men such as him and thousands like him. He was innocent of any crime—but in that instant he realized the extent to which he was condemned by the truths he had kept secret. And he could no longer keep silent.

Enzo returned to Palermo, where he gathered his family at the dining room table. He told them how he had been paying off the Mafia for years—and how his life had turned into a living hell.

"I've had enough," he said. "I want to go to the police. But I need to know what you think."

Weeping, Rosalia could only answer, "Whatever you think best."

Giuseppe asked, "What's going to happen to us if you go to the cops? Will the Mafiosi come after us too?"

Valentina settled the discussion. "Do it, Dad. Don't worry about us. You know it's right, and that's all that matters."

> He could no longer keep silent. "I've had enough," said Enzo. "I want to go to the police. But I need to know what you think."

Enzo Lo Sicco met with senior officers of Palermo's Squadra Mobile, the investigative squad, at a secret location in January 1997. As he began speaking, the burden of fear, pain and guilt lightened with every word. He talked for hours.

Names, dates, bank account numbers—over the next few weeks he provided police with a goldmine of information about the Graviano brothers' extortion racket.

Acting on the basis of his evidence, 20 members of the Graviano gang were tried in 1999 and sentenced to a total of just over 136 years in jail.

Enzo's family moved to another city under the Italian witness-protection programme. Enzo has had to start over again, struggling on a meagre government stipend that is a fraction of what he used to earn.

"Things aren't easy, but the family is united," he said recently, "and I can look at myself in the mirror again."

WELCOME TO THE
MARDI GRA EXPERIENCE

HUNT FOR THE
"MARDI GRA"
BOMBER

David Moller

The blackmailer's plan to extort money from Barclays Bank and Sainsbury's supermarkets had put fear into the hearts of London shoppers. Police drawn into a cat-and-mouse game with the ruthless extortionist had just one question: "Who is the 'Mardi Gra' bomber?"

Eddie, as his tenants called him, was hunched over the narrow workbench in his greenhouse. Obscured by climbing plants and shrubs at the end of the garden, the shed could hardly be seen from his council home in a quiet suburb of London. Paunchy, grizzled and bespectacled, Eddie would sometimes be in there until early morning, amid a jumble of screwdrivers, hacksaws, springs, timers, batteries and copper piping. Eddie had a plan and he wanted to make sure it worked.

His lodgers paid scant attention to the preoccupations of their eccentric, irascible landlord. One of them once asked him what he was up to, on finding him in the kitchen with an electric soldering iron and a circuit board. "Nothing," came the reply. "Just a little hobby of mine." The tenant thought no more of it. After all, this was the man who cooked a roast dinner at 6am, showed slightly too much enthusiasm for guns and associated with few people except his 66-year-old elder brother.

Today, in the greenhouse, Eddie put on rubber gloves, wiped the surfaces clean and carefully shaved the rough edges of the wooden mount he'd made.

On Saturday, November 15, 1997, a shopper picked up an abandoned carrier bag of groceries near the main entrance of Sainsbury's on The Broadway, Ealing, west London. Shortly after, at 2.19pm, the *Grand Canyon* film video inside went off in his hands. At 3.34pm, another device blew up in the Customer Service area of Sainsbury's in nearby Greenford after a customer handed in another video left behind in a bag.

It was only luck that prevented any serious injuries in either explosion, or when a third video, discovered earlier in the day, was detonated by police. The devices were constructed so that a spring-loaded bolt would slam into a shotgun cartridge, firing pellets at anyone opening the video cover. They were capable of killing.

Detective Chief Superintendent Jeffrey Rees listened as someone in the control room at Scotland Yard relayed the details of these explosions over the phone. The receiver crooked between his neck and shoulder, he stared out into his garden and knew he was taking on a major case. After 19 months of silence, the Mardi Gra bomber was back. The three devices left at Sainsbury's bore the trademarks of the unknown individual or group who, for nearly three years, had topped Scotland Yard's wanted list. Yet after 25 attacks, no one had even worked out the reason for the bomber's "Mardi Gra" signature—the misspelling of Mardi gras, the Shrove Tuesday festival.

On his hour's drive to Scotland Yard, the tall, lean, 50-year-old Rees reflected on the challenge ahead. A detective for some 30 years and a member of the elite Organized Crime Group, he knew about as much as there was to know about the dark world of extortion. But as Rees himself reminded colleagues that evening at a hurriedly convened meeting of 20 officers trained in organized crime and anti-terrorism: "On extortion, there are no experts."

No experts—just a few tried and tested rules. Rees knew that extortionists were usually people with no criminal record. When they referred to themselves in blackmail demands as a group, as the Mardi Gra bomber had done in earlier messages, they were often operating alone.

A neat, precise man, Rees expected even his deputies to call him "Sir" while working on an important case like this. In a voice that still carried slight cadences of the Welsh valleys, Rees stressed the importance of "covering the basics": house-to-house enquiries; scouring the neighbourhood for anyone who noted someone, or something, that seemed out of place.

Calling Card

Back in his box-like office on the fifth floor of Scotland Yard, Rees settled down to the computer files and the mound of documentation that had begun on December 6, 1994, when the first six Mardi Gra bombs had created panic at branches of Barclays Bank in north and west London.

Police presence—at the targeted supermarkets in west London, police stepped in to protect customers.

They had arrived in video cassette boxes, wrapped in blue Christmas paper with gold snowflakes. On each video sleeve was a photocopied logo of four men wearing dark glasses, suits and ties in an exaggeratedly cool pose reminiscent of the gangsters in the film *Reservoir Dogs*, and the now-ominous words: "Welcome to the Mardi Gra Experience".

Even those less powerful devices caused casualties. As Bali Hari, a part-time clerk at the Hampstead branch of Barclays, opened the video cover at 8.27am, the device exploded, burning her face and hands.

Two days later, a typed £1 million demand letter arrived at the Northampton headquarters of Barclaycard, again under the banner, "Welcome to the Mardi Gra Experience".

The police launched a major criminal investigation, but they found only dead ends. The extortionist had instructed Barclays to contact him via the personal column of *The Daily Telegraph* but then failed to respond. Teams of police fruitlessly followed hundreds of leads on disgruntled employees, ex-employees or aggrieved customers of Barclays. There were no fingerprints on any devices.

After several hours' reading, Rees rested his rimless glasses on a heap of files. The corridor outside his office was quiet. His wife, who was also a senior officer with the Metropolitan Police, knew full well about the need for long, late hours. But for his two daughters, now 10 and 12, it was to be another lost weekend.

Rees read on. After a five-and-a-half-month break, on May 19, 1995, Mardi Gra had begun a second, seemingly random phase, sending or planting 19 devices. The police had gathered some of the bomb recipients together at the St Ermin's Hotel, not far from Scotland Yard. They searched for any links they could have with the bomber, or each other. None could be found.

One target, Andy Bennett, landlord of the Crown & Anchor in Chiswick, west London, described how he narrowly escaped injury after unwrapping the brown paper on a double-sized video case. Bennett

No one paid any attention to the balding, ill-shaven regular sitting alone in the lounge bar.

couldn't think of anyone who had a grudge against him. A few days after the explosion when the pub was buzzing with speculation about why their local was a target, he had paid no particular attention to the balding, ill-shaven regular, sitting alone in the lounge bar with a glass of red wine, saying nothing but listening intently.

Elusive Prey

On April 3, 1996, Mardi Gra went public. The *Daily Mail* received a letter bragging of the "ability to strike and access to a constant supply of explosive material". The correspondent, who claimed to be representing "a small group of Barclays victims", warned that Barclays customers were now the target and included a photocopy of his latest 18-inch, double-barrelled shotgun device.

True to his word, on April 20 a similar device exploded in an alleyway near a Barclays in Ealing. Pellets shooting out peppered three people stood nearby.

Inexplicably, on July 11, 1996, Mardi Gra shifted focus again. Sainsbury's head office received a letter "welcoming" the supermarket group to the "Mardi Gra experience". It demanded £500,000. Despite two more threatening letters, there were no bombs for 16 months, until that afternoon of November 15, 1997, when the three devices were found at Sainsbury's.

As Detective Chief Superintendent Jeffrey Rees finally pulled himself up from his desk to go home, one word burned in his mind: extortion. While Rees sensed bitterness in the acts of violence, he also scented greed. *Maybe we can use his greed to entice him out.*

By the Monday morning of November 17, an operations room had been set up on the floor below Rees's office. On the walls of the 30-foot-long room, whiteboards displayed the chronology of each incident and photographs of the devices that had been disarmed or reconstructed. They included a suitcase bomb and a propane cylinder fitted with a timer.

With his deputy, Detective Superintendent Bob Randall, a hulking, fair-haired 45-year-old from the Anti-Terrorist Squad, Rees puzzled over the clustering of marker pins on a wall-map. The majority of incidents had taken place in the west or south-east of London. *But what on earth could be the connection between these two places?* mused Rees.

Lethal weapon—the bomber used this improvised shotgun device to cause maximum damage and destruction.

There were no obvious train or underground links; no direct roads.

"Maybe the bomber lives in one place and works, or has a girlfriend, in the other," ventured Randall.

In another room, officers scrutinized film taken from closed-circuit television cameras near the scenes of the latest bombings. As before, forensic evidence was lacking. Were the three-inch .410 Fioochi Italian cartridges and the 7.62mm Portuguese military rifle ammunition acquired abroad?

The edges of the wooden bases, on which a few devices were mounted, had been delicately shaved. To Rees, the attention to detail suggested someone of older years. But who?

There was nothing to focus police attention on a shadowy loner who made frequent trips from Chiswick across London to visit his ex-wife in Welling, south-east London. Nothing to make them take notice of his one indulgence: regular visits to France where he would buy crates of wine—and ammunition.

At 8am every morning, Rees held a meeting in the operations room so that his team could swap information and ideas. One day an officer asked: "Is there any way of tracing back one of these Sainsbury's carrier bags?"

It was a good question. Rees ordered the bomber's bags to be examined in the hope that they might contain a serial number which would indicate where they had come from. He was amazed to discover that all the numbers on the bags—which at any rate only indicated the manufacturer and batch—had been carefully cut out. This bomber was a real professional.

All the batch numbers on the bags had been carefully cut out. This bomber was a real professional.

Rees was concerned too that the devices were becoming increasingly sophisticated and that the latest three had an extra sinister touch. Each was contained in a video case which carried a sticker offering a £5 reward if the bag was returned to Sainsbury's. *Bombing by proxy*, Rees concluded grimly.

Acts of Destruction

A Sainsbury's bag full of groceries was left at a bus-stop in Ealing on December 6. Mrs Joan Kane, a 73-year-old widow, picked it up inadvertently with her own shopping bags and took it home.

"What do you think this is?" she asked a neighbour who was helping her unpack her purchases. In a vicious refinement, the bomber had stuck a small red sticker on the cassette case that housed the short, barrel-shaped device, proclaiming that it had been "checked by Sainsbury's staff". But the neighbour realized the danger: "Oh my God. It's a bomb. Get out."

From then on, the widow rarely left home. Often her family would find her sitting in her living room alone, staring at a blank television screen and crying. She died less than three months later.

Rees was formulating a plan to lure the bomber into the open. In a letter to

Sainsbury's sent in December 1997, the extortionist had proposed an ingenious deal. Sainsbury's was to arrange an offer of promotional cards in the weekly *Exchange & Mart* magazine. Only the bomber and Sainsbury's would know that the ostensibly fake cash cards had real magnetic information strips that could be activated with an agreed PIN number.

Using a cash dispenser, the bomber was planning to withdraw up to £10,000 a day for an unlimited period. Sainsbury's was to communicate details through the personal columns of *The Daily Telegraph.*

As a first step in his trap, Rees had to convince the blackmailer that Sainsbury's was cooperating and the police were out of the picture. His first cryptic message appeared in *The Daily Telegraph* on December 27, "M. Work will be completed and ready for London circulation on Thursday, March 26, 1998. This is the earliest possible date. Hope it meets with your schedule. G."

On January 16 Rees got his response: another bomb, followed by two more in February. There were no serious injuries.

Then at 5.45pm on March 4, 17-year-old Curtis Dennis, a keen runner and part-time worker with Sainsbury's, was walking past its store in Forest Hill, south-east London, when a shotgun device detonated inside a plastic bag, puncturing his thigh with shrapnel. The wounds required several hours of plastic surgery. "Another innocent victim," murmured Rees. *Someone just five years older than my eldest child.* Mardi Gra had to be caught before he killed.

On March 17 at 12.04pm on a crowded pavement in Eltham High Street in south-east London, a shotgun cartridge, activated by a timer, slammed into the metal post of a bus-stop.

A closed-circuit television camera picked up a man in a peaked hat and striped anorak crossing the street and leaving a black bin liner against the wall of a Sainsbury's store. Bending down, he gave a quick twist of his right wrist to align the barrel of the lethal homemade gun with a red dot on the bag and direct it at an angle of 45 degrees towards the glass bus-shelter. Viewing the video later in the operations room, Rees felt his blood run cold. Seconds before the blast, a young mother walked past with her child in a pushchair.

Uncannily, the bomber crossed the busy street without looking right or left. There was no front shot. Still, in the cat-and-mouse game they were playing, Rees sensed he was at last gaining on his prey.

The Sting

On April 14 Sainsbury's received a letter from the bomber, and on April 16 in *The Daily Telegraph* police communicated with him again. But would Mardi Gra come out to play?

On April 23 the tense waiting game began. By 7am, Rees was at his desk in

In the frame—police capture an image of the bomber planting a device at a bus-shelter in Eltham.

the operations room. By 8am—the earliest moment the plastic cards could be activated—nearly 1,000 highly trained detectives from the Organized Crime Group, the Anti-Terrorist Squad and the National Crime Squad were in place throughout London. Within minutes of the extortionist trying to use any of the cards, police would be notified in the operations room.

But on that first day: nothing. The minutes crawled by. At midnight, Rees left the operations room in charge of a detective inspector with instructions to rouse him at any hour.

On day two, Rees was back with a bundle of paperwork to distract him. Not all his colleagues were convinced that the bomber would show. "He'll be out," insisted Rees. Yet days three and four again brought nothing.

On day six, Tuesday, April 28, pressure on Rees was escalating. The operation, costing millions, was one of the most expensive in Scotland Yard history, and now there were only two days left to activate the cards. Then, at

347

6.14pm, a message was relayed to the operations room. Without a word, the officers looked at each other. The first cash dispenser hit.

Someone had taken out £100 using Mardi Gra's PIN number. An officer conveyed the information to surveillance teams: "Suspect has been to the Midland Bank cash dispenser at 108 South Ealing Road, London Whisky Five. Does anyone have him?" Officers on the ground reported no sighting. Rees felt his pulse racing.

Immediately, mobile surveillance teams raced to the area. At 6.38pm, there was a second machine hit less than a mile away from the first: £250 drawn from the Abbey National. Rees held his breath.

Finally, a message over the police radio: "Contact . . . Contact . . . Uxbridge Road, Ealing." Detectives had noted two men walking away from the Abbey National machine. They were moving towards a dark red Vauxhall Senator.

Only one person could give the order to arrest. Rees held back. The police needed cast-iron evidence of the suspects making withdrawals.

For another 50 minutes, police tracked the Vauxhall Senator on a tortuous route from west Ealing to Whitton, near Heathrow Airport. After parking in Bridge Way, two men walked from the car to the Nationwide Building Society. Both wore hats, tinted glasses, long coats. One held a clipboard—actually a mirror, to see who might be following.

At 7.34pm, the third machine was hit: £250 had been withdrawn. A minute later, another £100.

"Big mistake," murmured Rees. "Big, big mistake to use the same machine twice." A surveillance officer was able to record the two men on video.

Informed that the suspects were walking back to their car, Rees ordered in a specially designated arrest team. Over his mobile phone, he directed its leader.

"In your own time make the arrest."

As the two men reached their car, undercover cars squealed to a halt, blocking any exit. Police pulled the men from the Senator, pinning them to the ground. A police photographer and video cameraman recorded the moment when the men's hats, then wigs, were removed.

Both men were informed: "You are under arrest for demanding money with menaces, and also firearms offences."

During a thorough search, police found cash cards and £700 in cash—the entire proceeds of a three-and-a-half-year reign of terror.

Bitter Tale

Despite a surge of relief at Scotland Yard, Rees kept the surveillance operation on full alert: others could be involved in the scam. But there were no more cash-dispenser hits. At Walworth police station in south-east London, 60-year-old Edgar "Eddie" Pearce was claiming authorship of the whole enterprise. His elder brother Ronald, a retired tailor, said nothing.

At 1am, police forced entry into Edgar Pearce's three-storey, terraced council house in Cambridge Road North, Chiswick. Inside, they found two homemade pipe bombs, a host of other partly assembled bombs, a pistol, two crossbows, 272 shotgun cartridges, 410 cartridges for a specially adapted revolver, and a stun gun disguised as a mobile phone. Chillingly, there were also more than 100 pictures of customers with carrier bags outside various Sainsbury's stores.

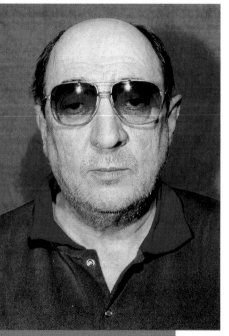

Edgar Pearce—he chose blackmail in the hope of a big payoff, and as a means of venting his anger.

But it was only with Edgar Pearce's lengthy statement the day after his arrest that Rees at last got some answers to the question that had played on his mind day and night for more than five months: who is Mardi Gra?

A bright boy from the East End of London, Pearce had started life full of promise, only to feel repeatedly thwarted. Sent to a private prep school in Oxford, he had to leave after three years when his tailor father ran out of funds. Later, he emigrated to South Africa with his wife Maureen and young daughter Nicola, but returned home, possibly angered by his continuing lack of success.

In 1982, after running a bistro on Hayling Island in Hampshire for eight years, he had to sell up when his wife became ill. He blamed Barclays and a local solicitor for a botched sale that eventually netted him £5,000, instead of the £20,000 he expected.

It was the start of a downward spiral. Pearce separated from his wife in 1987. After a stroke and a severe shoulder fracture in 1992, he was unable to work. As he grew more reclusive, embittered and alcoholic, his logic became twisted.

During the interview, he told detectives he stopped targeting Barclays because it was closing branches. He didn't want to be blamed for staff layoffs.

He chose Sainsbury's as an alternative when he heard that Tesco had become the country's most successful supermarket. He thought if Sainsbury's were struggling, it would be anxious to meet his demands.

He chose other bomb recipients randomly, coldly. At times during the interview, Pearce strove to give the impression that he realized the danger, but wanted to keep it to a minimum.

It was a claim that cut no ice with Rees. As he scooped the hundreds of pages of interview notes together, he reflected on the extensive efforts Pearce had made to extort funds, the casualness with which he had treated the lives of others.

Rees looked at his watch. It was late. Time to get back to his family.

With no evidence to implicate him in the blackmail campaign, Ronald Pearce was charged only with the illegal possession of a stun gun and sentenced to a year in prison. Since he had spent nearly that time in custody on remand, he walked free.

At the Old Bailey on April 7, 1999, Edgar Pearce pleaded guilty to 20 charges, including blackmail attempts on Barclays and Sainsbury's supermarket group, causing actual bodily harm and possession of explosives and firearms. He was jailed for 21 years. It was all a far cry from his goal of the fat payoff that had suggested his codename, the misspelling of Mardi gras, literally "Fat Tuesday" in French. Commented Deputy Assistant Commissioner John Grieve, head of the Anti-Terrorist Squad: "Edgar Pearce had a really good plan, but we had a better one."

Every effort has been made to trace the copyright holders of images in this book, but this has not always been possible. Anyone wishing to make a claim should contact the Picture Research Editor at gbeditorial@readersdigest.co.uk.

The publishers wish to thank the following people and organisations for permission to reproduce photographs belonging to them:
T = Top, C = Centre, B = Bottom, L = Left, R = Right.
2 L courtesy of Bernard Kerik; TR San Diego District Attorney's Office; BL Jackson Police Department; BR Candice DeLong; 2–3 © RD; 3 T Hinds County Sheriff's Office; B Barna-Alper Productions Inc./Thomas Fricke; 4 L Digital Vision; TR San Diego District Attorney's Office; BR © RD; 5 TR Jackson Police Department; BL & BR Candice DeLong; CL courtesy of Bernard Kerik; 8–9 Corbis/D Boone; 9 Ken Laffal; 11 C Getty Images Ltd; BL Corbis/Flip Schulke; 12 & 13 Corbis/Flip Schulke; 14 Corbis/Bettmann/UPI; 16 Corbis/Bettmann; 17 TL Corbis/Flip Schulke; TR & CR Jackson Police Department; 23 T & CL Jackson Police Department; 30 Hinds County Sheriff's Office; 33 David Rae Morris; 34 Robert Gumpert; CR Bournemouth News & Pictures; 36 Private Collection; 37 TL & TC Private Collection; BR Bournemouth News & Pictures; 41 San Diego Union Tribune; 43 San Diego District Attorney's Office; 46 Robert Gumpert; 47 & 48 San Diego District Attorney's Office; 50 Bournemouth News & Pictures; 52 TL & TR San Diego District Attorney's Office; 53 Robert Gumpert; 56 Nick Sinclair; 57–69 Icon Images/Peter Carrette; 71 courtesy of Concord Hospital; 72 Icon Images/Peter Carrette; 74 GettyOne Photodisc; 76–78 Patti McGowen; 82 Orange County Register; 84–85 Antonin Kratochvil; 89–97 courtesy of Bernard Kerik; 100–101 courtesy of Metropolitan Police; CL & CR The John Frost Historical Newspaper Service; 103 Terry O'Neill; 104 Mirrorpix; 105 Terry O'Neill; 106–7 The Press Association Ltd; 108 & 109 courtesy of Metropolitan Police; 111 The Press Association Ltd; 112 Corbis/Hulton-Deutsch Collection; 116 T & B Alex Waterhouse-Hayward;118 Alex Waterhouse-Hayward; 120 Trident Media Group; 121 Alex Waterhouse-Hayward; 122–135 Anastasia Vasilakis; 136–140 The Press Association; 138–140 The Press Association Ltd; 142 courtesy of Greater Manchester Police/Chris Oldham; 143–153 The Press Association Ltd; 154 Reuter Archive, Reuters Ltd; 155 The Press Association Ltd/Rui Vieira; 156 The Press Association Ltd; 158 © The British Museum; 161–164 Gus Alusi; 166–169 Richard Pierre; 170–172 courtesy of ROPE; 176–177 Corbis/Saba/Rea/Beniot Decout; 179 Getty Images Ltd/Reuters/Pascal Rossignol; 181 Corbis/Sygma/Orban; 184 TL & TR AP Wide World Photos/US Government; 185 Anna Mia Davidson; 188 L Brian Milne; BR Toronto Star; 194 Toronto Star; 201 Brian Milne; 206 Corbis/Bettmann; 207 & 208 CP Archive; 209 Barna-Alper Productions Inc./Thomas Fricke; 210 Toronto Star/John Mahler; 212 (Gunman) Corbis/The Garfield Studio; (Glass) Corbis/Walter Hodges; 215 & 216 Rocky Thies; 217 The Boston Globe; 219 Rocky Thies; 220 The Press Association Ltd; C Private Collection; 221 The Press Association Ltd; 223 Murdo MacLeod; 224 & 225 The Press Association Ltd; 226 Rex Features Ltd; 228 Alex Howe; 231 Rita Moreton; 234 courtesy of West Midlands Police; 236 Bob Severi; 237 & 239 Missy Anastasi; 240 Bob Severi; 246 (illustration) Martin O'Neill/courtesy of Hampshire Police; 247 & 248 courtesy of Hampshire Police; 252 Digital Vision; TR Daily News; CL New York Post; 255 New York Post; 256 Rex Features Ltd; 258 CR Henry Grossman; BL Daily News; 259 AP Wide World Photos; 260 John Harding; 262 TR Candice DeLong; C Corbis/Bettmann; 263 & 264 Candice DeLong; 274 Candice DeLong/Hyperion Books; 276–283 Alex Waterhouse-Hayward; 284 Network/Mike Goldwater; 286 Katz Pictures Limited/Headpress /Tim Bauer; 287 Jared Schneidman Design; 288 Munshi Ahmed; 292 Getty Images Ltd; 298 Corbis/Macduff Everton; 300 Andreas Ventura; 305 Corbis/Sygma/Lester Bob Larve; 307 Corbis/Sygma / Charles H Porter 4th; 310 AP Wide World Photos; 312 & 313 courtesy of Bill McVeigh & Lou Michel; 316 Corbis/Sygma; 326 SIPA/ Wichita Eagle/Jeff Tuttle; 327 Corbis/Sygma/Rocky Mountain News; 328 Corbis/SABA/Robbie McClaren; 330 merryweatherphoto.com; 332 © RD; 334 Corbis/Swim Ink; 335 & 336 The Press Association Ltd; 338 Corbis/John D Norman; 340–349 The Press Association Ltd.

Cover—background Getty Images Ltd. *Front cover* BL (illustration) Martin O'Neill/courtesy of Hampshire Police; BC (L) AP Wide World Photos; BC (R) Getty Images Ltd/Reuters/Pascal Rossignol; BR Network/Mike Goldwater. *Back cover* BL Gus Alusi; BC (L) Corbis/Sygma/Lester Bob Larve; BC (R) Hinds County Sheriff's Office; BR Richard Pierre.

Reader's Digest Crime Files was published by The Reader's Digest Association Limited, London.

Project Editors
Tim Bouquet, Anne Jenkins

Art Editor
Conorde Clarke

Picture Research
Julie McMahon

Copy Editor
Alison Bravington

Prepress/Image Controller
Egrette Rudder

Senior Production Controller
Sheila Smith

Originations: Colour Systems Ltd
Printed and bound at Mateu Cromo, Spain

ISBN 0 276 42810 2

BOOK CODE 400-017-01